THE
COVERT
ENLIGHTENMENT

Swedenborg Studies No. 17

THE
COVERT
ENLIGHTENMENT

*Eighteenth-Century Counterculture
and Its Aftermath*

Alfred J. Gabay

Swedenborg Foundation Publishers

Swedenborg Studies is a scholarly series published by the Swedenborg Foundation. The primary purpose of the series is to make materials available for understanding the life and thought of Emanuel Swedenborg (1688–1772) and the impact his thought has had on others. The Foundation undertakes to publish original studies and English translations of such studies and to republish primary sources that are otherwise difficult to access. Proposals should be sent to: Senior Editor, Swedenborg Studies, Swedenborg Foundation, 320 North Church Street, West Chester, Pennsylvania 19380.

Library of Congress Cataloging-in-Publication Data

Gabay, Al, 1946–
Covert enlightenment : eighteenth-century counterculture and its aftermath / Alfred J. Gabay.
    p. cm. – (Swedenborg studies ; no. 17)
Includes bibliographical references and index.
ISBN 0-87785-314-2
1. New Jerusalem Church–History. 2. Swedenborg, Emanuel, 1688-1772.
3. Mesmerism–History. 4. Mesmer, Franz Anton, 1734-1815.
5. Millennialism–United States–History–19th century. I. Title. II. Series.
BX8715.G33 2004   2004019561
289'.4–dc22

Cover credit: ©National Library of Medicine/Photo Researchers, Inc. Engraving of a drawing room wherein people are placing their limbs under bands of iron. This was one of the therapies advocated by Friedrich/Franz Anton Mesmer (1734-1815), seen at far left.
    Edited by Mary Lou Bertucci
    Designed by Karen Connor
    Set in Garamond by Karen Connor
    Printed in the United States of America.

Contents

For

Cherry and Darwin,
and the enlightenment
of all sentient beings

Acknowledgments

I am very pleased to acknowledge the help and encouragement of the following people and organizations: first, LaTrobe University, which granted two Outside Studies Programmes and funding that enabled me to do the basic research for this book; Dr. F. B. Smith, mentor and friend, who read the manuscript carefully and made many valuable comments; Dr. Erland Brock, whose academic and personal support has been invaluable; Leslie Price, who introduced me to new ways of understanding the material and to important new sources; and Carroll Odhner and the staff at the Swedenborg Library, Bryn Athyn, Pennsylvania, always ready to lend assistance and to share their extensive knowledge; the helpful staff at the British Library Rare Books section, who made the voyage of discovery both useful and pleasurable; Mary Lou Bertucci, senior editor at the Swedenborg Foundation, who gently and expertly guided the work to completion. Finally, I owe the deepest gratitude to my family for their many exertions on my behalf and their unflagging support throughout the lengthy process of research and writing.

ℐntroduction

Swedenborg, Mesmer, and the "Covert" Enlightenment

The European Enlightenment in the latter half of the eighteenth century heralded a grave conflict between theological and scientific modes of thought, starkly revealing the ancient tensions between spiritual gnosis and rational modes of knowledge. This conflict had complex sources, among them the fruits of the seventeenth-century revolution in methods of observation and the quantification of nature's phenomena and the resultant maxims of the rule of law, together with the rising cult of a confident progress. The reification of reason that took hold of peoples' minds set publicists like Voltaire (1694–1778) to explain Isaac Newton (1642–1727) to the masses, arguing for limited monarchy and religious toleration while condemning the clerics with "*écrasez l'infâme!*"[1]

The *philosophes* undertook the Baconian task of systematizing all knowledge through the *Encyclopédie*; and from the 1760s, political radicals, following John Locke (1632–1704) and Jean-Jacque Rousseau (1712–1778), began to strain against the *anciens régimes*. Various "benign" despotisms arose, while Thomas Paine (1737–1809) proclaimed the Age of Reason and urged the end of monarchy and American colonists and disaffected Frenchmen gave practical effect to democratic theories. In England, Jeremy Bentham (1748–1832) pondered utility, and Joseph Banks (1743–1820) promoted the scientific exploration of a New World in the southern seas. In these closing decades, Adam Smith (1723–1790), along with Anne-Robert Jacques Turgot (1727–1781) and the French Physiocrats, urged free trade based upon an analysis of the economic

---

1. Voltaire's *Lettres Philosophiques* [1733] linked the achievements of Newton to the milieu of intellectual liberty such as only existed in England. He offered English science and society as a universal model for enlightenment, and in his epic poem on Henry IV *La Henriade* [1728], Voltaire praised religious tolerance; see Jacob 1981, 101.

relations within human societies. Almost inevitably, in this developing atmosphere of free and rational inquiry, religion suffered casualties. Those in the West who rejected Christianity in the late-eighteenth century often found solace in Deism or in secular efforts to ameliorate the conditions of this life. A rejection of supernaturalism was thus a common feature of the Age of Reason.

There was another, a "covert" aspect to the High Enlightenment, bringing fresh perspectives on the soul, and by extension, on the human mind and on consciousness, in particular (Garrett 1975, chap. 6 and passim).[2] At this point, the dichotomy between science and religion was breached in a number of interesting and historically significant ways. In reaction to Newton's science and the mechanistic philosophy, numerous challenges were being posed to the religious, scientific, and medical establishments, and these would extend even to orthodox freemasonry. Through the increasing popularity of heterodoxy in religion, the line of a hermetic or "occult" tradition extending from Theophrastus Paracelsus (1493–1541) and Giordano Bruno (1548–1600) to Jacob Boëhme (1575–1624) and Emanuel Swedenborg (1688–1772) was revived among the literate, especially in Britain and France. Another challenge was posed to the medical arts by the Austrian physician Franz Anton Mesmer (1734–1815), who claimed to have discovered, or rediscovered, a universal fluid which he called "Animal Magnetism," which promised a panacea for diseases.

Finally, within the murky world of freemasonry, numbers of aristocrats and *haute bourgeoisie* adopted a rational religion, claiming an *antient* lineage to Hermes or even earlier which soon, however, abandoned its early occult connections (Jacob 1991, 22). A breakaway reforming trend was observed, especially in France over the last decades of the century, that reconstituted its votaries into new quasi-Masonic societies. Their syncretic program involved a millenarian outlook and incorporated a wide range of ritual and theoretical as well as practical elements, drawing upon a variety of sources: Catholic and Talmudic theology, mysticism and Renaissance

---

2. The term "covert" or "mystical" Enlightenment was first used by Clarke Garrett (1975) and most recently by Robert W. Rix and other historians; see R.W. Rix, "William Blake and the Radical Swedenborgians," *Esoterica* 5 (2003): 96–137.

Introduction

hermeticism, and especially on the teachings and practices of Swedenborg and Mesmer. These quasi-Masonic societies, while at times sharing a common membership, had different concerns and outlooks from what might be called the mystic materialism of Mesmer or the religious dispensationalism of Swedenborg. In the closing decades of the eighteenth century, new groups were established like the Avignon Society, which, though small in numbers, had a disproportionate influence upon the religious and cultural life of its votaries and a far more permeating influence upon later generations than has generally been recognized. They comprised the substance of what some historians have called the "mystical" or "covert" Enlightenment (Garrett 1975, passim).

In Paris, London, and Stockholm and in provincial centers like Lyon and Avignon, the Swedenborgian, mesmeric, and other intellectual currents then circulating among the European intelligentsia became manifest in different ways. Specifically, these amalgamations of ideas and practices, through Mesmer's theory of "crises" and Swedenborg's teachings on an afterlife produced a hybrid, having firm roots in the Enlightenment and in particular in its covert aspects, that would hold considerable importance for later generations, firstly in the magnetic movement, then in spiritualism. This hybrid was the mediumistic séance, a nineteenth-century phenomenon through which it was claimed that "sensitives" could transcend the liminal zone between this world and a putative Other World.

The application of the language and methods of science to metaphysical concerns was one attempt at *rapprochement* between empirical and theological modes of knowing; its most characteristic expression would be found in nineteenth-century America. The chief postulate of this study is that the principal features of the mystical Enlightenment were attempts at just such a *rapprochement*, as those who could accept neither religious orthodoxy nor the mechanistic philosophy nor yet the glittering generalities of orthodox freemasonry began to organize themselves into para-Masonic, mystical, and millenarian societies, drawing upon the vast fundament of eighteenth-century learning. The result was no less than a new formulation concerning the nature and purposes of the human experience; this cultural transformation and its aftermath in Europe and North America constitute the principal focus of this book. It is within this

Introduction

context of change and discovery, during the covert Enlightenment, that the lives and labors of Swedenborg and Mesmer are best understood, both in the relation of their ideas to each other and in their broader significance to the era.

As exploration increased in the world at large, some thinkers were exploring the interior regions of the human psyche. At least one, Emanuel Swedenborg, advanced the boldest of claims, that he was the instrument of a new Christian Dispensation, a revelation for humanity based upon reason, which entailed direct knowledge of an afterlife, of its inhabitants and their conditions. One unintended result of Swedenborg's writings was the amazing profusion of spiritisms, occultisms, and Masonic-style societies they inspired throughout the Atlantic world over the closing decades of the eighteenth century. This was apart from the gradual establishment of the New Church based upon Swedenborg's theology and moral philosophy. One central feature of these developments was a new attitude toward an afterlife. It was above all else this hypothesis, the "proof" of the continuance of life beyond the grave, that would spur the growth of spiritualism from the 1850s, and a generation later would bring into existence the Society for Psychical Research (S.P.R.), the first scientific society formed specifically to investigate these supernatural claims. Frank Podmore (1963, 1:15), better known as an original Fabian socialist, was among the core workers for the S.P.R. Writing in 1902, he asserted that:

> The idea of intercourse with distinctively human spirits, if not actually introduced by Swedenborg, at least established itself first in the popular consciousness through his teaching. E. Swedenborg is therefore deservedly ranked as the first Spiritualist in the restricted sense in which the term is here used.

While the New Church and her unwelcome stepdaughter spiritualism would have severe differences, it was on this point, the accessibility of an afterlife, that Swedenborg established the first element of what in the spiritualist movement would evolve into a plebeian cosmology for the latter nineteenth century.

Introduction

Swedenborg believed in contact with the spirits of those who had once lived as men and women, although this interaction was authorized to him alone as agent of the Lord and was subsumed within his broader message of spiritual regeneration. He taught that the future life is a state much the same in variety, character, and circumstances as life on earth. These became the two chief articles of the spiritualist creed. Podmore observed that "[Swedenborg's] special contribution to the Spiritualist belief consists in his conception of a future life," though Swedenborg, unlike the spiritualists, populated his heaven not only with the spirits of the departed, but also with demons and angels (Podmore 1963, 1:15).[3]

In most other societies, and in Europe's own past culture, belief in spiritual influences has figured prominently, these being associated with and frequently deemed accessible through the induction of altered states of consciousness.[4] During the Christian era, spiritual manifestations were understood principally as demonic possession, and those branded as *diabolos* were dealt with accordingly. In the persecution of unfortunate medieval "witches," in seventeenth-century Salem or in the Cévennes, the shared assumption of both persecutors and persecuted was that spiritual beings exist, but that they are not human spirits:

> The nuns of Loudun were possessed by demons, the Tremblers of the Cévennes had claimed inspiration by a divine afflatus, the Rosicrucians and Paracelsus believed they were dealing with elemental creatures. (Podmore 1963, 1:14)

At least until the age of the baroque, deviance from accepted norms was condemned according to religious and canonical understandings

---

3. On the structure of the heavens, see Swedenborg, *Divine Love and Wisdom*, §140; and *Heaven and Hell*, §§449, 450. As is customary in Swedenborgian studies, the numbers following titles refer to paragraph or section numbers, which are uniform in all editions, rather than to page numbers.

4. On traditional initiations of the Australian Aborigines employing the special use of crystals to induce hypnoid states, see Ellenberger 1970, 34; and Elkin 1977, passim. On the shamans in North America and Siberia, where both hypnosis and traveling clairvoyance figured in initiatory personations, see Holtved 1967, 26 and passim. Porphiry's life of his master Plotinus gives an account of an attempt to contact the sage's "tutelary spirit," in *Plotinus: The Enneads* 1969, 85–90. And on Socrates' *daimonion* and the Delphic Oracle, see Sauvage 1960, 92–93.

Introduction

incorporating a complex demonology. However with the advent of the age of the individual reason, as the mechanistic philosophy infused order into the universe, along with those among the European educated elite who sought better to understand society and to probe the human mind were many persons in the West also thinking differently about the nature and purposes of the human experience in its spiritual aspects. This was apart from and sometimes in opposition to the accepted church views.

Three major trends can be identified in England and on the Continent up to the early eighteenth century that helped to transform attitudes to the Christian message, setting the stage for the radically new understandings of the covert Enlightenment. These were millennialism, based upon biblical exegesis, and in particular prophecies as to the Last Days; popular millenarianism, comprising small but influential movements usually grouped around a charismatic leader; and the rising organization and influence of freemasonry and quasi-Masonic societies.

These trends became manifest in many forms throughout this century of Enlightenment. Some turned to biblical prophecy and the millennial predictions of impending doom during the Last Days; others joined freemasonry, claiming to possess secret knowledge reaching back to Egyptian or other antiquity, and rendered obeisance to the rational worship of a Great Architect. Still others in England and on the Continent, in small but increasing numbers, grew in sympathy with the "new" Christianity, like that exhibited in the ecstatic visions and inspired writings of the German mystic Jacob Boëhme. Over the last decades of the eighteenth century, many of these same people adopted a new revelation and Christian Dispensation as proclaimed in the writings of Emanuel Swedenborg. These trends were in evidence throughout Europe and when in the 1780s was added the potent influence of the new magnetic techniques of Mesmer and the Marquis de Puységur (Jacques Armand de Chastenet, 1751–1825), all the principal elements of the occult revival were in place.

The occult revival was due in part to the same forces that in the broader Atlantic community gave rise to romanticism: a breakdown of intellectualist, rational explanations that was given its dominant impetus from J. J. Rousseau and the nature philosophy (Brooke 1994, 94–97). To

Introduction

better understand these transformations in attitudes, it is necessary first to examine the various heterodoxies that flourished at the advent of the Enlightenment and to connect them to the more diverse trends that emerged at the end of the eighteenth century in Europe and North America.

The great swell of sectaries following the English Civil War produced numerous sects such as the Quakers and the Muggletonians, who continued in small but devoted groups into the new century. In England, as J. F. C. Harrison has argued, this millennial inheritance from the seventeenth century produced an intellectual milieu favorable to the eschatological interpretation of events (Harrison 1979, 14). Aided by a free press, millenarian and prophetic traditions flourished in England as they had never done in France, due to the pervasive influence of the Catholic Church on the populace (Garrett 1975, 166).

The Muggletonians and numerous other sects proclaimed the imminent end of the world. The six principles of Lodowick Muggleton (1609–1698) include the belief that God and the man Jesus Christ are synonymous expressions. Around the same time, the Philadelphian Society, named after the sixth of the seven churches in Asia mentioned in Revelations, flourished in London. It was headed by Jane Lead (1623–1704), author of *A Fountain of Gardens*, a chiliastic spiritual diary that drew substantially on Boëhme's ideas (Harrison 1979, 23–24). Unlike Swedenborg, whose message was based on a new revelation and a personal witness to the continued existence of humans beyond the grave, these seventeenth-century mystic millenarians did not recast the Christian message to proclaim a new dispensation; rather they placed their faith in the private spiritual insights of their leaders and founders. They did, however, provide a receptive environment for Swedenborg's teachings, inasmuch as his insistence that Jesus Christ is God echoed the views of Muggleton, while his symbolic interpretation of biblical stories was a strong feature of the chiliasm of the previous century.

The rising interest in the millennium was not limited to the broad populace. Millenarians were found primarily within popular culture throughout the eighteenth century; they awaited more direct manifestations, as shown by the appearance of various sects centered on individual prophets. The archetype of the millennial philosopher was William Whiston (1667–1752), Newton's successor at Trinity, Cambridge, while the Camisards, and arising out of their influence, the Shakers, represented the interests of the humbler classes. In general, millennial ideas were more prevalent among the educated class, and largely concerned with various schemes of biblical prophecy as to the Last Days, the breaking of the Seven Seals and so forth. The Bible was used in a variety of ways: as literal and divinely inspired, as a guide to contemporary events, or as allegory, where stories would be interpreted as internal states of the human mind (Harrison 1979, 14). Swedenborg would continue the latter trend after his illumination in 1745. He brought a new and deeper interpretation of the Bible based on the doctrine of correspondences and degrees, believing that he had been permitted by divine favor to understand these truths, thence commanded to convey them to humanity at large. After 1745, Swedenborg taught the arrival of an "internal millennium"; this was in stark contrast to contemporary understandings of the millennium, those awaiting an apocalyptic conflagration to be followed by a thousand years of peace. Yet such beliefs did urge among many in Hanoverian England and elsewhere a loss of faith in orthodox Christianity, at the same time as the Act of Settlement and other measures flowing from the Glorious Revolution strengthened the established Church and secured its relation to the Crown.

The most radical millenarians were the Camisards, or French prophets, a breakaway sect of Jansenism strongest in southeast France, and especially in Lyon. They taught the impending arrival of the millennium, to be preceded by the conversion of the Jews and their return to the Holy Land (Garrett 1975, 21). Resulting from the tensions that followed Louis XIV's revocation in 1685 of the Edict of Nantes, thereby withdrawing a guarantee of religious freedom to French Protestants, there was official oppression of sects like the Quietists and the Jansenists. After revolts in 1702 and 1705 stemming from this new environment of persecution, the Camisards fled to England (Harrison 1979, 25). Their three principal prophets, Élie Marion (1678–1715), Jean Cavalier (1681–1740), and Durand Fage were filled with the spirit; when they arrived in London in 1706 from the Cévennes, where the Huguenots were in rebellion, they preached an imminent millennium. Brooking no disagreement with their prophecies and visions, which were often accompanied by tremblings and seizures, they denounced all those who rejected their authority. Inspired by the sermons of the Huguenot pastor Pierre Jurieu (1637–1713), then living in the Netherlands, they understood their struggle in apocalyptic terms, with the French monarchy and its armies seen as serving the Great Beast in Revelations. They departed after six years, leaving many followers like John Lacy (b. 1664), James Cuninghame, and Richard Roach (1662–1730), who became known as the English Prophets (Garrett 1975, 147; Rousseau 1988, 94, 98).

Although numbering only in the hundreds, the Camisards were a significant bridge between French and English cultures. In their style and in their eschatology, they continued in the tradition of the seventeenth-century sectaries. Richard Roach, rector of St. Augustine's church in Hackney, was a follower of Jane Lead. He regarded them as God's instruments, and as yet another sign of the millennium approaching; in London, the Camisards joined with Philadelphians to announce that the Last Days had begun in 1700 (Harrison 1979, 27). Élie Marion, an unlettered peasant, delivered thunderous addresses under inspiration, where he promised the common people, "*Je vengerai mes enfants ma cause; votre sang sera vengé. . . . je vous éléverai sur des trônes, je mettrai ma force en Sion. . . . C'est la forteresse de l'éternel, ton Dieu, qui doit défendre son peuple d'entre les mains du diable du monde*" (I will avenge my children, my cause; your blood will be avenged. . . . I will raise you upon thrones, I shall apply my force in Zion. . . . It is the fortress of the eternal, your God, who will defend his people from entering into the hands of the devil of the world). Such zeal cost three of their leaders a sentence at the pillory in 1707 (Podmore 1963, 1:6; Rousseau 1988, 94).

In England, Dr. George Cheyne (1673–1743), author of *The English Malady*, reflected a rising interest among the educated in the French prophets. This trend was augmented by his concurrent interest in Jacob Boëhme's hermetic treatises, recently translated into English by the mystic William Law (1686–1761), that were popular among intellectuals, but not confined to them. Frequently the sort of people interested in Boëhme later adopted Swedenborg's writings. Ralph Mather (1750?–1803), an

Introduction

early Swedenborgian missionary from Bolton evangelizing in various corners of England during the 1780s, confirmed that, among the artisan class, many of those who sought "inward religion" had already been influenced by the works of Boëhme and Law (Harrison 1979, 21). John Wesley (1703–1791) had been an early student of William Law, while Boëhme's works exercised a more lasting effect on mystics like Thomas Tryon (1634–1703), as later they would influence the Reverend John Clowes (1743–1831), an Anglican clergyman with a deep and lifelong interest in the theology of Emanuel Swedenborg (Garrett 1975, 145).

Cheyne's interests in the mystical millennium and his association with Prophets and Quietists were not aberrant among educated men in his era. In speaking of those like William Law, Thomas Tryon, and others greatly influenced by Boëhme (Rousseau 1988, 101), as well as those like Nicholas Fatio (1664–1753) and Dr. Cheyne himself, "stricken" by the French and English prophets, G. S. Rousseau mildly rebukes traditional historians of the Enlightenment for failing to recognize this perpetual interest in heterodoxies of all kinds, a lacuna whereby "Enlightenment scholars have remained largely oblivious to this huge underbelly of their so-called Age of Reason" (Rousseau 1988, 117). This "underbelly" and the momentous events flowing from it form the principal focus of this study.

The other main current among the educated of the early eighteenth century—millennialism—drew on speculations about biblical prophecies that were being fulfilled in current events, as advanced earlier by Thomas Brightmann (1562–1607) and Joseph Mede (1586–1638). These ideas were taken up by Newton and William Whiston, and by the Unitarian theologian and scientist Joseph Priestley (1733–1804) (Garrett 1975, 126). Steven Bullock (1996, 10) notes the irony that Newton "drank deeply from the mysteries of alchemy and biblical prophecy, even as he forged many of the concepts that underlay the later mechanistic science that ultimately denied these occult connections." Fatio, Newton's disciple, enlisted himself in the service of Élie Marion, and it seems that, for a time, Newton was not averse to the Camisards (Rousseau 1988, 94). William Whiston also had a visit from the French prophets, but he rejected their version of the Last Days; and from his own calculations, he predicted in 1712 that a comet would soon destroy the world. Whiston listed ninety-nine signs preceding the restoration of the Jews to the Holy Land, an important precondition to the millennium, which he set first at 1736, then 1766 (Garrett 1975, 153–154; Rousseau 1988, 95).

The third significant aspect of the "underbelly" of the Enlightenment was freemasonry. While more elusive to the historian, the freemasons' status and undoubted permeation of European society in this century make the movement more than a mere adjunct to any study of the Enlightenment, and more especially to a deeper understanding of its covert aspects. This holds true because freemasonry, despite claims to an *antient* and venerable lineage, was itself a product of the Enlightenment. By 1789 there were between six and seven hundred lodges in France, and some thirty thousand members (McIntosh 1975, 19). Its popularity reflects a current dissatisfaction with religious orthodoxy among the aristocracy and *haute bourgeoisie*. More directly, not only were many of these same individuals involved in freemasonic lodges, Swedenborgian study groups, and mesmeric conclaves, but, as we shall see, there was a continuity with Masonic forms of organization, and other features like its exclusivity and secrecy, that are found again in the rash of societies that grew from the 1780s, whose aspect was often syncretistic and millenarian. One contributing factor to this spilling out of Masonic-like associations was a schism occurring within freemasonry itself. An urge for reform from the 1730s resulted in the "Scottish" rites, and later still in other reformed fraternities like the Templars or "Strict Observance" Masons (Jacob 1991, 59; Weisberger 1993, 72). As orthodox freemasonry steered further from occultism, other groups deriving from mesmerism and a host of other practices devoted to chiliastic pursuits and often borrowing from Swedenborgian theology arose throughout Europe. While they retained the quasi-secret and hierarchical Masonic structures, groups like Mesmer's harmonial societies, the Exegetic and Philanthropic Society in Stockholm, and the *Illuminés* at the Avignon Society became virtual clearinghouses for heterodox ideas of all kinds. It was especially within these cultural trends of the 1780s and beyond, that the melding of Swedenborgian and mesmeric influences was to figure prominently.

THE
COVERT
ENLIGHTENMENT

1

EMANUEL SWEDENBORG:
THE ALTERNATE-REALITY PARADIGM

> Since the Lord cannot manifest himself in person . . . he is going
> to do this by means of a human being who is capable not only of
> intellectually receiving the teachings of this church but also of
> publishing them in print. I testify in truth that the Lord has man-
> ifested himself to me, his servant, and sent me on this mission . . .
>
> *True Christianity* ƒ779

The Covert Enlightenment

Emanuel Swedenborg was not the first seer to claim contact with a higher
reality. Yet he holds a singular importance for historians with an interest in
the cultural changes wrought by the Enlightenment in all its phases,
principally because the diffusion of his teachings was a major contribution
to the occult revival at the end of the century. Unlike Jacob Boëhme, his
seventeenth-century predecessor in mystical religion, Swedenborg made
that knowledge accessible to a very wide public. His detailed descriptions
of the spiritual worlds and their inhabitants attracted numbers of
adherents among both the curious and the bereaved. Nor was he like
Boëhme, an unschooled mystic. Prior to his illumination in 1745 at the age
of 54, Swedenborg had acquired a distinguished reputation as both
scientist and statesman in his native Sweden and throughout Europe. His
labors in all fields were characterized by variety and originality. A pioneer
in several fields of science, he arrived at the nebular hypothesis before
Immanuel Kant (1724–1804) and Pierre Simon Laplace (1729–1827),
and for sheer brilliance of mind he ranks with his friend Carl Linnaeus
(1704–1778), by whom he was presented to the Swedish Academy of

Science. Perhaps most remarkable among Swedenborg's many anticipations of later theories was his localization of the motor centers in the cerebral cortex, at least 150 years before any other scientist. Swedenborg made this discovery while seeking to locate the soul within the body (Jonsson 1988, 30; Block 1984, 4, 14). In these and other attainments, he bears comparison with that other eclectic genius, Leonardo da Vinci (1452–1519).

This extraordinary man, whom Ralph Waldo Emerson (1803–1882) called "the last of the great Church Fathers," was raised within a pious evangelicalism, the third of nine children (1980, 93). His father Jesper Svedberg (1653–1735), professor of theology and then Lutheran bishop of Skara, was deeply involved in current debates within the Protestant churches concerning the sufficiency of faith or the need for works to attain salvation. Svedberg insisted on works as the primary motive and made a large personal expenditure in translating the Bible into Swedish (Williams-Hogan 1988, 5; Trobridge 1992, 3).[1] He also provided an indirect connection with America. In June 1697, Reverend Svedbeg induced King Charles XI of Sweden to send three missionaries to America, Andreas Rudman (1668–1708), Erick Tobias Biorck (1668–1740)and Jonas Auren (1666–1730), in response to the needs of Swedish Lutherans settled on the Delaware River. Svedberg also conversed with angels, heard voices, and practiced a form of hypnotic healing. These interests are evident, for instance, in an article he wrote concerning a servant girl who apparently took no nourishment and communicated with spirits (Sachse 1895, 93; Schuchard 1988, 369; Block 1984, 4). Thus, in the home there was a strong attachment to the Bible as the Word and a family tendency to mystical reverie. Through royal patronage, the Svedberg family was ennobled to Swedenborg.

As a student, Swedenborg showed a particular aptitude for science, his studies being especially strong in mathematics and mechanics. He wrote poetry in Latin and became fluent in French, German Dutch, English, and Italian. In 1718, he published the first book on algebra to be written in Swedish (Suzuki 1996, 5). On the tour of the Continent usual for young

---

1. Like his father, Swedenborg was opposed to a theology that discourages works and intuition (Block 1984, 4).

aristocratic men in his era, he did not waste his time in dissipation, and already he lived by the moral "doctrine of uses" that he would expound in his mature theology. During the first of many sojourns in London, he perfected his command of a number of crafts, including engraving and glass-grinding, and studied varied scientific disciplines (Block 1984, 5; Keller 2000, 27–28). While working with John Flamsteed (1646–1719), the eminent astronomer royal, Swedenborg discovered new methods for observing the moon, stars, and planets, and for calculating the terrestrial longitude by means of the moon.

On his return to Stockholm, the king appointed him assessor for the Swedish Board of Mines, where he remained, with frequent absences abroad, relinquishing the post only after his illumination twenty-five years later. An extraordinarily prolific worker, Swedenborg had published over 150 papers in seventeen disciplines, written in the scholarly Latin of his day, before he abandoned science for theology in 1745. His rank entitled him to a seat in the Riksdag, the Swedish House of Nobles, where he applied himself with characteristic industry. He presciently championed the decimal system and produced weighty papers on finance and currency reform. His career brought him success, even eminence in the world of European science. An omnimath and true son of the Enlightenment, Swedenborg's interests covered a wide field (Trobridge 1992, 9–10; Block, 1984, 8).

As Helen Keller (1880–1968) lyrically phrased it, "He was as familiar with forge and quarry, workshop and shipyard, as he was with the stars and the songs of birds in the morning" (Keller 2000, 28). He attempted to construct a universal musical instrument, drew up plans for drawbridges and for a flying machine, and among his proposals was what sounds like a steam engine, in which "the wheel will . . . revolve by means of the fire, which will put the water in motion" (Trobridge 1992, 10; Block 1984, 5). At the Board of Mines, he perfected a technique for extracting salts from minerals and showed his gifts as military engineer in 1718 when he devised a means of carrying a ship fourteen miles over mountainous terrain between bodies of water, thus helping the Swedish navy surprise and defeat the Danes at Frederikshald. He also had a plan for a canal to connect the North Sea and the Baltic.

The Covert Enlightenment

Returning to England in 1734 to study mining and manufacturing, Swedenborg published his first great scientific work, the *Principia*, the first of his three volume opus *Opera Philosophica et Mineralia*. His next venture was into anatomy and physiology, for at this time he was determined to discover the soul within the human organism. That there was no sharp demarcation in his life before and after his illumination, that his thoughts were already turning to higher things, is indicated in his prologue to *The Animal Kingdom* (§19): "Thus I hope, that by bending my course inwards continually, I shall open all doors that lead to her, and at length contemplate the soul herself: by the divine permission" (Swedenborg 1960, 1:12; Block 1984, 6–8; Suzuki 1996, 20).

Commencing in 1743 when he was 54, Swedenborg's life took a dramatic turn with the first signs of his illumination. What he experienced over the next two years was no less than a transformation that, ever the precise scientist, he carefully recorded in a special diary. His mental suffering was undoubtedly very severe. He fasted and prayed, had strange dreams and fantasies, tremors, prostrations, trances, sweatings, and swoonings (Block 1984, 11). At last, in a grand vision in April 1745, the "Lord God" appeared and commanded him to explain to the world the spiritual sense of Scripture (Trobridge 1992, 41). Swedenborg's life entered a new phase, and a new state of consciousness was opened within him where he was fully awake in both worlds at the same time. He describes this momentous event in his life:

> From that day I gave up the study of all worldly science, and labored in spiritual things, according as the Lord had commanded me to write. Afterwards the Lord opened, daily very often, my bodily eyes, so that in the middle of the day I could see into the other world, and in a state of perfect wakefulness converse with angels and spirits. (Tafel 1875–1877, I:36)

There was nothing in Swedenborg's personal appearance to suggest a revelator. A typical eighteenth-century aristocrat, he appeared at formal functions in black velvet and fine lace, sporting a jeweled sword and a gold-headed cane (Block 1984, 9). He lived a quiet bachelor's existence in unprepossessing style, eating little animal food, only sometimes "a few eels." His chief sustenance was cakes, tea, and exceedingly sweet coffee, and he drank volumes of water. Swedenborg's main vice was taking snuff (Hindmarsh 1861, 19). He has been described as "tall and spare in person, with . . . blue eyes, a wig to his shoulders, dark clothing, knee-breeches, buckles, and a cane"; his character was "placid, serene, and ever ready for conversation . . . but he was afflicted with a stammer which hindered his enunciation" (Doyle 1926, 1:14). John Christian Cuno (1708–1796), a friend in Amsterdam, recounted how "when he gazed on me with his smiling blue eyes, which he always did in conversing with me, it was as if truth itself was speaking from them" (Tafel 1875–1877, 2:445).

In obedience to the Lord's command, Swedenborg set about conveying in numerous heavy, Latin tomes, written in the language of dry scientific discourse, what had been revealed to him regarding the "inner" sense of the Bible and the destiny of humankind. Accordingly, the *Secrets of Heaven* (*Arcana Coelestia*) in eight quarto volumes was published between 1749 and 1756, followed by *Heaven and Hell* (*De coelo et ejus mirabilibus . . .*), perhaps his best known work, and *Marriage Love* (*Delitiae Sapientiae de Amore Conjugiali*), which was to cause some dissention within the New Church because of views expressed therein on marriage and "concubinage." Swedenborg believed the revelation vouchsafed to him would rejuvenate the Christian faith. He never wavered from the task of expounding a theology that he claimed was received through inward illumination as he read the Word. In *True Christianity* §508 (*Vera Christiana Religio*), his last published work and the most important work theologically because, according to Swedenborg, the completion of its first draft on June 19, 1770 signaled the commencement of the era of the "New Jerusalem," he asserts, "Permission has been granted to explore with the intellect and delve deeply into all the mysterious teachings of the church." After the appearance of that book, Swedenborg wrote to Gabriel Beyer on April 30, 1771, "[T]he Lord will operate both mediately and immediately establish the New Church, which is founded on this Theology, throughout Christendom."[2] The Enlightenment in theological matters had arrived,

---

2. *Small Theological Works and Letters of Emanuel Swedenborg* (London: Swedenborg Society, 1975), 255.

for in a vision, he had seen inscribed over a temple portal the inscription *Nunc Licet*: "Now permission has been granted." (*True Christianity* §508).

In 1749, the same year that John Wesley's *Plain Account of the People Called Methodists* was given to the world, Swedenborg was in London, where there was no literary censorship, overseeing the publication of the first Latin volume of the *Arcana*. John Lewis (fl. 1750), bookseller, printer, and early convert, placed advertisements in London newspapers. The following year the second volume was published, and Lewis produced the first English translation.

The New Church did not come into existence until some years after Swedenborg's death, because of the tendency by acolytes to permeate existing communions, especially in England. Receivers of the "Heavenly Doctrine" (as it is known) during Swedenborg's life included the Reverend Thomas Hartley (1709–1784), M.A., rector of Winwick parish in Northamptonshire, and a Dr. Hampe of London, philosopher and preceptor to King George II (Hindmarsh 1861, 2). Swedenborg was not concerned about the small numbers of his followers, believing that the establishment of the New Church was inevitable, since it had been divinely mandated (Brotherton 1860, 6). According to Robsahm's memoirs, he did not proselytize or argue his experiences with anyone (Tafel 1875, I:34). Like Nostradamus (1503–1566), Swedenborg foretold the exact date on which he would die, and expressed great delight at the prospect. He sent a short note to John Wesley inviting him to pay him a visit as "I have been informed in the world of spirits that you have a strong desire to converse with me." The astonished Wesley wrote back confirming that he had indeed been wanting to speak with him, but could not as he was then leaving on a month's journey. Swedenborg replied that this would not do, since he expected to "go into the world of spiritis [sic] on the 29th day of the next month, never more to return" (Tafel 1877, 2:565). Swedenborg died quietly on March 29, 1772, in his lodgings, no. 26, Great Bath Street, Cold Bath Fields, in Clerkenwell, London (later demolished). He was buried in the vault of the Swedish Church. In 1908, the seer's remains were removed to his native Sweden, where they were interred in Uppsala Cathedral (Block 1984, 17; Suzuki 1996, 47; Trobridge 1992, 49, 51).

Swedenborg's Essential Teachings

Swedenborg's widespread and diffuse influence was spread initially through private study groups and via the slow dissemination of his published works, both in England and in the New World. The Lutheran clergy had them proscribed in Sweden for a generation. From the early 1780s, the Reverend John Clowes (1743–1831) sparked interest among working-class adherents in Manchester and Bolton. Meanwhile, a Theosophical Society (not to be confused with the venture of H.P. Blavatsky [1831–1891] a century later) was inaugurated in London, which included among its membership the sculptor John Flaxman (1755–1826); William Sharp (1749–1824), the radical engraver; the brothers Robert Hindmarsh (1759–1834) and James Hindmarsh (1731–1812); Dr. Benedict Chastanier (c.1728–1806); General Charles Rainsford (1728-1809), afterwards governor of Gibraltar; the merchant James Glen (?1750–1814); and the painter Philippe-Jacques de Loutherbourg (1740–1812) (Hindmarsh 1861, 21). Over time, these believers coalesced into the New Church, attracted by the seer's promise of a regenerated Christianity and his special insights into the Word. A second and far wider circle was drawn to Swedenborg's pronouncements regarding the spiritual and celestial worlds he claimed to have directly experienced. Hence two inherently conflicting trends are already discernable: while the New Church grew unremarkably in the latter half of the eighteenth century, the *dilletanti* throughout Europe, generally educated and of aristocratic birth, were affected principally by Swedenborg's claims to being a seer and by the general resemblances they might have inferred between Swedenborg's system and hermetic and other occult wisdom.

Two branches of the occult revival can be discerned in both France and England: what may be called the Masonic branch, where current ideas were diffused through the interconnected European lodges, and a popular occultism, deriving especially from English working-class culture. Many seekers had already been made familiar with hermeticism via the popular translations of Boëhme, as well as through the French and English Prophets and a native tradition of millenarianism drawing upon the seventeenth-century sectaries. It was in this environment that, from the 1770s, Swedenborg's message began to appeal to modest but growing numbers of the disenchanted within the orthodox communions. These were drawn equally by his descriptions of the heavens he claimed to have visited regularly over more than twenty-five years, as by the Swedish seer's promise of a new Christian dispensation.

At this distance, through the penumbra of our knowledge of spiritualism and New Age philosophies, one needs to emphasize the radical nature of Swedenborg's teachings regarding contact with an afterlife. But he discouraged others less well protected than himself, as instrument and agent of the Lord, to endeavor such contacts.

Helen Keller, a distinguished receiver of the Heavenly Doctrine, described Swedenborg's system as encompassing three main ideas: God as divine love, God as divine wisdom, and God as power for use (Keller 2000, 148). This neatly encapsulates Swedenborg's theology and moral philosophy, whose first and fundamental principle is that the Lord Jesus Christ is God, sustainer of all life in all the spheres every instant of existence through the constant emanation of his divine influx. This doctrine, while monistic, escapes mystical pantheism since it preserves the essential dualism between the Creator and the creation. In *Divine Love and Wisdom* §283 (*Sapientia angelica de divino amore*), Swedenborg wrote that, ". . . even though God did create the universe and everything in it out of himself, yet there is not the slightest thing in the created universe that is God (Block 1984, 40). God cannot be known *in esse*, but his effects are revealed in this world through love and wisdom, whose representations are heat and light, two aspects of divinity constantly referred to in various ways throughout Swedenborg's writings. The regeneration of humans, the final purpose of the spiritual life, is achieved by opening their "interiors" to the reception of "influx," its power depending on the moral quality of the individual's inner life. Through the performance of uses, to the neighbor and to God and by eschewing the selfish love of self, regeneration is made possible.

There is an intimate connection between Swedenborg's moral doctrine and his spiritual ability as seer. Through personal experience after the opening of his "inner eye," he claimed direct witness to the truth of his central proposition, the existence of a causal link—in Swedenborgian parlance, a "correspondence"—between the interior morality of human beings and the environment they thus create, physical, emotional, and spiritual. This symmetry extends also to the world of spirits and angels, whose direct influence is given through what Swedenborg called their "exhalations" into the interiors of like-minded humans on earth. In *True Christianity* §475, he wrote, "From hell's side, evil radiates into this intervening area in complete abundance; and from heaven's side in turn, goodness flows into the area, also in complete abundance." Cosmology is essential to Swedenborg's moral and spiritual purposes of regeneration. Hence the geography of heaven, which he describes in meticulous detail, places the spiritual and celestial angels, all of whom are former human beings, in closer proximity to the Source as they are able to live according to "the Good of faith and the Truth of knowledge," symbolized as heat and light, respectively.[3] This too is allied to correspondences and degrees. The quality of one's moral life is integral to the level of illumination, or inner understanding, one receives. In *Heaven and Hell* §533, Swedenborg explains that ". . . it is simply a matter of recognizing, when something attractive comes up that we know is dishonest or unfair, that this is not to be done because it is against the divine commandments." In establishing such a habit of mind, one is "gradually united to heaven. To the extent that we are united to heaven, the higher levels of our minds are opened." Swedenborg insists that humans are able to enter into this state because of their freedom of action, and thus to do virtuous acts becomes for the individual "the delight of his love."

Perhaps the key to Swedenborg's theology and moral philosophy is his notion of equilibrium, incidentally an important eighteenth-century concept in general. Swedenborg taught that, owing to a lack of equilibrium created over time between the heavens and the world of spirits, an inordinate number of souls was populating this intermediate region between heaven and earth, thus impeding the reception of influx to the earth and making a final judgment necessary. According to Swedenborg, this judgment occurred in 1757 and was sealed through two events: the

---

3. See *True Christianity* §§1, 392; *Heaven and Hell* §468; and *Other Planets* §§123, 135 for variations on these images.

reception of his revelation concerning the condition of humans and their relation to an afterlife and the opening of the Bible as Word to deeper meanings (Trobridge 1992, 58). These esoteric meanings had been understood in the so-called "ancient" churches but were hidden from the Christian churches in his time because of their incapacity to receive the requisite understanding through influx. The notion of an equilibrium has another function, that is, between the "exhalations" of good and evil spirits. Swedenborg taught that these exhalations emanate through the "interiors" of humans to affect their conduct and therefore constitute, according to one's true nature, the channel through which moral choices are exercised. Thus, absolute free will being molded by moral inclinations is a fundamental aspect of Swedenborg's regenerative theology. He believed that the human being is free to draw his or her spiritual sustenance from either—that is free-will. Regeneration is effected entirely by the Lord through divine influx, but is dependent on the individual's cooperation. A person can be saved only insofar as he or she chooses the good and struggles actively, with the Lord's help, against temptations.

A deeper interpretation of the inner sense of the Word comprised Swedenborg's primary mission to the world, to indicate "where its holiness and divinity lie concealed"; this was why he understood the new dispensation as the Lord's Second Coming, as the advent of an "internal millennium." Through a deeper understanding of correspondences and degrees, the representations of the spiritual and the celestial within the natural world, the Word could be profitably studied, and thus a deeper comprehension of its inner sense could be attained with faith and diligence. Swedenborg taught that biblical stories speak to humanity on several levels of meaning simultaneously, made comprehensible to the human reason through the science of correspondences and degrees in the first instance, and ultimately by the gift of inward illumination. Thus, for instance, with the benefit of Swedenborg's insights, an historical account of the Creation can be understood also as a commentary, or correspondence, on the necessary path to individual regeneration. Similarly, Psalm 78 is at once a historical record of the experiences of the Israelites in Egypt and their pilgrimage to Canaan, but it is also a parable of our own individual exodus from materialism and ignorance, and the slow, difficult progress to a happier life, symbolized by Canaan (Williams-Hogan 1988, 16; Block 1984, 27; Keller 2000, 55–61).[4]

Among Swedenborg's most curious teachings was that the Last Judgment occurred in 1757, at which date an immanent spiritual millennium had commenced (Garrett 1984, 68). His theology can be located both within the Rational Enlightenment, in the idea that the deepest mysteries might be comprehended by the unaided reason, and as part of the lineage of earlier biblical millennialists, except that his soteriology involves the regeneration of humans within the Christian faith, requiring no external apocalyptic events. Sharing with Methodism an emphasis on practical piety and on the emotional and spiritual dimension of enlightenment, Swedenborg laid great emphasis on the possibility of human improvement in this world. Through reason, piety, and hard work, this world could be made better, at the same time that the spiritual worlds grew more accessible (Garrett 1984, 69; Trobridge 1992, 59–60).

The Alternate-Reality and Alternate-Consciousness Paradigms

It was, however, as a seer of spiritual and celestial spheres rather than as theologian and moralist that Swedenborg's views exerted the widest influence on outlooks. In the nineteenth century, this permeating influence would be based on a popularized idea of the spiritual worlds he had described principally to emphasize his message of regeneration.[5] In a

---

4. The six days, or periods, of Creation are according to Swedenborg successive states in the regeneration of the human being. The first state, including infancy, relates to the "void," "emptiness," and "thick darkness," whereupon the Lord's mercy is manifest in "the Spirit of God moving upon the face of the waters." The second state occurs "when a distinction is made between those things which are of the Lord, and those which are proper to man," and so on up to "the sixth state when, from faith, and thence from love, he speaks what is true, and does what is good: the things which he then brings forth are called the 'living soul' and the 'beast.'" And as the individual then begins to act at once and together from both faith and love, he or she becomes a spiritual person, who is called an "image." See *Secrets of Heaven*, §§6–13.

5. Bernhard Lang notes that Swedenborg's heaven is anthropocentric, with four main characteristics: (1) only a thin veil divides heaven from earth; (2) life in heaven is not the opposite of life on earth, but a continuation and fulfillment of earthly existence; (3) heaven is not a realm of repose and contemplation, but dynamic and motion-filled; and (4) the focus is on human love expressed in communal and familial concerns, not in a beatific vision like that of the scholastics; see Lang 1988, 309–310.

letter to Prelate Friedrich Christoph Oetinger (1702–1782) dated September 23, 1766, Swedenborg wrote, "I can solemnly bear witness that the Lord Himself has appeared to me, and that He has sent me to do that which I am doing now, and for that purpose He has opened the interiors of my mind . . . which [privilege] I have had now for twenty-two years" (Tafel 1875–1877, 2:249).

Swedenborg's intromissions and visions had revealed to him that, at death, no radical change takes place either in the individual or in the lived environment. He held that the soul enters the world of spirits where it lives in society, experiences thoughts and feelings, and functions for a time just as it did on earth (Lang 1988, 312). The world of spirits, while not heaven per se, serves as a middle ground between the heavens and the earth. Swedenborg described a strongly human-centered world with flowers, temples, and gardens, and the continued enjoyment of food and bodily pleasures, including the marriage of true "conjugial" partners. Among the most controversial of Swedenborg's teachings was his portrayal of marriage and sex in heaven, which completely separates his visions from the static heaven of the Scholastics and from most of his contemporaries (Lang 1988, 314, 329).[6] While it horrified the clerics, this was to prove the most popular feature of his writings, drawing from Plato's *Symposium* the idea that "two real lovers are not separated by the death of one, since . . . they again meet and are reunited, and love each other more tenderly than before" (Doyle 1926, 1:10; Lang 1988, 325). Swedenborg's doctrine of the afterlife was extremely popular with the bereaved and unique in promoting the love of a man and woman as the foundation of all other love.

Some have credited Swedenborg with the discovery of both mesmeric phenomena and traveling clairvoyance more than a century before Mesmer. In *Secrets of Heaven* §1883, he speaks of two kinds of vision which he had been permitted to experience. The first he calls "being taken out of the body," where the individual is:

---

6. Medieval theologians like Thomas Aquinas, strongly disposed to Aristotle's idea of the *Primum Mobile*, believed that, at the end of time, the universe will stand still since movement implies a cycle of growth and decay. Rejecting also the Lutheran doctrine of soul sleep between death and the Last Judgment, Swedenborg describes instead another world: "As we did in our former world, we see, hear, and speak; as we did in our former world, we walk, run, and sit; . . . we lie down, go to sleep, and wake up; . . . we eat and drink; as we did in our former world, we enjoy making love to our spouse—in a nutshell, we are human in each and every way" (*True Christianity* §792).

... brought into a certain state that is midway between sleep and
wakefulness. . . . All his senses are as fully awake as in the highest
wakefulness of the body: the sight, the hearing, and, wonderful to
say, the touch. . . . In this state also spirits and angels have been
seen to the life, and also heard, and . . . have been touched, and
almost nothing of the body then intervened.

As we shall later see, this state has resonances with that which Andrew
Jackson Davis (1826–1910) later termed the "Superior Condition." In
Secrets of Heaven §1884, Swedenborg describes another kind of vision,
"being carried by the spirit into another place," which he illustrates from
his own experience. Once, when he was walking to the country, he was
suddenly

... in the sight of the body, and became aware that I was in another
place. Greatly amazed at this, I perceived that . . . while this state
lasts there is no reflection concerning the way, even if it be many
miles; nor is there reflection concerning the time, even if it be
many hours or days; nor is there any feeling of fatigue.

The experience of seeing one's own body and being led to distant places
with no recollection of time or fatigue was reported from the first by
somnambules and later by mediums. Swedenborg states that he was
permitted to experience these states on three or four occasions each, but he
insisted that, by contrast, the scenes he had habitually witnessed over
twenty-five years were not visions "but sights seen in the highest
wakefulness of the body, and this for several years" (*Secrets of Heaven*
§1885).

An idyllic heaven presages the covert Enlightenment, harmonizing well
with the current romanticism, for instance, in J. J. Rousseau's belief that
human beings are fundamentally good and worthy of salvation.
Swedenborg's accounts of the highest sphere, the celestial kingdom where
the angels are naked, a correspondence with their spiritual purity and
innocence, foreshadows the natural philosophy and the concept of the
noble savage (Lang 1988, 320–321). Swedenborg admired the African

races, and these views would yield among some of his Swedish followers a fervent opposition to slavery, which led to the formation in 1786 of the first organization to work against the slave trade. To a Bible-loving people, Swedenborg gave new hope and a new interpretation of the Word, together with the certainty that good works and a good will would have their just rewards in the hereafter. As Margaret Block notes, it was Swedenborg's teachings regarding the afterlife that made the greatest number of converts to the New Church, while his views of heaven greatly affected the success of spiritualism and had deep implications for religion in general (Block 1984, 35–36).

It was not Swedenborg's principal message of a regenerated Christianity, but his assurances concerning the accessibility of the higher spheres—and by implication the existence of augmented senses to perceive them—that fed into what I have called the ontological or alternate-reality paradigm. Allied to Mesmer's complementary paradigm of alternate-consciousness (a term proposed by the psychotherapist Adam Crabtree [1993, 87–88]), this would result over the next century in no less than the bold claim of a scientific "proof" for a continued existence beyond the grave, a claim that would give hope of an afterlife for many thousands of spiritualists and other believers.

2

FRANZ ANTON MESMER
AND ANIMAL MAGNETISM

Autrefois Moliniste
Ensuite Janséniste
Puis Encyclopédiste
Et puis Economiste
A présent Mesmériste [1]

Over the early decades of the nineteenth century, the New Church based on Swedenborg's writings would grow increasingly critical of mesmerism, and later of spiritualism. This was partly because of Swedenborg's exclusive claim to illumination and his warnings of the dangers of unwanted influences from spirit intercourse. The popularized versions of animal magnetism (later known as mesmerism or simply magnetism) extant from the late eighteenth century both drew upon Swedenborg's writings and introduced new and, from a New Church perspective, dangerous innovations. This was one reason, as we shall see, that, in 1787, the Exegetic and Philanthropic Society in Stockholm established contact with the mesmeric harmonial societies. Around the same time, through the work of an Austrian doctor, Franz Anton Mesmer, a revolution was being inaugurated in current concepts of mind from which a psychological lineage can be traced that extends back to Paracelsus and forward to Sigmund Freud (1856–1939) and the psychotherapists. It was Mesmer

---

1. Formerly Molinist / Later Jansenist / Then Encyclopedist / And then Economist / Now Mesmerist. Quoted in Darnton 1970, 39.

who provided the other fundamental element, the paradigm of alternate-consciousness, in the gradual transformation from the covert Enlightenment to popular spiritualism.

Mesmer and Animal Magnetism

The pioneering historian of dynamic psychiatry Henri Ellenberger has compared Mesmer to Columbus: "Both men discovered a new world, both remained in error for the remainder of their lives about the real nature of their discoveries, and both died bitterly disappointed men" (1970, 57). Franz Anton Mesmer was born in 1734 in Iznang, Germany, son of the gamekeeper to the bishop of Constance. After making a start in theology and the law, Mesmer found his vocation in medicine, graduating from the University of Vienna in 1766, at the age of 33, with an M.D. dissertation titled "A Physical-Medical Treatise on the Influence of the Planets" upon human diseases (Crabtree 1985, 2). At a monastic school at Dilligen in Bavaria, where he studied philosophy for four years, Mesmer had gleaned from Descartes what was to be of immense importance to his later thought: the conviction that medicine could be turned into an exact science by extending cosmological laws to the physiology of the human body (Buranelli 1976, 31).

Setting up in private practice, and with the leisure to pursue research made possible by his fortunate marriage to the wealthy Maria Anna von Posh (b. 1724), ten years his senior, Mesmer soon became involved in "alternative" forms of cure that eschewed the heroic drugging, purgatives and bleeding then common to his profession (Darnton 1970, 15). He claimed instead to have discovered, or rather rediscovered, a universal fluid he called "animal magnetism," by which he believed he could cure most maladies that affect the nervous system (Crabtree 1985, 3). But he was no mystic; the purpose of Mesmer's dissertation on the influence of the planets upon the human body was to explain, in a strictly scientific manner, the specific effects of gravitation on human physiology. He posited forces that operate through a superfine universal fluid interpenetrating and surrounding all bodies, and he maintained that within this fluid all things are immersed as in a cosmic sea. According to

Franz Anton Mesmer and Animal Magnetism

Mesmer, animal magnetism was another of its aspects; and when stored in copious quantities within the physical organization of a healer and combined with a "crisis," this fluid could produce seemingly miraculous cures. Later he theorized further that the fluid must exist as the medium of gravity and that it provided an explanation also for magnetism, electricity, light, and heat (Buranelli 1976, 35; Darnton 1970, 3).

Theories about cosmic fluids and the use of magnets were not new; Plutarch (c. 46–after 119) records that Pyrrhus of Epirus (318–272 BCE) cured cases of colic by touching the sufferer with his big toe, and Paracelsus used magnets to concentrate healing properties on patients' cosmic fluid. In a later era, experiments by Franciscus Mercurius van Helmont (1614–1699) in Brussels and William Maxwell (fl. circa 1676) in England further elaborated the theory of a healing cosmic fluid. Indeed some of Mesmer's critics accused him of plagiarizing from Maxwell's work (Buranelli 1976, 20; Goldsmith 1934, 5). Two individuals were important to Mesmer's elaboration of the fluidic theory: the Jesuit astronomer with the unlikely name Father Maximilian Hell (1720–1792) and the Swabian faith healer and exorcist Johann Joseph Gassner (1727–1799). From the first, he learned of the influence of magnets, which he soon abandoned; from the second, he developed his theory of crises, which remain as Mesmer's specific legacy to psychology.

In 1773, Mesmer and Hell conducted a magnetic clinic (Darnton 1970, 47). The following year, drawing on their experiments Mesmer began treatment of Fraulein Francisca Oesterlin (b. 1746), a patient in her twenties suffering from a variety of ailments, including hysterical faints and trances. Mesmer induced an "artifical tide," whereby the patient was made to swallow an iron preparation as he attached magnets, one to her stomach, and two to her legs. Oesterlin soon felt the flow of a mysterious fluid through her body and eventually was reportedly cured; indeed, later she married into Mesmer's family. From these effects occurring first on July 28, 1774, an important date, Mesmer concluded that the cause could not have been the magnets alone but an "essentially different agent," the animal magnetism accumulated in his own person, the magnet being an auxiliary means of reinforcing the fluid and giving it a direction (Ellenberger 1970, 59).

Mesmer's curative regimen quickly abandoned the use of magnets for the "gaze" and the passes. Under Gassner's tutelage, Mesmer had found that he could cure disease by manipulating the fluid without magnets and that Gassner produced many of the same effects he had previously observed with Oesterlin (Darnton 1970, 48). Gassner would treat patients by means of exorcism, invoking the name of Jesus; if the condition grew worse, he would attribute its cause to demonic influence; but if no worsening of the condition occurred, he would conclude that the causes were physical and that he could do nothing further. His model was the "intrusion" paradigm, whereby external forces and entities are deemed responsible for disease (Ellenberger 1970, 57). The following year, 1775, they had a falling out, mainly because of Mesmer's rejection of faith in Jesus and his insistence that his cures were based on scientifically verifiable laws. Nevertheless, it seems clear that Mesmer adapted Gassner's methods in his evolving theory of crises.

Mesmer was an accomplished musician, and he delighted in the Viennese culture. He commissioned his friend, the young Wolfgang Amadeus Mozart (1756–1791) to write the opera *Bastien und Bastienna*, the first performance given at Mesmer's home in September 1768. Christoph Willibald Gluck (1714–1787) and Joseph Haydn (1732–1809) also came often to the fashionable house in the Landstrasse. In 1790, enjoying a mild jest at the expense of his old friend, Mozart put a direct reference to Mesmer in *Cosi fan Tutte* (Goldsmith 1934, 52; Buranelli 1976, 56).[2]

Mesmer's reputation for magical cures was growing rapidly. After a triumphant demonstration of his powers in Munich, Mesmer was elected a member of the Bavarian Academy of Sciences. Emboldened by his previous successes, he returned to Vienna where he endeavored to cure Fraulein Maria Theresa Paradies (b. 1759), a young musician who had been blind from the age of three.

---

2. "Despina, disguised as a doctor draws a huge magnet from under her robe and makes mysterious passes at Ferrand and Guglielmo, who are supposed to have swallowed poison out of unrequited love for Dorabella and Fiordiligi. The woodwinds sound their vibratory theme, which signifies the flow of animal magnetism from the magnet along the patients' nerves to the stricken area of their anatomy. The libretto was written by Lorenzo da Ponte: Here and there a touch/Of the magnet,/The stone of Mesmer,/Who was born and bred /In Germany,/And became so famous/In France." Quoted in Buranelli 1976, 56.

Franz Anton Mesmer and Animal Magnetism

Paradies, a gifted pianist, was born into a highly influential family. Her father was private secretary to the empress, her godmother, after whom she was named. Normal for her first three years, she awoke blind one morning. After repeated bleedings, purgings, and blisterings without success, in desperation her parents agreed to try Mesmer's cure (Buranelli 1976, 72). A few sessions of magnetic treatment partially restored her vision, but Mesmer's growing number of enemies pointed out that she could see only when Mesmer was present. This led to an acrimonious conflict with the medical faculty and the establishment of a commission in Vienna, whose conclusion was a denial of the reality of the cure. Paradies was taken off the treatment, partly it seems because the restoration of her sight might have meant the withdrawal of the pension the Empress Maria Theresa (1717–1780) had endowed upon her goddaughter. After this the young musician permanently lost her sight (Ellenberger 1970, 60). It was the first of Mesmer's many conflicts with medical officialdom. He now believed that the effects on his patients were produced by the force of the accumulated fluid in his own person, discharged with curative benefits according to the principles he had worked out regarding polarity and other factors. Oesterlin had been cured and married into Mesmer's family; the Paradies case was more problematic.

Henceforth, Mesmer devoted the best part of his life to "an earnest, passionate, often belligerent, and sometimes petulant campaign" to have his discovery recognized by the medical profession (Buranelli 1976, 39). Although his sincerity as physician was never in doubt, there was always more of the magus than the rational therapist about Mesmer, while his insistence on the physical nature of the alleged fluid drew accusations of materialism. An arrogant and opinionated man, throughout his life he "adhered with bulldog tenacity to a body of doctrine which changed but little, and then only in inessentials" (Gauld 1995, 16).

Paradoxically Mesmer's doctrine was based primarily on his intuition of being the bearer of a mysterious fluid, for which he devised rational theories to explain its nature and action. His true genius, however, lay in a recognition of what modern psychologists term the therapeutic benefits of "abreactive induction" in combating illness. The crises he induced, drawing on Gassner's methods and on analogies given by contemporary discoveries in the field of electricity by Luigi Galvani (1737–1798), Benjamin Franklin (1706–1790), and others, were in truth the beginning of psychotherapeutics; Henri Ellenberger and Robert Fuller have argued that his elaboration of crises constitutes the basis of their claims for Mesmer's ultimate significance as a pioneer of psychology (Ellenberger 1970, 63; Fuller 1982, 2 and passim).

In one of his early experiments, Mesmer invited the Dutch physician Jan Ingenhousz (1730–1799), the discoverer of photosynthesis, to observe Oesterlin. As she drank from a cup Mesmer had earlier magnetized with his finger, she suffered a fainting fit: ". . . then Mesmer pointed his finger dramatically at his patient lying there. She moved convulsively as if in great pain and arched her body . . . into a rigid position until he released her" (Buranelli 1976, 64). Ingerhousz was noncommittal, and he remained a skeptic. Buranelli (66) explains that Ingerhousz believed her reaction to have been not to the universal cosmic fluid, as Mesmer theorized, but to the power of suggestion, for Mesmer had unwittingly made a far more significant discovery: how to put a patient into a hypnotic trance. With this latter development, Mesmer's work transcended the physicalist assumptions with which he imbued his scientific practice and entered imperceptibly into the psychological, without his apparent realization of the subtle yet far-reaching implications this change in emphasis betokened (Buranelli, 72). Vincent Buranelli puts it best:

> Mesmer understood full well that his will dominated the will of the patient . . . Moreover, that the subject in trance could obey his commands because something deeper than ordinary consciousness was at work. He did not at once grasp the concept of the unconscious mind or realize that he was probing into deeply hidden parts of the psyche. Only after Mesmerism developed along unexpected lines, in his own hands and in those of his followers, did he comprehend the meaning of the trance. (115–116)

Mesmer understood the need to create a rapport with his patient, thus anticipating Freud and the psychoanalytic school; it is in this sense also that he was an unwitting contributor to psychology. However it would be left to his disciple, the Marquis de Puységur, to recognize the psychological nature and significance of these techniques. Alan Gauld has cautioned against "the urge to make a psychiatrist out of Mesmer," which in some writers is "so strong that they present him as someone whose psychological intuitions, though unformulated, were so powerful that they in fact guided the therapeutic procedures which he thought he was basing on quite other principles" (Gauld 1995, 16–17). Expelled from the Vienna medical faculty because of his rigid adherence to an idea, Mesmer left for Paris in 1778. It was now only five years since he had made his momentous discovery at the age of forty. If Mesmer was not a mystic, neither was he a materialist: "He felt the pulsations of the cosmic fluid, suffusing and uniting all things, especially all living things, and he felt it flow with peculiar strength through him. He knew the theory to be true, and facts, observations, cases were simply fitted to it" (Buranelli 1976, 92).[3]

Paris in the 1780s

When Mesmer arrived in Paris with much fanfare in February 1778, the High Enlightenment, with its ambience of discovery, was at its peak. Voltaire and Rousseau had both died that year, and Denis Diderot (1713–1784) had just published the final volume of the great *Encyclopédie*. Confidence in newness and discovery was everywhere; Laplace was pondering the origins of the solar system, the element oxygen had recently been discovered by the chemist Antoine Lavoisier (1743–1794), while

---

3. It seems that, on his way to Paris, Mesmer retreated into Nature to seek an answer to his many perplexities. For some three months, he wandered alone in a forest like a Rousseauite savage. Three years later, he would write concerning this event, "I felt closer to nature there. . . . O nature, I cried out in those paroxysms, what do you want of me?" In this inspired state, he managed to erase from his mind all ideas acquired from society, to think without using words "and to imbibe the pure philosophy of nature" (quoted in Darnton 1970, 117). Gradually his duty became clear–that he ought to share this momentous discovery of animal magnetism, and "pass on to humanity, in all the purity that I had received from Nature, the inestimable benefaction that I had in hand." In this interlude, if it was not mere mythologizing after the fact, we can see the influence of the natural philosophy and a religiosity based on the "Presences" more eloquently expressed in Wordsworth and Coleridge's *Lyrical Ballads* two decades later. At any rate, it puts pay to the notion that Mesmer was an unreconstructed materialist.

The Covert Enlightenment

George Buffon (1707–1788) was probing natural history and Joseph Lagrange (1736–1813) was working out his algebraic equations (Buranelli 1976, 92). Many reasons have been advanced as to why pre-Revolution Paris was receptive to Mesmer's ideas: a large, wealthy and indolent class of aristocrats, a current vogue of occultisms, the great prestige of science, along with a degree of intellectual freedom (Gauld 1995, 4). As Robert Darnton has eloquently observed, "In the 18th century, the view of literate Frenchmen opened upon a splendid, baroque universe, where their gaze rode on waves of invisible fluid into realms of infinite speculation" (1970, 44). Even Jean Sylvain Bailly (1736–1793), the author of a report condemning Mesmer, held embarrassingly similar theories (Darnton 1970, 38).[4] It was a time of great enterprise, and the shadow of the French Revolution was yet distant. Perhaps the current mania for flight contributed most to an environment favorable to the reception of Mesmer's ideas so quickly and comprehensively. If a man could fly like a bird, then all things became possible.

In June 1783, at a time when Mesmer enjoyed his greatest popularity, the Montgolfier brothers (Jacques-Etienne, 1745–1799; Joseph-Michel, 1740–1810) astounded cosmopolitan Paris by sending a balloon six thousand feet high. That August, Jacques Charles (1746–1823), pouring oil of vitriol over iron filings, held a hydrogen balloon aloft over the Champs de Mars for forty-five minutes (Lopez 1967, 215). Not to be outdone, the Montgolfiers, using a rarefied air balloon, then achieved the first manned flight on October 17, 1783; the balloonist François Pilâtre de Rozier (d. 1785), sitting in the attached wicker basket, offered two observations: "What a wondrous sight!" and "How priceless this would be during a battle" (Darnton 1970, 18; Lopez 1967, 217).

Preceded by a reputation for magical cures, along with the taint of occultism and the calumny of his erstwhile colleagues in newspapers, journals, and private letters, Mesmer set up a clinic at the Place Vendôme (Darnton 1970, 117). He was introduced to Parisian high society via the Comte Charles-Philippe D'Artois (1757–1836), younger brother of the

---

4. "Science had captivated Mesmer's contemporaries by revealing to them that they were surrounded by wonderful, invisible forces: Newton's gravity, made intelligible by Voltaire; Franklin's electricity, popularized by a fad for lightning rods. . . ." (Darnton 1970, 10).

king, probably through his personal physician Charles D'Eslon (1750–1786), an early convert to Mesmer's curative system (Darnton 1970, 48). With the benefit of these influential contacts, Mesmer acquired a thriving practice among the *noblesse* and the *haute bourgeoisie*.

By 1784, Mesmer's *séances* (literally, events, a term created by him that would assume varied meanings later) were so popular that they were now dramatically organized. He invented the *bacquet,* a circular oaken tub around which thirty or more seated persons could be magnetized simultaneously. By means of iron rods attached to a floor covered by powdered glass and iron filings, magnetism was conducted to the hands of patients who, linking thumbs and index fingers, were arranged in several rows around the bacquet:

> In subdued light, absolutely silent, they sat in concentric rows, bound to one another by a cord. Then Mesmer, wearing a coat of lilac silk, and carrying a long iron wand, walked up and down the crowd, touching the diseased parts of the patients' bodies. (Lopez 1967, 170–171)

Soft music was performed by pianoforte, armonica or wind instruments, in a richly carpeted salon decorated with elegant furniture and adorned with copious and strategically placed mirrors. Astrological symbols and the attending *valets toucheurs* in livery created a subdued effect, and all these together contributed to a hushed and expectant atmosphere as the cream of Paris society, resplendent in their powdered wigs, silks, and satin, awaited results. The master's iron wand augmented the mystery further. There was an adjoining mattress-lined "crisis room," and a separate *bacquet* was reserved for the lower classes, free of charge; but the majority of his patients came from among the nobility and the intelligentsia. Many of them, like the Marquis de Lafayette (1779–1849), not long returned from his triumphal support of the American revolutionists, became members of the Harmonial Society founded soon after to teach and promote Mesmer's system.

The Covert Enlightenment

Described as "a tall, handsome, imposing man," Mesmer would sometimes magnetize with his eyes, by fixing his gaze (Lopez 1967, 171; Darnton 1970, 8), or make use of the famous passes. Or he might lay his hand on the affected part, in a manner similar to the seventeenth-century Irish adept Valentine Greatrakes (1629–1683), who had cured the scientist Robert Boyle (1627–1691) and the poet Andrew Marvell (1621–1678) by "stroking with his hand the part affected, by which means the pain was gradually dislodged from the diseased part, and ultimately driven to the extremities . . . and so out of the body" (Podmore 1963, 1:48; Owen 1971, 170). Normally the work was done by his *valets toucheurs*, but with unusual or difficult cases Mesmer might place himself *en rapport* with a subject seated opposite, positioned foot against foot, and knee against knee (Lopez 1967, 171). To dislodge obstacles to the flow of the fluid, he focused his treatment at the poles of the small, natural magnets ostensibly located throughout the body, the most stable of these being in the nose and fingers. He carefully avoided the north pole at the top of the head, which he held to be the recipient of sidereal influence, along with the south poles at the feet, the natural receptors of terrestrial fluid (Darnton 1970, 4).

Mesmer was an "animal magnet." Often the mere proximity of the bewigged master's imperious gaze and potent finger might, by being directed at a patient, be sufficient to induce a trance-like state. This would evoke a "crisis," an emotional upheaval such as he had first observed in Gassner's patients; after this, a transformation might result with a temporary—and not infrequently a permanent—disappearance of symptoms. The Comtesse de la Malmaison was one aristocratic success story; having suffered paralysis from the waist down after falling out of her carriage, she recovered her health through Mesmer's therapy and produced a supportive testimonial. The crisis was specific; for instance, asthmatic or epileptic attacks when repeatedly provoked became less severe and would eventually disappear (Buranelli 1976, 107; Ellenberger 1970, 63). Viewed from a psychotherapeutic perspective, it is reasonable to infer that the emotional responses of patients to Mesmer constituted a form of "transference" relation (Owen 1971, 173). Insights like the influence of the physician on a patient, and the nonsomatic origins of many diseases belong to the later era of Jean Martin Charcot (1825–1893), Pierre Janet

(1859–1947), and Freud. But in Mesmer's era, these were still radical concepts.[5] While Mesmer himself concentrated on his physical fluid, his disciples Puységur, the Chevalier de Barberin, and Louis Claude de Saint-Martin (1743–1803) would open a whole new avenue of investigation that led straight to the unconscious, whereupon they believed they had discovered the soul.

Significantly, in consideration of the development of the complementary ontological paradigm I am proposing, not all crises took a violent form. They might develop into a deep sleep, while some claimed that this enabled communication with dead or distant spirits, who utilized the fluid to send messages directly to the patient's internal sixth sense (Darnton 1970, 6). Mesmer denied that there was anything supernatural about his cures, and he regarded these manifestations as minor epiphenomena of his curative techniques (Fuller 1982, 4). Indeed, Mesmer continued with great energy and resource, if some Teutonic arrogance, his endeavors to force acceptance of his discovery by the medical and scientific authorities. His system was a synthesis along rationalist lines, explicable not by "spiritual beings acting by arbitrary will," but by "effluences radiating under ascertainable laws" (Podmore 1963, 1:48).

Soon, however, the hostility of the Paris medical establishment, receiving negative reports from their Vienna colleagues, and the extreme popularity of his *bacquet* sessions brought a certain notoriety to Mesmer. To critics like the Baron Friedrich Melchior Grimm (1723–1807), his cures were simply "*la charlatanry du thaumaturge allemande*" (the charlatanery of German thaumaturgy) (Grimm 1830, tome X). He was suspected of simply putting older women to sleep and of inducing in the younger ones *titillations délicieuses*. Along with suspicions about mesmerism (as it was now being called) as sexual magic and as a threat to morality, the police became interested in the preponderance of political

---

5. In this regard, at least, the development of modern dynamic psychiatry can be legitimately traced to Mesmer and animal magnetism. A magnetizer is the therapeutic agent of cures; he or she needs to establish a rapport with the patient, and healing then occurs through crises. Most dramatic in the nineteenth century was the relation of hysteria, and the demonstrable curative power of hypnosis on hysterically-produced somatic symptoms, to such phenomena as "hysterical blindness" (Ellenberger 1970, 69).

radicals in the harmonial societies that had now spread to many provincial cities. A secret government report warned that several mesmerist pamphleteers were mixing radical political ideas with their pseudoscientific discourses (Darnton 1970, 52, 62). Mesmer became embroiled in a bitter quarrel with D'Eslon, his erstwhile supporter, which led Nicholas Bergasse (1750–1832) and others to seek to protect these "secret" teachings from the vulgar through the formation of harmonial societies, where a stiff subscription fee and grades of initiation ensured their exclusiveness. Jacques Mallet du Pan (1749–1800) complained that "*une foule des gens de tout état . . . se presentent journellement avec des merveilles de toute espèce*" (a great mass of people of all classes . . . present themselves daily to experience all sorts of marvels) (Darnton 1970, 27). Among Mesmer's early supporters was the venerable Protestant theologian and freemason Antoine Court de Gébelin (1725–1784), author of *Le Monde Primitif,* an erudite search through ancient languages for traces of lost primitive sciences. It was de Gébelin who had presented the tarot, a French invention, as an occult device to the public. Unfortunately for Mesmer's reputation, de Gébelin died while receiving treatment in a mesmerist *bacquet* (McIntosh 1975, 12; Darnton 1970, 38, 116).[6]

The scientific rationale for Mesmer's praxis was now threefold: the dislodgement of blockages, somewhat like the Chinese concept of *chi*; the replenishment from his own ample store of the magnetic fluid; and the inducement of crises. This last feature would, in a therapeutic sense, long outlive Mesmer's other ideas about fluids and the like. In a *Memoire*, Mesmer explained that "Animal Magnetism is a fluid universally diffused; it is the medium of a mutual influence between the heavenly bodies, the earth, and animated bodies. . . . [E]verywhere it continues, so as to leave no void; its subtlety admits of no comparison." To explain the existence of this fluid, which is invisible and has no interstices, he used the analogy of fish, "who would protest against the one among them who tells them that the space between the bottom and the surface of the sea is filled by a fluid in which they live" (Mesmer 1957, 11). Mesmer also compared magnetism's

---

6. Gebelin's *Le Monde Primitif* (1773) was a dictionary that examined nouns, verbs, and adjectives from Chinese, Hebrew, Greek, and Latin. There is also a lengthy section on the Eleusinian mystery cult, drawing similarities with modern Masonry (Weisberger 1993, 100).

relation to the bodily organs, as the wind is to the windmill. Animal magnetism served to galvanize the organs so as to push the fluid through the neural channels—hence, the need for a crisis (McIntosh 1975, 33; Buranelli 1976, 107).

Perhaps the greatest perceived threat to officialdom in Mesmer's hugely popular *bacquet* sessions was his notion of physical causation. Mesmer's claims were nothing if not grandiose. Taking his lead from Newton, who had spoken of an ether, a "most subtle spirit which pervades and lies hid in all gross bodies" (Darnton 1970, 11), Mesmer held that, in the elaboration of his curative technique, he had at last come upon that primordial ether, the gossamer medium through which sensations of every kind, such as light, heat, magnetism, and electricity, were able to pass from one physical object to another (Ellenberger 1970, 59). In his 1799 *Memoire*, Mesmer staked his large claim: "I dare to flatter myself that the discoveries I have made will push back the boundaries of our knowledge of physics as did the invention of microscopes and telescopes for the age preceding our own" (1957, 22; Gauld 1995, 11). If a magnetic fluid could be transmitted between humans, then the possibilities of other unrecognized forces or fluids were also opened up—hence this continuing paradox where the magician and the scientist lived in apparent harmony.

The 1784 Commissions

Throughout the early 1780s, the mesmerists enjoyed a high public profile. Queen Marie-Antoinette (1755–1793) became interested, probably through her courtier the Comte Louis Ségur (1753–1830), a member of the Harmonial Society. At the urging of convinced mesmerist courtiers like Princesse Marie Thérèse de Lamballe (1749–1792) and the Duchesse Marie-Louis de Chaulnes (1718–1787), she offered Mesmer an annual pension of 20,000 livres, plus 10,000 for the rent of a building to house a school of animal magnetism. In return, he would accept three pupils named by the government. Mesmer turned down the offer in high dudgeon, among his objections being what he interpreted as the surveillance of government "pupils" to be forced upon him. He insisted on official endorsement and a free hand to choose his own pupils. This ended the affair, and a vaguely insulting letter to the queen, lecturing her on the "austerity of my principles" concluded the interest of the French aristocracy in Mesmer and his theories (Buranelli 1976, 138).

Over these years, mesmerism was "debated and investigated, . . . ridiculed several times on the stage, burlesqued in popular songs, doggerels and cartoons, practiced in a network of masonic-like secret societies, and publicized by a flood of pamphlets and books" (Darnton 1970, 40–41, 51). Claude-Anne Lopez, in her biography of Benjamin Franklin, has exactly caught the mood of Paris in 1784:

> The issue which was agitating the minds of Parisians in 1784, dividing them into quarreling factions [was] whether Mesmer was a genius or a quack. A genius, proclaimed such a blue-blood as the Comte D'Artois; a benefactor of mankind, insisted such a hero as Lafayette; a saint, said the throngs of people who crowded his clinics or obtained initiation, at a price, into his secret societies. An impostor, maintained the respected Lavoisier; a charlatan, declared the majority of Parisian doctors; a threat to decency and public order, grumbled the more conservatively inclined. (1967, 168–169)

After only five years, Mesmer's clinic in Paris was attracting a great deal of attention, not all of it favorable. In 1784, two commissions were established by the government of Louis XVI (1754–1793) to investigate Mesmer's cures and to test the efficacy of his new "fluid." The eminent Benjamin Franklin, oracle on electricity and ambassador from the American republic to the French court, was asked to serve on the first commission, where he threw his considerable status as scientist behind a rejection of Mesmer's claims to have discovered a new fluid. There is a certain irony in that this "tradesman in the Age of Reason" and recent leader of a revolution, while striking a blow against what he believed to be mere superstition, was probably also helping to put an arresting constraint on a potentially dangerous political movement (Wright 1986, 325–326). Among Mesmer's early partisans were several future leaders of the French Revolution such as Lafayette, Jean-Louis Carra (1743–1793), and

Franz Anton Mesmer and Animal Magnetism

Nicholas Bergasse. The appeal of Mesmer's universal fluid to radicals was firstly in its democratic implications and its ready "scientific" political theory, while it served also as a weapon against the medical establishment (Darnton 1970, 164). Before long, through the efforts of the energetic lawyer Bergasse, harmonial societies were being established in Paris and other cities. There these future *revolutionnaires* "perceived their own insides while in somnambulist trances . . . and the means and date of their recovery while ill" (Darnton 1970, 45). Bergasse also had mixed motives, including a need for public recognition. Along with Francois Jean Chastellux (1734–1788), Guillaume Kornmann, Jean-François Duport (1759–1798), Jean-Jacques d'Eprémesnil (1745–1794), and others, he soon seceded from the society; they now called themselves political mesmerists and were soon joined by Jacques Pierre Brissot (1754–1793), future leader of the Girondins (Darnton 1970, 54; Buranelli 1976, 177).

Nor was Mesmer the only topic of controversy. In England, there were numerous freemasonic and other channels to provide a ready conduit for fructifying heterodoxies, which created an atmosphere favorable to Swedenborg's teachings. In France, the pervasive influence of the Catholic Church meant that freemasonry and other deviations from orthodoxy remained the province of the wealthy, while the 1738 papal bull condemning freemasonry made it even more attractive to the privileged classes, who dominated its leadership (Bullock 1996, 46).

Until the Revolution, Paris was the mecca of the marvelous in eighteenth-century Europe (Darnton 1970, 47; Garrett 1975, 155). This was where Count Allesandro Cagliostro (1743–1795), originally Giuseppe Balsamo from Palermo, who had given himself a title, apparently enjoyed some genuine success as a faith healer. Entering in flowing robes and a tall turban, he would use a piercing glance and gaze into crystal balls. Like Faust, he believed that he could summon beings from the nether world, and he was the founder in France of the Council of Egyptian masonry. Giovanni Casanova (1725–1789) was another wandering occultist, as was the alchemist the Comte de Saint Germain (d. 1784), engravings of whom were hawked on Paris streets (Buranelli 1976, 130). Saint Germain also awarded himself a title, and as he traveled through Europe, trailing debts that remained unpaid, rumors abounded that he could restore youth through a magical elixir. He persuaded Madame de Pompadour (1721–1764), Louis XV's mistress, about his elixir of youth, and he was given a laboratory and pension; but having produced neither elixir nor gold, he was eventually discovered as a fraud. He continued his travels and died in Germany in 1784. As the *Journal de Bruxelles* commented with evident disdain, there was then in Paris a plethora of "hermetic, cabalistic, and theosophic philosophers, propagating fanatically all the old absurdities of theurgy, of divination, of astrology etc." (Darnton 1970, 33). The Comtesse d'Houdetot (Elizabeth Françoise de Bellegarde, 1730–1813) wrote to the elderly Benjamin Franklin about Mesmer's cures that "Versailles is buzzing with this miracle" (Lopez 1967, 173).

Benjamin Franklin, then aged 78 years, was in the twilight of a brilliant and varied career as scientist, inventor, and statesman. From 1778 he did considerable work in cementing the crucial relationship between the American revolutionary elite and their French allies. He found time also to imbibe French aristocratic culture, making a variety of useful contacts and pleasant liaisons. He moved in a rarefied world, a member of the circle of the philosopher Hélvétius (1715–1771), where he became intimate with the leading figures of the High Enlightenment, who regarded him as a sort of rustic philosopher from the American frontier. Franklin was also *vénérable*, or grand master, of the Masonic Lodge of the Nine Sisters. Founded in 1776 to foster the study of the arts and sciences, it was in this lodge that in 1778 Franklin led the aged Voltaire to his initiation (Weisberger 1993, 5; Lopez 1967, 249; Bullock 1996, 36, n. 61).

Franklin and Mesmer met at least once, ostensibly for musical rather than scientific purposes. Franklin had been partly responsible for the invention of the glass armonica, on which Mesmer was an acknowledged virtuoso.[7] In 1779, Franklin with bluestocking friend Mme. Anne Louise Brillon de Jouy (1744–1824) paid Mesmer a visit, but they became somewhat uncomfortable as their host promoted his medical theories,

---

7. The armonica consisted of several glasses blown in the shape of hemispheres, with 3-inch to 9-inch diameters, and an iron spindle passing through holes in the middle of each glass. Sitting before the instrument, the player revolved the spindle with a treadle like that on a spinning wheel and touched the edges of the moving glasses with his fingers to produce different pitches of sound (Lopez 1967, 22).

while his guests attempted to keep the conversation on music. Mme. Brillon, herself a musician and fond of speculating on heaven, wrote to Franklin that "in heaven, Me Mesmer will content himself with playing the armonica and will not bother us with his electrical fluid!" (Lopez 1967, 170).

The Franklin commission was charged with assessing the curative efficacy of Mesmer's techniques, while the *Societé Royale* was to test the hypothesis of a new fluid. The participation of distinguished scientists like the astronomer Bailly and the chemist Lavoisier attests to the degree of controversy Mesmer had aroused at the highest levels of French society (Fuller 1982, 7; Ellenberger 1970, 65). With the revolution, tragedy would befall these members of the commission, who both perished at the guillotine, while ironically another member, Dr. Joseph-Ignace Guillotin (1738–1814), barely escaped the instrument bearing his name, which he had earlier promoted as the most humane form of execution.[8] Political mesmerists like Brissot and D'Eprémesnil were also beheaded, while out of disgust, Lafayette deserted to the enemy Prussians and Austrians when the revolution soon lurched toward the *Terreur*.

The Franklin commission worked with Dr. Charles-Nicholas D'Eslon (1750–1786), since Mesmer himself declined to participate, refusing to reveal the secrets of his system now protected by graded initiations. He felt also, probably with justification, that the commission was greatly biased against him. A defiant letter from Mesmer warned Franklin that "whatever the test, Monsieur, like you, I have the world for a judge, and while they may forget the good I have done and prevent the good I wish to do, I will be vindicated by posterity" (Buranelli 1976, 167). At Franklin's estate at Plessy, tests were carried out by Franklin, Lavoisier, and others. D'Eslon, representing the *Faculté de Médecine*, brought forward a magnetic subject, a twelve-year-old boy, to be experimented upon. A certain tree on the estate had earlier been magnetized by D'Eslon, and now the "boy sensitive" with eyes bandaged was asked to find this tree. After feeling varying sensations near several trees, he fainted at the foot of the wrong (unmagnetized) tree,

---

8. Though not its inventor, he was linked to the apparatus that bears his name since, as a humanitarian, he advocated its use as less barbarous than the hatchet (Lopez 1967, 171; Buranelli 1976, 183).

some twenty-eight meters away. The experimenters also tricked sensitives by giving them ordinary water, supposedly magnetized beforehand, and observed as the subjects fell into the expected crises. The commissions did show bias, and they ignored hundreds of claims to cures effected through the employment of Mesmer's methods (Darnton 1970, 64). They concluded that the magnetic fluid as such did not exist and that the convulsions to which patients fell prey were the products of overactive imaginations. Unfortunately, as Robert Fuller notes, they did not pause to reflect upon just what a wondrous faculty the mesmerists had shown the imagination to be (Fuller 1982, 8).[9]

Twenty thousand copies of the Franklin report were published and eagerly received. Thomas Jefferson (1743–1826), who had just taken over Franklin's ambassadorial role in France, noted with satisfaction in his February 1785 journal: "Animal Magnetism dead, ridiculed" (Lopez 1967, 174; Darnton 1970, 66). Yet despite the ritual humiliation suffered by Mesmer at the hands of officialdom, numerous others in Paris and throughout the provinces remained deeply interested, and some used mesmerism as a stepping stone to more mystical speculations. *Les Illuminés*, a play staged in 1788, defends mesmerism: "It is the true system of the Universe, the mover of all things" (Darnton, 38). The legal philosopher Joseph-Michel-Antoine Servan (1737–1807), a friend of Voltaire and Buffon, had been amazed by the balloon flights, but "never have the effects of mesmerism struck me so. . . . [I]t speaks to me Mesmer's language about nature, and I listen to it with ravishment" (Darnton, 60).

Part of Mesmer's appeal was that his doctrine could harmonize with a variety of outlooks. He presented his theory as "the remnant of a primitively recognized truth" (Darnton 1970, 117) and, paradoxically,

---

9. The aged Franklin's own attitude to marvels can be gauged by the trick he played when out walking on a stormy English day in 1772, as a guest of Lord Shelbourne. He boasted that he could quiet the waters in the stream that coursed through the estate; and walking ahead some 200 paces, he "made sweeping passes over the water with his bamboo cane. To the astonishment of his companions, the stream became as smooth as a mirror. Franklin then revealed that he had concealed in the hollow cane enough oil to do the trick" (Wright 1986, 7). Franklin's opinion of Mesmer was clearly unfavorable; in a letter he notes dryly, "[I]f these people can be persuaded to forbear their drugs in expectation of being cured by only the physician's finger or an iron rod pointing at them, they may possibly find good effects tho' they mistake the cause"(Lopez 1967, 172).

also as an exercise in Newtonian physics. Having refused the queen's offer of a clinic and a life pension and having been rejected once again by the medical and scientific establishment, Mesmer was now an embittered man, a *philosophe manqué*. He left Paris for the shores of his native Lake Constance around 1785, never to return. He lived until 1815, propounding what he still regarded as his great discovery. Mesmer never achieved the recognition in scientific circles that he believed his discovery merited. In these, its first stages, mesmerism expressed the Enlightenment's faith in reason taken to an extreme. Later this provoked a movement toward the opposite extreme in the form of romanticism (Darnton 1970, 39). For the moment, the fortunes of animal magnetism took a decided turn with the practice of his disciple the Marquis de Puységur.

Mesmerism and Somnambulism

In the wake of Mesmer's disputes with d'Eslon regarding the ownership and completeness of the therapeutic system of which he claimed to be the sole originator, Nicholas Bergasse had founded the *Societé de l'Harmonie Universelle* at Paris. Bergasse, a lawyer from Lyon, was a political activist and vague theorist who dreamt of regenerating humanity by applying Rousseau's concept of "nature" into the spheres of government, society, and education. In the early 1770s, along with his brother, he had been a member of the mystical Catholic masonic lodge *Les Amis de la Vérité* [The Friends of Truth] at Lyon (Garrett 1975, 26). After being cured of a pathological depression by Mesmer, Bergasse became convinced that this was the key to his Rousseauist paradise (Buranelli 1976, 147). In May 1789, he was elected a deputy of the Third Estate to the *Estates Général* at Versailles, where he would demand the eradication of aristocratic privileges.

Before a further split which sent him and others like Lafayette in a more political direction, Bergasse did most of the teaching at the *Societé*.[10]

---

10. A further split occurred in mid-1785 when Bergasse and Kornmann were ejected from the harmonial lodge and established a political group including Lafayette, d'Eprémesnil, Sabathier, and Brissot (Darnton 1970, 78).

Reflecting the vogue of illuminism and religious mysticism that was partly a reaction against atheistic rationalism, he taught paid-up initiates in kabbalistic signs, symbols of the pure doctrine Mesmer claimed had been communicated to him during a fabled three-month retreat in the wilderness prior to descending on Paris and following his humiliation at the hands of the Vienna faculty; this aspect of the magus seems to have been reserved for his entourage in the *Societé Harmonique*, whose specific aim was to counter D'Eslon and other "traitors," so as to protect their master's esoteric system (Darnton 1970, 115).[11]

A strange mixture of business enterprise, private school, and Masonic lodge, the harmonial societies thrived in their pre-Revolution heyday, in Paris and in around twenty-four provincial centers (Ellenberger 1970, 65). There were harmonial societies also in Turin, Berne, and Malta; and a society was founded in the French West Indies by Puységur's brother (Nelson 1969, 50). The most influential provincial lodges were at Strasbourg, where the Marquis de Puységur was the leading figure, and at Lyon, where Jean-Baptiste Willermoz (1730–1824) and the Chevalier de Barberin promoted mesmerism, together with a *mélange* of Masonic and mystical tenets. Entrance fees were stiff, and new members had to pledge clean living and abstinence from tobacco, as Mesmer taught that snuff upset the nose's magnetic balance (Lopez 1967, 173; Darnton 1970, 4). By 1789, the Paris society had 430 members, many of whom were of eminent birth, including a number of powerful aristocrats. Among the forty-eight gentlemen were such luminaries as the Duc de Lauzun (Armand-Louis de Gontaut Biron, 1747–1793) and the Comte de Ségur, the Baron de Talleyrand, brother of the statesman, along with a number of doctors, bankers, merchants, and clergymen. At the close of their initiation, acolytes were placed *en rapport* with the director of the ceremony, who embraced them, saying "*Allez, touchez, guérissez*": "Go, touch, heal" (Darnton 1970, 74–76).

The phenomena of magnetic sleep provided the common ground between explorations of consciousness and explorations of invisible

---

11. Charles D'Eslon's star fell dramatically, from being *médecin* to the Comte d'Artois, to being struck off the *Faculté's* roll for supporting Mesmer. In another sense, he was perhaps the first martyr for the cause since in August 1786, like Gébelin, he died while being mesmerized (Darnton 1970, 48).

realms, both central concerns of the covert Enlightenment. While the framework was understood as being essentially physiological, it had been assumed that the observed somnambulistic phenomena were related to the passage of the "fluid," or the "nerve fluid" as it was known in later formulations, that awakened an "internal sense." The subtle fluid to which this sense responds produced a "critical sleep"; and because it had complete extension, it could project to any distance, thus also becoming the conduit of "rapport," occasioned by a merging of fluids between magnetizer and subject (Crabtree 1993, 65). But this could not adequately explain the deeper states, when mesmerized subjects claimed the ability to see inside their own bodies and those of others and to prognosticate the path and resolution of ailments. More spectacularly, some so-called "sensitives" claimed that, on occasion, they would traverse to distant places, describing with uncanny accuracy places they had never visited in the body, foretelling future events, and relating accurately past events unknown to them in the normal state; at times, some even claimed to communicate with departed spirits and angels (Crabtree 1985, 17). While the induction of an artificial somnambulic state and the crisis were probably Mesmer's most important contributions, credit for the recognition of the psychological basis of these practices and their therapeutic elaboration belongs to Puységur. He took magnetic healing in a wholly new direction, one leading straight to the subconscious mind (Fuller 1982, 10).[12]

Armand Jacques Marc de Chastenet, Marquis de Puységur, was the scion of an ancient aristocratic family. He had served with distinction as an artillery officer in the French army and was involved in the siege of Gibraltar (Crabtree 1985, 4). Following his discharge, he came to Paris where he joined Mesmer's Harmonial Society. It was only when he returned to his family estate at Buzancy and began applying Mesmer's techniques that Puységur accidentally made a discovery that would have

---

12. Mesmer referred to the phenomenon of artificial or induced somnambulism as "critical sleep," related to an "internal sense," a human species of instinct most awake when the reason is dormant and thus the five senses are not in the forefront. He explained that it is this internal sense that enables *somnambules* to perceive the nature of a disease and is the basis also of rapport, since the subtle fluid to which this internal sense responds can extend any distance, and may thereby provide a conduit for the "merging" of fluids between the magnetizer and subject. But he insisted that it was not occult (Crabtree 1993, 65, 67).

stupendous importance both in the short term for the fortunes of the covert Enlightenment and in the long term for the study of the human mind.

A.L. de Jussieu (1748–1836), a dissenting member of the 1784 commission, was perhaps the first to record his observations of certain puzzling phenomena, which Mesmer and his early disciples attributed simply to side effects of the induced crisis (Podmore 1963, 1:56). While treating Victor Race (1760–c. 1818), a young shepherd on his estate who suffered with a chronic chest infection, Puységur stumbled upon some of the same phenomena noted by Jussieu. Attempting to induce a crisis in Victor, he found instead that the young servant went into a "lucid slumber," a hypnotic somnambulism followed by amnesia of these events. He could not wake Race, who in this state would stand, sing, or dance as ordered, or perform the simulated movements of the hunt when this was suggested to him (Owen 1971, 174; Crabtree 1985, 4). Having faithfully applied Mesmer's techniques only to have his patients fall into unusual, sleeplike states of consciousness, Puységur took the matter further. He found that in this state subjects were not only malleable to suggestions, but that they could also perform spontaneous feats of thought reading, clairvoyance, and precognition (Fuller 1986, 30; Podmore 1963, 1:60). More intriguing still, when in a somnambulistic trance, Victor was far brighter than in the waking state, able to diagnose his own disease, to foresee its course and prescribe a regimen of treatment, which in his case led to a full recovery. Eventually Puységur concluded that the real agent in the cure was the magnetizer's will. He carried out further tests on Victor and other peasants from surrounding estates, with often similar results (Ellenberger 1970, 102, 189).

Puységur called the new phenomenon "magnetic sleep"; its most important aspects were mental rapport and the existence of a separate chain of memories for both waking and magnetic states. Soon this was compared to the suggestible state of sleepwalking and became known as induced or "artificial somnambulism." It seemed he had uncovered a new order of vision (Crabtree 1985, 5, 17). In rare instances, a state of ecstasy was achieved, in which state the inhabitants of sublime realms were revealed. Thus, Puységur's discovery had implications both spiritual and psychological; he had in truth unearthed the subconscious mind, and he became among the first to recognize at least two levels of consciousness existing within human beings. Imbued with the beliefs and assumptions of his era, he believed he had discovered the soul (Ellenberger 1970, 119; Crabtree 1993, 67).

As a psychological phenomenon, artificial somnambulism was enthusiastically appropriated in the provinces, but not by Mesmer, who saw it as a danger to his precious theories. When Puységur brought Victor Race to Paris to demonstrate these new wonders, the master showed little interest (Gauld 1995, 43). Puységur still held to the theory of a sensible fluid, but seen now in psychological rather than physicalist terms: through the establishment of "rapport" between magnetizer and patient and the resultant mingling of fluids in a conjoint circulation, the will of the operator was able to control the phenomena; "*Croyez et veuillez*" are the key words, said Puységur: "believe and will" (Gauld, 47).[13] How much in these cures still depended on the physical rejuvenation afforded by animal magnetism is a moot point. Puységur concluded that "animal magnetism lies not in the action of one body upon another, but in the action of the thought upon the vital principle of the body" (Fuller 1982, 11). For him these remarkable phenomena implied psychological rather than physical causality. It was a *power* transferred from the robust to the ailing, which had the significant effect of controlling the will of the magnetized subject. As we shall see, it was this aspect that worried the ever free-willing Swedenborgians of the Exegetic and Philanthropic Society, who as moralists were concerned, as the medical establishment would continue to be, about the possibilities of abuse from such a degree of control over the minds of subjects.

However, the immediate ramifications of Puységur's discovery would be to change the praxis of mesmerists and even the focus from curative techniques to the exploration of the somnambulistic states as ends in themselves, so as to glean spiritual insights. How this new emphasis came about can be gauged somewhat through the activities of the provincial

---

13. There was a magnetic effluence from the sun, and yet another, differing in glory, from the earth, which Puységur identified with the "dephlogisticated air" given out by plants under the rays of the sun (Podmore 1963, 1:62) .

harmonial societies and similar gatherings in France and throughout Europe. In their dissemination of Puységur's insights, which occurred rapidly, the various freemasonic societies with which the harmonial lodges were loosely connected, often with the same persons participating in both, had an undoubted role. Not only were these new manifestations drawing attention away from the cure of disease, but the very concept of an universal fluid was being challenged by some of Mesmer's own disciples.

Artificial somnambulism or magnetic sleep (or simply magnetism) encouraged an approach based upon a belief in the psychogenesis of many conditions, relying on the rapport between hypnotist and patient as therapeutic channel. In time, magnetism revolutionized psychology and psychosomatic medicine, but this became possible only when the fluidic theory was abandoned. The insight that unknown psychological forces were at work and the induction of the trance states of magnetic sleep to explore unknown psychic functions as well as to serve therapeutic ends heralded a sea change in the practice of numbers of mesmerists (Ellenberger 1970, vii, 102; Buranelli 1976, 105). At the Lyon society, the Chevalier de Barberin dispensed with any material sort of fluid. Extending the notion of rapport, he diagnosed by "feeling" patients' diseased states within himself and prescribing accordingly. Religious mysticism

> had flowed through the age of reason, from the convulsionaries to the mesmerists, like an underground stream. When it broke through to the surface after 1789, it had been swollen by Swedenborgianism, martinism, Rosicrucianism, alchemy, physiognomy, and many other currents of spiritualism; but the mesmerist current was one of the most powerful . . . in the transition from the Enlightenment to romanticism. (Darnton 1970, 127)

Thus by 1789, an eclectic, spiritualistic form of mesmerism was established and was rapidly spreading throughout Europe. Mesmer's ideas "had escaped his control and had run wildly through supernatural regions where he believed they had no business" (Darnton 1970, 71). It was during this next phase—the transformation from Enlightenment speculations to the fantastic and overarching romantic vision of a world soul and other effluviae—that another close link was provided with Swedenborgian concepts and from which can be discerned the logical connection between fluidic therapeutics and supernatural manifestations. Rather than being the mere side effects of a rationally applied fluid, the new manifestations themselves slowly emerged as the central focus of experimental psychology for at least a generation. From the 1850s, James Braid (1796–1860), James Eisdale (1808–1859) and others would begin to refer to these phenomena as hypnosis. In this transition, a major aftermath of the covert Enlightenment, the work of the Marquis de Puységur was to be of incalculable importance.

3

THE MARQUIS DE PUYSÉGUR: THE ALTERNATE-CONSCIOUSNESS PARADIGM

Dieu seul sait mes tourments et mes inquiétudes,
Le but mysterieux de mes jeunes études.
Tout jeune, j'ai cherché sur les pas de Mesmer
A sonder le sommeil, cette profonde mer.

Alphonse Esquiros, *Chants d'un prisonnier* (1841)

(God alone knows my torments and my anxieties
the mysterious aim of my youthful studies.
As a young man, I sought, following Mesmer,
To plumb the unfathomable sea of sleep.)

Mesmer and Puységur

We now leave the urbane world of Mesmer and his direct cohort for the French provinces, where a third interrelated development arose in the covert Enlightenment with the organization of various quasi-Masonic societies during the 1780s and 1790s. Their conceptions were liberally adapted from the current vogue for Swedenborg and a host of other mystical systems. It was the first grand conjunction of Mesmer and Swedenborg's systems in Europe that was also to have important ramifications for the development of alternative realities in England and in the New World.

The three major trends of the covert Enlightenment were the recovery of ancient knowledge, the millenarian imperative, and the alleged contact with a higher reality. To each of these trends, the insights and teachings of Swedenborg and Mesmer contributed significantly. Swedenborg's works contain an elaborate exposition of the history of the churches seen in relation to the revelation Swedenborg claimed to have brought to humanity. As was discussed previously, he taught that an "internal" millennium had arrived in 1757, that it was a second coming taking the form of a deeper penetration of the Word through the science of correspondences, with a new theology based on the ineluctable moral and spiritual influence of the spirit and angelic realms upon human beings.

Mesmer avowed that in animal magnetism he had rediscovered an ancient form of healing long abandoned, but he insisted on its physical provenance. The occult implications of his discovery constituted Mesmer's indirect contribution to the covert Enlightenment, mainly through others, in the fresh application of his theory of crises. First his disciple the Marquis de Puységur and then a multitude of mesmerists and occultists extended the practice; their manipulation of somnambulistic phenomena went beyond a therapeutic technique, rapidly evolving into a vehicle for communication with a higher reality or realities. Thus within European high culture, the concepts of both these Enlightenment thinkers were perceived as being interrelated and were to assume vast significance in the broader atmosphere of cultural debate.

In the efforts of Saint-Martin, Willermoz, Barberin, and others in the French provinces, where, after Mesmer's departure from Paris, the movement thrived until the revolution, the fluidic theory began to decline in popularity. Medical historians like Ellenberger and Crabtree have recognized in Puységur's activities the advent of the first dynamic psychiatry, whose basic features were the use of hypnotic trance as an approach to the subconscious, based on the evolving concept of a dual model of the mind comprising a conscious and an unconscious ego. Of especial importance was the impetus that artificial somnambulism gave during the 1780s to these emerging views of the mind and its modalities of consciousness. France was then the center for such interests, and in addition to the existing Societies of Harmony, specific magnetic societies were formed in Paris, Rennes, Troyes, Caen, and Rheims. Apart from disputes over the reality or otherwise of the phenomena, "a second consciousness had been discovered—a consciousness with properties very different from ordinary waking consciousness. Puységur had discovered it and the later magnetizers confirmed it" (Crabtree, 1985, 20; see also Owen 1971, 175).

In the long term, as Crabtree asserts, the alternate-consciousness paradigm did make it possible "to conceive of a subconscious or unconscious life in human beings and thereby provided the foundation for all modern psychotherapies that recognize the existence of a hidden arena of dynamic mental activity" (Crabtree 1993, 88). With the hiatus of the French Revolution and the changing focus of the magnetizers toward metaphysical enquiries, these new discoveries were being channeled in somewhat different directions, reflecting the altered priorities of the troubled 1790's decade throughout Europe. Along with the proliferation of interest in mesmerism and the brief period of wide exposure afforded through the harmonial societies, something new was occurring: a noticeable shift from animal magnetism as curative panacea to the new phenomenon of somnambulism as a means of divination and spiritual communication. Darnton thus expresses the changing focus of mesmerism: "As the Revolution approached, mesmerists tended increasingly to neglect the sick in order to decipher hieroglyphics, manipulate magic numbers, [and] communicate with spirits" (1970, 70).

Strasbourg and Lyon

The most successful of the provincial harmonial lodges, the *Societé Harmonique des Amis Réunis* at Strasbourg, was founded by Puységur with some of his former army colleagues. Enjoying the protection of authorities who were also participants, the Strasbourg society became an *entrepôt* for other forms of heterodoxy, especially German mysticism, which poured into France prior to the revolution. As Swedenborg's teachings were spreading in England during the 1770s and 1780s, his ideas were propagandized in Germany via translations of his works by Immanuel Tafel (1796–1863) and F. C. Oetinger. A disciple also of the mystic philosophy of Jacob Boëhme, Oetinger suffered persecution for his radical theological views. At the same time, Jacques Cazotte (1719–1792) was spreading German mystical doctrines in France (Gauld 1995, 145; Block 1984, 56; Darnton 1970, 70).

At Strasbourg and Lyon especially, new associations were being made between the harmonial lodges and other Masonic and occult societies.

Many of these have not survived in historical memory, but one may glean their current import, for instance, in a letter from Thomas Duché (d. circa 1789) to his father in England, written during a six-month tour of the continent, that he had found "great Openings of this Kingdom everywhere unconfined to any religious Sects and Denominations" (Garrett, 1984, 76). Around the same time, the egregious Count Tadeusz Leszczy Grabianka (1740–1807) was visiting many societies in England and on the Continent, including Jacob Duché's Swedenborgian group in London, to gather like-minded acolytes for what he believed was the advent of the millennium.

By 1789, the city of Strasbourg, situated on the Rhine border, with a population of fifty thousand supported some twenty-nine Masonic lodges, counting 1,500 members. Strasbourg was a connective link between orthodox Paris Grand Orient freemasonry and the more mystical German versions extant in Berlin and Vienna. Some lodges drew their membership from specific professions, like medicine or the arts; there existed a few Protestant lodges, but most Masonic fraternities were Catholic. Lodges were also divided along class lines, being predominantly bourgeois or aristocratic. *La Candeur* (Honesty) was the most eminent of the Strasbourg lodges, conservative, Catholic, and exclusively aristocratic (Jacob 1991, 186, 181). At *La Candeur*, members like Friedrich Rodolphe Saltzmann (1769–1845), who also participated in Willermoz's various mesmeric and masonic organizations in Lyon, were intent upon reforming the Catholic Church. These reformers held gatherings with, among others, Count Cagliostro. A mystical freemason and a Catholic, he was known to hold séances with Cardinal Louis Rohan (1734–1803) in these lodges during the 1780s in a search for regeneration of the Church, a term loosely adapted from Swedenborgian theology. Cagliostro set himself up as high priest of the Temple of Isis, on the Rue de la Sondière in Paris. He was later arrested by the Inquisition while living in Rome and died in prison (Jacob 1991, 184; McIntosh 1975, 31).

Among the Masonic-style societies that grew in Strasbourg was Puységur's *Societé des Amis Réunis*, which had strong associations with *La Candeur*. It was a specifically medical and mesmerist society, its most visible membership comprising doctors and surgeons; somewhat unusual for the era, it included women as full members. The reforming impulses of genteel womanhood could find expression in such a society; their zeal for "*le premier bonheur de l'humanité*" was centered around the charitable thought that animal magnetism was needed because medicines for the poor were rare. Though not as exclusive as *La Candeur*, the Strasbourg Society with its initiation fee of 100 louis [600 livres] would certainly have excluded entry by the humbler classes, and applications for initiation were received from all over France and Germany. The aristocrats of *La Candeur* were also represented among its membership, along with women. The *Societé des Amis Réunis*, like other societies that sprang up in this decade should not be seen as aberrations, but as integral to the Enlightenment, whose ambiance, as Margaret Jacob has noted, was simultaneously rationalist and theosophic; rather than simply representing the "end" of the Enlightenment, she argues, "the mystical could express concrete social and ideological postures" (Jacob 1991, 186–187, 199)

The *Societé des Amis Réunis* was the most influential of the provincial harmonial lodges outside Paris. We note again the interrelation between conventional Masonic societies and more mystical and mesmeric gatherings. At Puységur's Buzancy estate, mesmerism was being practiced on a huge scale, with the support of local officials in nearby Bayonne. By 1786, as Darnton notes, the Strasbourg Society was wading into the deep waters of spiritualism under the protection of A. C. Gerard, the head of the local magistracy (Darnton 1970, 53, 67).

Puységur had inadvertently discovered the phenomenon of induced somnambulism, with a corresponding shift from a strictly fluidist framework to one based upon psychological precepts, especially regarding the importance of the magnetizer's will and the rapport between subject and operator. This had the added effect of diminishing the employment of the *bacquet* for mass magnetization in favor of individual treatment, although for the lower classes in his region, Puységur would magnetize an old oak tree and connect patients to it *en masse* by ropes. This shift in focus heralded the genesis of a curative psychological paradigm still employed in modern psychotherapies. Moreover, Puységur and philosophers like J. C. de Saint-Martin, both of whom had trained in Paris with Mesmer and brought these practices to the provinces, kept in contact with one another.

Saint-Martin returned to Lyon, where with J. P. Willermoz, he founded the Lyonnaise Harmonial Society. He was among those who believed that the fluidist theory was inadequate to account for the observed phenomena and that an undue emphasis on it could lead to materialism (Darnton 1970, 68–69). Of Mesmer he said:

> It is Mesmer—that unbeliever Mesmer, that man who is only matter and is not even a materialist—it is that man, I say, who opened the door to sensible demonstrations of spirit. . . . Such has been the effect of magnetism. (Crabtree 1993, 68).

Saint-Martin brought an occult flavor. From the founder of Martinism, Jacques Martinès de Pasqually (c. 1715-1779), he had learned of the evil influence of "astral intelligences." Pasqually was founder of the Order of the Elect Cohens, after the Hebrew word for priest, who practiced ceremonial magic. Martinism like its contemporary the Avignon Society preached cabalism, Talmudic tradition, and a mystic Catholicism based on Cornelius Agrippa von Nettesheim (1486?–1535) and other occult writers. They were forbidden to consume the blood, fat, or kidneys of animals or to indulge in fornication. Louis Claude de Saint-Martin, then a young army officer, became a disciple. Pasqually died in 1779; among his chief disciples was J. B. Willermoz, who then went over to the Rite of Strict Observance (McIntosh 1975, 20, 24-25). Saint-Martin became a sort of metaphysical consultant to the mesmerists, especially to Puységur and Barberin. He directly influenced Puységur's idea that magnetic somnambulism provides a direct link to the spirit world and that these phenomena are tantamount to proof for the spirituality of the soul—the final destruction of materialism. Later Saint-Martin, writing as "*Le Philosophe Inconnu*" would evolve a unique mystical synthesis, weaving varieties of mesmerism with Martinism, in a philosophy strongly influenced by Boëhme and Swedenborg. He died in 1803 and remained a strict Catholic all his life (Darnton 1970, 69–69; Crabtree 1993, 68, n. 6).

Such views were reinforced by the increasing diversity of phenomena, and the new methods that were being developed among the second wave of mesmerists. To a considerable degree they incorporated the insights and techniques of the fluidists into their own, often Masonic, practices. In relation to induced catalepsy, Jacques Henri Desiré Pététin (1744–1808) recorded that, at times, patients could see their own insides. A leading figure at the Lyonnaise Society was the Chevalier de Barberin, who "practiced a unique technique of locating a patient's disease, without touching him, from the sensations felt by the mesmerizer" (Darnton 1970, 68). Along with Barberin, men like J. P. Willermoz, Jean-André Perisse Du Luc (b. 1738), Bernard de Turckheim, and Rodophe Saltzmann of *La Candeur* were all united by Masonic ties, and they were also involved in the Lyonnaise Harmonial Society, called *La Concorde*.

J. B. Willermoz, a Lyon silk merchant, was the most respected figure in French mystical Masonry, a chief disciple of Pasqually and member of the Order of the Elect Cohens. With his fraternal colleagues at Lyon, he initially concentrated on mesmerism as a healing technique. By the autumn of 1784, they were enthused by Puységur's technique of induced somnambulism. Willermoz and the others placed a succession of ladies into a trance, who would prophesy and bring news from the spirit world. The following year the energetic Willermoz organized the "Workers of the Eleventh Hour," a select band of mystics who studied messages from heaven transmitted by automatic writing through a noblewoman of his acquaintance (Garrett 1975, 110–111). This was possibly a different and more select group than those at *La Concorde*, and its membership interpenetrated with his other Masonic venture, the *Loge Élue et Chêrie* (the Lodge of the Elect and Beloved).

There was a plethora of similar associations at this time. In addition to the messages received through the *somnambules* of *La Concorde*, Willermoz's secret *Loge Élue et Chêrie* propagated what was regarded as the true primitive religion, from hieroglyphic messages conveyed to him from God in unspecified ways (Darnton 1970, 68). The use of Talmudic and kabbalistic magic was also a feature of the Order of the Elect Cohens and of the Avignon Society. Willermoz's Harmonial Society, having many members in common with his Masonic ventures, blossomed with Rosicrucians, Swedenborgians, alchemists, cabalists, and assorted theosophists recruited largely from the orthodox Masonic *Ordre des Chevaliers Bienfaisants de la Cité Sainte* (Crabtree 1993, 68). For instance,

Joseph de Maistre (1753–1821), who followed the ideas of Saint-Martin, Swedenborg, and Willermoz, believed that the theory of mesmerism had already been formulated in Swedenborg's writings (Darnton 1970, 139).

In late 1784, they secured local veterinarians for experimentation on animals, to prove that curative effects were not dependent on the expectations of the patient. Mesmer was invited to Lyon to witness these experiments. Willermoz magnetized a horse, which trembled and gave hacking coughs when he concentrated on the area of the throat; an autopsy later revealed a diseased larynx. In 1841, the French magnetizer Charles Lafontaine (1803–1892) would attract considerable attention with a similar feat, by mesmerising a lion in the London Zoo, which sparked the interest of James Braid in the phenomena. Willermoz, being a devotee of animal magnetism but also of occultism, greatly disappointed Mesmer, who regarded him as a mere seeker after arcane philosophy too closely connected to the Martinists, a dabbler in Rosicrucian symbols, and a speculative Freemason; to Mesmer, Willermoz represented a new and unhealthy trend, which promoted unscientific opinions built up from these dubious sources (Goldsmith 1934, 209; Buranelli 1976, 170–171).

In his 1799 *Memoire*, Mesmer attacked the notion that somnambulism is connected in any way to occult forces. He insisted that everything is explicable by the "mechanical laws of nature" and explained, not very helpfully, "that all the effects appertain to changes of *matter* and *movement*." He related these phenomena to an "internal" sixth sense, which he characterized as a human species of instinct:

> In that sleeping state of crisis, those persons are able to foresee the future, and bring the most remote things into present time. Their senses can extend to every distance and in all directions, without being checked by such obstacles. . . . [T]he more common phenomenon consists in being able to see the interior of their bodies, as well as those of others, and of judging with extreme accuracy the nature of diseases, their progress, the necessary treatment, and the results. But it is rare to find all these faculties combined in any one individual. (32)

Mesmer urged that oracular statements, prophecies and divination, magic, even the demonology of the ancients, and in his day phenomena like convulsions and possession "should be considered only as variations of the condition called somnambulism" (Mesmer 1957, 30).

At this early date, a large part of the repertoire of the nineteenth-century séance was already manifest; "mediums" produced trance and automatic writing, but also prophecy, retrocognition, and medical clairvoyance, which included the diagnosis of disease by direct perception into the internal organs and functions of the body. Willermoz, like Saint-Martin, was an admirer of Pasqually and a former member of the Elect Cohens, whose lodges in various cities maintained contact with the Mesmeric societies. Its members were reported to fall into trances and to enjoy visions of angels (Buranelli 1976, 171).

These practices of the latter 1780s reinforced what may be called the metaphysical rather than the strictly curative aspects of the new science. The new channel for investigation provided through *La Concorde*'s *somnambules* and other mystical Masonic gatherings, together with the experiences of Puységur with Victor Race and others, were changing the emphasis of these practices. Soon the new *pratique* of induced somnambulism was incorporated for even more daring metaphysical flights by esoteric societies like that at Avignon, which were influenced also by Swedenborgian conceptions and maintained close contact with Puységur and the Strasbourg society. In some ways these permutations were part of a wider reaction against Enlightenment rationalism and materialism; the slow rise of the "irrational" against the reified reason of previous decades. On the eve of the revolution, this eclectic spiritualistic form of mesmerism was in ample evidence at Strasbourg, Lyon, and elsewhere, and it even exercised an impact upon West Indian religions, through the mesmeric society founded there by Puységur's brother.

The Diffusion of Animal Magnetism throughout Europe

Among both the humble and the privileged in France, millennial ideas held strong sway at this time, and by the 1780s Mesmer's new science seemed for some to hold the key to solving nature's secrets (Garrett 1975,

20). As in England, the new millennial influences were felt in Masonic institutions like those already outlined. From the 1730s, mainstream freemasory had been drawing away from the occultism of the first generation, following its reorganization in England in 1717. The generation after Newton had already begun moving away from occult beliefs, and "the ancient mysteries lost their intellectual respectability, as science and social thought grew increasingly mechanistic and rational" (Bullock 1996, 11). The "Scottish" reforms of Chevalier Andrew Michael Ramsay (1686–1743) and others had the effect of producing new elitist lodges, like the Templars and the *Amis de la Vérité*. Other directions for nonformal masonry included the Avignon Society, and the most public of the new movements, the Fareinists, who moved away from the Masonic fraternal codes into millenarian and millennial directions.

The increasing social tensions created by the events leading up to the French Revolution had varied effects. In this process, both mesmerism and Swedenborgianism had a significant role. As Garrett writes concerning this trend in freemasonry in the closing decades of the eighteenth century:

> There was great interest among some masons in varieties of mysticism that were sometimes esoteric and sometimes Catholic. Aided by cabalism, astrology, prophetic lore, and the trances of mesmerized mediums, lodges throughout France prepared for what they believed was an approaching age of spiritual revelation and worldwide unity, perhaps in the near future. (1975, 20)

A Catholic form of mystical masonry surfaced mainly in France. From the 1760s, *La Candeur* had been steering toward more mystical and Germanic forms of freemasonry (Jacob 1991, 195). In 1773, a group of pious Catholics formed *Les Amis de la Vérité*, claiming about a thousand members at Lyon, with another two hundred members in Toulouse and a smaller group at Grenoble. They met each month to offer an office for the conversion of the Jews and the renovation of the Church; the Bergasse brothers, included among the early membership, would later describe themselves as "Christian mesmerists" and later still as "political mesmerists" (Garrett 1975, 26).

The Marquis De Puységur: The Alternate-Consciousness Paradigm

The pattern of Masonic-style institutions was maintained in the harmonial lodges and also in the various mystical para-Masonic societies like Avignon and the *Amis de la Vérité*. Over time, these new associations melded the numerous extant philosophic currents, especially the teachings of Swedenborg and Mesmer, into syncretic organizations concerned with the dawning of the millennium. After Swedenborg's death in 1772, his teachings survived through small groups in London and Manchester and also a few individual adherents throughout Sweden and Germany. The American colonies sustained small study groups and convocations like that of Jacob Duché (1738–1798), which probably arose from the one instigated in 1697 by Bishop Jesper Svedberg, Swedenborg's father, through royal patronage. Not until the 1780s was the New Church organized in England; and during that same decade, Swedenborg's writings were already being appropriated by chiliastic sects such as Antoine Joseph Pernety's (1716–1796) society at Avignon, based on biblical, Talmudic, and alchemical lore.

Hence the therapeutic interests of Mesmer and his core disciples were giving way in the latter half of the 1780s to a more metaphysical intent and a spiritual focus, especially among the antifluidists at the Strasbourg and Lyon societies. The discovery of the somnambulic trance and the unwonted influence of mystically minded adherents like Saint-Martin and Willermoz, had pushed forward a new therapeutic praxis as well as new theories concerning these wonders. This changing view of Mesmer's important discovery would, by the end of the decade, have a considerable, if somewhat foreshortened, influence throughout Europe, even in the sedate Swedish kingdom.

Following Mesmer's downfall at the hands of the commissions in 1784 and his subsequent return to the shores of Lake Constance, interest in mesmerism declined rapidly in the French capital, although as we have seen, it flourished in the provinces. Among the higher classes, one could find a certain *ennui*, a weariness of the rational and a presentiment of the romantic, as in a 1784 pamphlet by a Lamartine, a harmonial lodge member, proclaiming that the reign of Voltaire, of the Encyclopedists, is collapsing; that one finally gets tired of everything, especially of cold reasoning; that we must have livelier, more delicious delights, some of the sublime, the incomprehensible, the supernatural. (Darnton 1970, 151)

By 1788, other harmonists like the minor satirist Louis Mercier (1740–1814) had moved on from Mesmer to a belief that the world was full of invisible ghosts (Darnton 1970, 38). Yet mesmerism continued to exert a potent influence on the practices and, to some extent, on the theories of the second wave led by Puységur, Barberin, and Willermoz in the provinces. For his part, Puységur was sympathetic to the Martinists of Lyon, to Cagliostro in Paris, and to the freemasons and Swedenborgians in Germany and Sweden (Crabtree 1993, 70). To "*la Psychologie Sacrée de Lyons*" and its fellow travelers in other parts of Europe, mesmerism had proven the fundamental truth, the continued existence of the soul. Not the least among the complex influences that opened such a possibility to their minds were the insights of Emanuel Swedenborg.

Although they rejected the Swedenborgian theory of disease as emanating from the "exhalations" of angels and spirits, the new generation of magnetizers did not shun the possibility of contact between the spheres, even though Swedenborg himself had discouraged it. Correspondence in the late 1780s between the Exegetic and Philanthropic Society in Stockholm, the Strasbourg Society, and small conclaves like that of the Reverend Jacob Duché in London are among the many indications of the close connections between and among harmonial societies, Swedenborgian churches, and Masonic or quasi-Masonic organizations throughout western Europe. The best evidence for the complex traffic among these organizations in the 1780s and beyond relates to the Avignon Society and signals for the first time the wider diffusion of Swedenborg and Mesmer's key concepts. The crucial point is that, despite Mesmer's disclaimers, the era of the fluidists was over, and what might be called the "spiritists," or more neutrally the "vitalists" such as Puységur, were in the ascendant.

In France this was a period of proliferation in the vogue of quasi-Masonic societies, as at Strasbourg and Lyon, where their millenarian sympathies formed part of the occult revival. Combined with the ideas of spirit contact and an afterlife derived from the works of Swedenborg and frequently those of Jacob Boëhme, there were practices of thaumaturgy, kabbalism, and induced somnambulism, or as we might now call it, mediumistic trance.

Already in the previous decade of the 1780s, contacts had been established between Swedenborgian societies in England and the French sects, where the spread of mesmerism, now with more positive attitudes toward spirits, was manifest in numerous small but influential societies. The best known was the Avignon Society, which until its forced demise during the revolution served as a sort of clearing house for hermeticism, mesmerism, and occultism. During its relatively brief existence, it enjoyed a constant flow of visitors, who formed a network with like-minded persons on the Continent and in England. The ambit of influence extending from Avignon to other societies with a more strictly mesmerist intent like Strasbourg and to the Exegetic and Philanthropic Society in Stockholm illustrates the considerable traffic between quasi-secret societies in the last two decades of the covert Enlightenment.

The Avignon Society

The Avignon Society was "only one of the many shoots in the lush undergrowth of mystical Masonry in the 18th century" (Garrett 1975, 99). At a time when Deism and conventional freemasonry "with its tidy generalities" were losing the interest of the educated classes, groups like the Avignon Society were becoming attractive to many seekers. The society was organized like the harmonial and other Masonic-style associations, according to degrees of inititation. Its mystical Catholicism, especially the cult of the Virgin Mary, was grafted onto numerological, Swedenborgian, mesmeric, and other conceptions. In a letter dated February 12, 1787, to the Swedenborgian Robert Hindmarsh, the group intoned:

> For very dear Brethren, the angel that stands before the face of the lamb, is already sent to sound his trumpet on the mountains of

Babylon, and give notice to the nations that the God of heaven will soon come to the gates of the earth, to change the face of the world, and to manifest His power and glory. (cited in Hindmarsh 1861, 47)

Although not part of mainstream freemasonry, through its founder Dom Antoine Pernety the Avignon Society enjoyed considerable legitimacy in freemasonic circles; they were respectable enough to send delegates to International Masonic conferences at Wilhelmsbad in 1782 and Paris in 1784. According to scholars of freemasonry, Frenchman Antoine Pernety was already a high-degree Mason, having written in the 1750s the most highly elaborated hermetic degree in the Masonic repertoire, the *Chevalier du Soleil* (Knight of the Sun), part of the Rite of Perfection. Pernety was also deeply interested in Swedenborg, producing a French translation in 1782 of *Heaven and Hell* (*Les Merveilles du Ciel et de l'Enfer*). At the 1784 conference, the Avignon delegates proclaimed that the reunification of the Christian churches and the promulgation of a new doctrine for the entire world were now imminent; as with Willermoz's hieroglyphics, this intelligence was based on kabbalistic numerology, alchemical lore, mesmerist séances, and Swedenborgian spiritualism (Brooke 1994, 96; Block 1984, 59).

Part of that shadowy European world of occult freemasonry, mesmerism and spiritualism flourishing during the 1780s and 1790s, the activities of the Avignon *Illuminés* reveal how the currents of mysticism and occultism within freemasonry contributed to the dissemination of millenarian ideas. They would come to recognize the cataclysm of revolution as lending a special urgency to their mission (Garrett 1975, 14–15). The sect originated in Berlin in 1779 under the leadership of Dom Pernety, a former Benedictine monk and sometime librarian to Frederick II of Prussia (1712–1786). Pernety was an adventurer who had accompanied Louis-Antoine de Bougainville (1729–1811) in the early 1760s as chaplain on his expedition to the Falklands. On his return, Pernety abandoned the monastic cowl and went to Avignon in 1765, then a center of Jacobite émigrés, where he introduced a Masonic rite for a schismatic lodge, the *Séctateurs de la Vertu* comprised exclusively of nobles, which was reorganized on the basis of this hermetic rite (McIntosh 1975, 26, 29).[1]

Pernety was deeply influenced by works like *L'Histoire de la philosophie hérmetique* (1742) by the Abbé Nicholas Langlet Dufresnoy (1674–1755). In 1758, Pernety penned *Les Fables égyptiennes et grecques* and later the *Dictionnaire mytho-hérmetique*, both of which became popular expositions of occult wisdom, propagating the view that the bulk of ancient literature was disguised hermetic lore. Pernety claimed to draw on secret Greek and Egyptian sources in formulating the rite of the *Chevalier du Soleil*, later divided to form the twenty-seventh and twenty-eighth degrees of the Scottish rite (Garrett 1975, 99–100; McIntosh 1975, 30). However Avignon was papal territory, where the papal bull forbidding Masonic practices was enforceable. Pernety moved to Berlin, where for a time he worked at the Prussian court, enjoying the protection of Frederic II's brother Prince Henry (1726–1802), who was deeply interested in occult mysteries. Pernety brought in others like the French priest Guyton de Morveau, known as Brumore, along with Morinval, Melle Bruchier, Countess Stadniska, the Count and Countess Jean Tarnowski, and others. In 1778, with the arrival of Count Grabianka, the *Illuminés* were formally constituted (Garrett 1975, 101; Harrison 1979, 70).

"Count" Tadeusz Grabianka, not really a count but a very wealthy Polish nobleman, was largely responsible for introducing a millenarian emphasis into what had heretofore been mainly a thaumaturgic society and Masonic lodge. In his youth, he had frequented fortune tellers; through contact with Sabbatean Jews in his native region of Podolia, he became familiar with the apocalyptic prophecies of the seventeenth-century "Messiah," Sabbatai Zevi (1626–1676). Nursing a desire to succeed to the elective Polish throne, an honor that was to be denied to him, he became increasingly convinced that the millennium was approaching and that he would in due course be placed upon the throne of Israel as well, another dream never to be realized. Grabianka, with his own grandiose aspirations, was a significant precursor to the apocalyptic Englishman Richard

---

1. The first lodge was that of Saint-Jean d'Avignon, comprised entirely of nobles; in 1749, a separate lodge was founded for the bourgeoisie, and the two later fused as the lodge of Saint-Jean de Jerusalem.

Brothers (1757–1824) in his wish to establish an Isrealite kingdom. In Warsaw, Grabrianka had joined the reformed order of "Templars" or "Strict Observance" Masons, founded around 1760 by Baron Charles Hund (d. 1776) and, through that connection, he met Pernety in Berlin in 1778 (Scholem 1961, 287–296; Garrett 1975, 102).

The *Illuminés* practiced the "true science of numbers" and posed questions to a divine intelligence whom they called "*Sainte-Parole*" (divine or holy word), who gave enigmatic responses, much in the manner of the Delphic oracle, although it is not clear whether these responses came through *somnambules*, as with the pythonesses at Delphi, via hieroglyphs, automatic writing, numerology, or other means. The *Illuminés* had frequent contact with Strasbourg. Each member had an occult number, Pernety's being no. 135. When consulted by Brumore concerning Grabianka, known as "Dear King 1.3.9," *Sainte-Parole* intoned: "*O mon fils, son cœur est pur. Ne crain pas de mêler ton encens avec le sien, parce qu'il deviendra un jour sept fois plus grand que toi!*" (O my son, his heart is pure. Do not fear to mix your incense with his, because one day he will become seven times greater than you!) (Bricaud 1927, 46; see also 43; Harrison 1979, 71).

Bricaud writes that Pernety believed he was guided by an angel called Assadai, "*un esprit supérieur*" or an angel of the first degree, who watched over and helped him and who promised never to ascend to the ethereal regions until Pernety had discovered the secret of their "great work." In 1782, he issued a divine command that the society should be relocated from Berlin. Ironically, Avignon, the place of the greatest schism of medieval Christianity, was chosen wherefrom to proclaim their message of unity. Assadai, the guiding angel of the society referred to as *Sainte-Parole*, declared that each would be consecrated there in an occult way, to be regenerated and become a "child of Sabaoth."[2] Guided by visions, they held the fervent conviction that they were embarked on a "*Grand Oeuvre.*" Through Pernety's friendship with the Marquis de Vaucroze (d. 1786), the

---

2. Bricaud writes: "*Pernety etait guidé dans ses recherches par un esprit supérieur, un ange du premier degré, Assadaï, qui veillait sur lui, l'aidait de ses conseils, et ne devait gagner les régions éthérées que lorsque Pernety aurait découvert le secret du Grand Œuvre*" (Bricaud 1927, 38; see also 45).

society was installed on his Avignon estate. Among the prominent *Illuminés* were the Chevalier Marie Daniel Bourrée de Corberon (1748–1810); a Dr. Bouge; Jean Pierre Moët (1721–1806), the Marquis de Thomé; and Esprit Calvert, a professor of physiology at the Avignon medical faculty (McIntosh 1975, 29; Garrett 1984, 76). Now established as a freemasons' lodge with the grandiose title *L'Académie des Illuminés Philosophes*, they soon attracted seekers from all over Europe. Their doctrines have been described as a blend of Swedenborgianism and Roman Catholicism, salted with occultism. As J. F. C. Harrison notes, their interests were indeed varied:

> To the cold intellectualism of the Swedish visionary was added the veneration of the Virgin Mary and recital of the Athanasian creed; while individual members studied Renaissance alchemy, the theurgy of Alexandria, hermetic authors, the philosopher's stone, the divine science of numbers, and the mystical interpretation of dreams. (1979, 70)

In their early alchemical endeavors they sought the philosopher's stone, consulting *Sainte-Parole* about every detail, the furnace to be used, the crusets and alambics, all evidently needed to produce the "powder of projection" (Bricaud 1927, 44). A visitor in 1792, A.-H. Dampmartin (1755–1825), marshal of the king's armies, has left an account of the society in a *memoire*. Dampmartin recalled that many notable persons had become zealous disciples, and they had great confidence in the divine voice of *Sainte-Parole*, who guided their activities. In the midst of the revolutionary "abomination," as he terms it, the brethren had remained calm, practicing virtuous deeds; and fed by their abiding piety, they continued to live in the manner of the primitive Christians (Bricaud 1927, 92). They offered a contrast to the tumultuous events that before long would inexorably engulf both them and their chronicler. Dampmartin had wished at first to join the society. Through their auspices, he had received prophecies of the terrifying events to follow, activities in which he would become mired in succeeding years, as the *Terreur* and the Directorate spread in France. But he does not explain why he did not join; perhaps the demands of war were of greater moment.

Though never exceeding one hundred members, the *Illuminés* maintained a considerable network among the mystical Masonic groups advancing the idea of an impending millennium and the establishment of a true, unitary church, to be presided over by Jesus Christ. Thus would they form the basis of "the new people of God." There existed in France at this time numerous other mystical and quasi-Masonic orders, like the *Rite des Philalèthes*, formed in 1775 by Savalette de Langes, keeper of the royal treasury, which comprised twelve degrees and combined the doctrines of Pasqually and Swedenborg. At Avignon, Pernety's numerological and alchemical interests were now being overshadowed by Grabianka's concern with preparations for the millennium, which confirms the historical opinion that the Avignon society's activities "reveal how the currents of mysticism and occultism within the world of freemasonry contributed to the dissemination of millenarian ideas" (McIntosh 1975, 30; Garrett 1975, 14–15). It was through his participation in the earlier freemasonic lodge at Avignon that Dr. Benedict Chastanier had first discovered Swedenborg. Another close adherent was the Marquis de Thomé, royal librarian at Versailles and another French translator of Swedenborg, who introduced a reformed system of Masonry in 1783 called "the Rite of Swedenborg" (Block 1984, 58). Through Pernety's Masonic ties, many freemasons were drawn to Avignon, like the ubiquitous General Rainsford, who figures in almost every Masonic organization of the period. Chastanier, a French doctor and longtime resident of London, like his friend William Bousie joined Jacob Duché's Swedenborgian study group; both men later became members of the New Church.

The most colorful of these converts was the ardent freemason and anti-Catholic aristocrat, the Chevalier Borrée de Corberon. During his early travels in Russia, he had encountered Cagliostro in St. Petersburg, and he was as incessant in his accumulation of Masonic degrees as in his study of systems of philosophy, magic, and alchemy (Bricaud 1927, 86). Deemed a qualified "seer of spirits" by Empress Catherine II (1729–1796), on his return to France in 1780, he was introduced to Swedenborg's writings, and he entered into correspondence with Pernety on the matter. While living in Paris in the mid 1780s, Corberon joined Mesmer's Harmonial Society. It was there that he met Count Grabianka and learned of the Avignon

Society. Soon after, in a letter to a fellow German freemason, Corberon expressed his enthusiasm for the doctrines of the *Illuminés*, his fervent wish to be admitted into the society and to live with the acolytes; thus would he avoid human distractions, so as to realize *"l'étude sublime et consolante de la religion et de la nature."* He corresponded also with Grabianka and other members such as Louis-Michel Gombault, Count Pasquini, the brothers Bousie and Duvigneau, Picot, and La Richardière (Bricaud 1927, 90, 88).

With his great intellectual drive and spiritual curiosity, Corberon imbibed the currents of alchemy and mesmerism along with Swedenborgian theology. Nor was he alone in his high expectations. A Colonel Count Thiroux also yearned for the truths discovered by the brothers in their communications with *"Très-Haut"* (the Most High), probably *Sainte-Parole*. If they could give him that sublime proof of immortality, Thiroux assured them in his application for membership, it was "this conviction which he desired more than anything men may wish for, more than knowledge of the philosopher's stone." Thiroux, like Corberon, was admitted soon after into the Avignon Society, celebrating the initiatory rites on the hill named Tabor in June 1790 (Bricaud 1927, 91).

Following the divine call, in 1782 Abbé Pernety had relocated the society, producing in the same year a translation entitled *La Sagesse Angélique d'Emanuel Swedenborg* (Block 1984, 56; Garrett 1975, 104). Though he had been responsible for introducing the Avignon Society to England, Dr. Chastanier's enthusiasm waned as his dissatisfaction increased with the Pernety translations and with the new premillennial direction the society was taking. Since Grabianka's arrival, the efforts of the society were being increasingly redirected to preparations for the millennium. As a result, Chastanier resigned. He was among the first to join the New Church in England, being present at the first public meeting in 1783 when the Theosophical Society, its precursor, was organized. The Avignon Society fell out with the New Church also over Swedenborg's work *Marriage Love*, which they considered a "damnable book" for its expressed views on "concubinage," and Chastanier, now a leader of the New Church and for some years custodian of some of Swedenborg's original manuscripts, repudiated his connection with the Avignon Society (Block 1984, 59, 66).

61

According to its members, the Avignon Society had been formed by Jesus Christ to advance an impending millenarian regeneration of humanity and the establishment of a true, unitary church. Acolytes were initiated on a nearby hill Pernety had named "Tabor," an initiation that extended over nine days. There they would first form a "circle of power," then burn incense and vow to consecrate themselves to God's service. In return, this covenant with the eternal would bring a special grace, which they called "*faire un Jêhovah*" (to construct a Jehovah); they might be favored also with a vision of their guiding angel. Along with hermeticism and Hebrew Sabbatarianism, they now drew on the apocalyptic aspirations of Grabianka to become king of Poland and a second Solomon in Jerusalem, with Pernety mooted as the pontiff (Bricaud 1927, 45–47). Their tenets and practices, a strange mixture of Masonry, spiritism, Jesuitism, Swedenborgianism, and the teachings of Saint-Martin have been described as "mystico-cabalistic Magnetical" (Brooke 1994, 96; Block 1984, 59). The *Illuminés*, like Willermoz at the *Loge Élue et Chérie* in Lyon, were also committed to a secret Masonic form of organization; and like the harmonists at *La Concorde*, they applied the new insights being spearheaded by Puységur and Barberin toward metaphysical rather than therapeutic pursuits, employing mesmeric methods to direct the minds of subjects. To be sure, they connected these to their other, more esoteric beliefs and practices.

From the foregoing, it is at least clear that the emphasis of the Avignon Society gradually became millenarian in intent. They studied Swedenborg both for his allegorical interpretation of the Bible and for his pronouncements concerning the world of spirits, the same aspect also drawing Saint-Martin and the Martinists. It was believed that what Swedenborg had taught on the divisions of the heavens into spiritual and celestial degrees drew upon a previously secret hermetic wisdom of correspondences, and this appealed to their gnostic sensibilities.

Connections with Swedenborgian Churches in England

After Swedenborg's death in 1772, his doctrines were studied by small groups, the best known being centered on the evangelical efforts of the

Reverend John Clowes in Manchester and in nearby Bolton, and another group was formed in London and led by the printer Robert Hindmarsh. The New Church was organized first in Manchester, then in London. Richard Houghton of Liverpool introduced the Reverend John Clowes to Swedenborg's writings. Somewhat later, the London Theosophical Society grew out of the Swedenborgian discussion group held on Sunday evenings at the Lambeth residence of the Reverend Jacob Duché, chaplain of the female orphan asylum. It quickly became a meeting point for mystics, millenarians, and reformers of all kinds.

The Reverend John Clowes, for some sixty years rector of St. John's Anglican Church at Manchester, never left his Anglican communion; yet throughout his life, he worked tirelessly to promote Swedenborg's teachings. Clowes's dedication was genuine; he translated Swedenborg's works and to devote himself to his Swedenborgian labors refused a bishopric offered by William Pitt (1759–1806) (Block 1984, 65). His conversion had occurred in the mid-1770s when, coming across a Latin copy of Swedenborg's *True Christianity* and feeling at first a strong distaste for it, he left it unread. Then taking it up casually one day, he opened the book and was struck by the words *"Divinum humanum,"* which seemed to possess an inner glow. Later he had a profound transcendental experience, his mind seemingly impressed by a kind of internal dictate, and he recorded that "the glory (connected with the *Divinum humanum* phrase) lasted a full hour" (Brotherton 1860, 48).[3]

Clowes was familiar with the lineage of Christian mysticism and hermeticism, for his appointment to St. John's had been endowed by a wealthy benefactor interested in propagating the ideas of William Law, the English translator of Boëhme's works, who before he turned thence, had been a confidant of John Wesley (Knox 1961, 433–434). Clowes had been chosen from a number of applicants because of his interest in Boëhme and Law (Garrett 1975, 156).

His enthusiasm for Swedenborg was evidently not shared by some of Clowes's parishioners. A letter dated August 30, 1783, from "a Layman" to the local bishop accused him of "Hypocrisy and Dissimulation" in

---

3. According to Odhner 1904, I:111, the first New Church society was formed in Manchester in 1778 through Clowes' influence.

spreading "the absurd and heretical tenets of E. Swedenborg, in this town." He was accused not only of having "disseminated them publickly [sic] in print, but also introduced and recommended them in his public preaching and chatechising, and more particularly and familiarly in the numerous classes, which he assembles at his own house and in the neighbouring parishes, of the converts to his delusion" (Porteus Papers, 18:210ff). Nothing came of the complaint, probably because Clowes enjoyed the bishop's patronage and was the well-regarded rector of a working-class congregation in the north of England, where a widespread interest in Boëhme, Law, and other types of "mystic divinity" was of long standing.

Though it is not clear why he remained an Anglican and refused a bishopric, Clowes was a sincere and ardent devotee of the Swedish seer. For his part, Clowes was at a loss which to admire most in Swedenborg, "the solid learning, the deep investigation, the mature judgment, or the unaffected piety of the philosopher." In his *Outlines of Swedenborg's Doctrines*, he explained several key concepts. Swedenborg's philosophy "enlightens the understanding, and improves the heart" by referring natural phenomena to spiritual agency. He opens the mind "by teaching it to consider all the visible universe . . . as a theatre and representation of that invisible world from which it first derived its existence, and by connection with which it continually subsists" (Clowes 1873, 5–6). Clowes dilates on the central doctrines of correspondences and influx:

> Every individual human body . . . consists of several orders of forms, distinguished from each other according to degrees of purity, wherein the lowest degree is the basis or receptacle of one still purer and more interior; and this again of a higher degree, which is the most pure and inmost. In this highest degree the human spirit hath its residence; being a *spiritual organized form*, corresponding to that of the body, and communicating life thereto; whilst the spirit itself receiveth life from the spiritual world . . . by continual influx from the Father of Beings. (7–8)

Clowes sought to comprehend Anglican theology according to the deeper penetration of the Word afforded by Swedenborg's works. In relation to the atonement, he argues, for instance, against the common view of a wrathful God, insisting that the disposition of the universal Father towards humankind is one of love and mercy. Since Swedenborg had taught that God is unchangeable goodness and truth, true atonement consists not in appeasing his wrath, but "in changing the state of man, by removing from him the powers of hell and darkness wherewith he was infested in consequence of transgression." Only thus could a human being experience "a real renewal and regeneration of all the parts, powers and principles of his life, both in soul and body" (Clowes 1873, 34–35).

From around 1782, Clowes began to form Swedenborgian study groups, riding out regularly to manufacturing villages around Manchester. Some hearers were reportedly "visited by angels" thereafter (Garrett 1984, 74). At this early stage of the Industrial Revolution, with an outlook less rigid than in the later factory system and with the presence of a strong local Dissenting population, factory owners often permitted their workers to leave work in order to hear his discourses on Swedenborg. Another group was started by lay leader Samuel Dawson in nearby Bolton, where the Shakers also originated, and counted among its converts Samuel Crompton (1753–1827), inventor of the spinning mule (Garrett 1975, 156).

The origins of the New Church in London centered on a small group led by Robert Hindmarsh, who met from 1783 at Clerkenwell Close to study Swedenborg's writings. On December 5, 1783, the first public meeting was held at the London Coffee House, then adjourned to the Queen's Arms Tavern, where the Theosophical Society was inaugurated. Among those present were the Hindmarsh brothers, the disaffected *Illuminé* Dr. Chastanier, the sculptor John Flaxman and the wealthy planter James Glen (1750?-1814). It was Glen who the following year, 1784, would be responsible for spreading Swedenborg's works to America, in the same year that Lafayette brought animal magnetism on his triumphal return to the now-independent United States. The Theosophical Society was loosely attached to Jacob Duché's discussion group at the Lambeth Orphan Asylum, and in 1788 the first Swedenborgian chapel was founded at Great East Cheap. They chose by lot, and James Hindmarsh, Robert's brother, thus became the first New Church minister (Harrison 1979, 75; Garrett 1975, 159; Brotherton 1860, 7–8).

That there were already small groups studying Swedenborg in America before Glen's tour is indicated by the activities of the Rev. Jacob Duché, who provides an important connecting axis between European mystical freemasonry and occultism and Anglo-American Swedenborgianism. Jacob Duché was part of the pre-revolutionary social and intellectual elite. Born into a prominent Philadelphia family, he became rector of the leading Church of England congregation in that city, serving as chaplain to the first two Continental Congresses. Like his colleague the Rev. John Clowes, Duché was deeply interested in mysticism, hermeticism, and related topics; and also like Clowes, he remained within the Anglican communion while tirelessly promoting Swedenborg's works. As early as 1767, Duché was also reading William Law's translations of Jacob Boëhme. His early interest in Quietism grew out of his proximity to the Quakers, living in their colonial capital Philadelphia; this interest is indicated by his 1772 poem on the Ephrata cloister, the German sect of "Dunkers" who had settled in western Pennsylvania earlier in the century. He also joined with a group of men and women who met regularly for prayer and Bible discussions, led by Carl Wrangel, provost of the Swedish Lutheran mission on the Delaware River (Garrett 1984, 71–72).

This was the same mission for which Bishop Svedberg had earlier provided three pastors. It is likely that this group discussed Swedenborg's writings and that this was also the source of his acquaintance with the famous Ephrata cloister. As hostilities increased with England, Duché became the first Anglican clergyman to omit prayers to the king from the liturgy. However, he soon grew dissatisfied with the American Revolution and wrote to George Washington (1732–1799) about his concerns, gratuitously advising him "to represent to Congress, the indispensable necessity of rescinding the hasty and ill-advised declaration of Independency." It was a mistake at this time to confront the Revolutionary elite, and Duché quickly became *persona non grata*, forced to flee to England where he lived for the next fourteen years (Garrett 1984, 70).[4]

---

4. Rev. Jacob Duché to George Washington, Philadelphia, October 8, 1777 (*Collected Tracts*, British Library).

European Masonic Societies

Fortunately, the loyalist Duché had a patron in the bishop of London. In 1782, he was appointed chaplain of the Asylum for Female Orphans at St. George's Fields, Lambeth. He was well regarded as a pastor, and subscribers to his American sermons published in 1789 included Hannah More (1745–1833) and William Blake (1757–1827). Jacob Duché had a deep and abiding commitment to Swedenborg's teachings. In a letter to his mother-in-law in May 1785, Duché advised her to "Look Henceforth for an Internal Millennium" (Garrett 1984, 72–73). For several years, Sunday evening discussions of Swedenborg's writings were held in Duché's apartment at the asylum. Robert Hindmarsh attended, as did John Flaxman and William Sharp (1749–1824), who probably on occasions brought his friend, the fellow engraver and radical William Blake. In April 1789, Blake and his wife attended the first General Conference at the chapel in Eastcheap and signed the register as visitors (Rix 2003, 96). The Swedenborgian Robert Hindmarsh recalled many occasions when, together with upwards of thirty persons, male and female, he had "spent Sunday evening together in a truly delightful manner, receiving from his [Duché's] lips the most impressive lessons of instruction" (Hindmarsh 1861, 40; Garrett 1975, 158–159; Harrison 1979, 75).

Duché's circle also attracted many foreign visitors. Various dabblers in alchemy, kabbalism, and mesmerism were involved, like Dr. Chastanier and the freemasonic gadfly General Rainsford, who was attracted to Swedenborg's experiences "as one more confirmation of the existence of truths beyond the reach of the five senses" (Garrett 1984, 75). At this time, Count Grabianka was touring various mystical Masonic organizations throughout Europe and England, seeking like-minded societies to merge with the Avignon Society, for which as we have seen, he set a new agendum in preparations for an imminent millennium and the reign of Christ on earth (Garrett 1975, 104). Spending the year 1786 in London for that specific purpose, Grabianka was a "frequent and welcome" visitor to the Swedenborgian gathering at Duché's rooms. Hindmarsh found him "a man of great ability and the most engaging manners," whom he describes as "particularly desirous of celebrating the Lord's Supper, eating bread and drinking wine at each of our houses." He recounts also, with evident horror, Grabianka's custom of embracing "each individual after the manner of foreigners, and to kiss, first on the right cheek, then on the left, and lastly on the lips of the mouth" (1861, 41).

Grabianka wished to create a sort of millenarian international. In his letter of thanks to Duché following his departure, he asserted that several other similiar societies existed with whom he was in contact and that all were preparing for the divine command (Garrett 1975, 109).[5]

Apart from the worship and discussions, there was a strong element of mystical freemasonry in the sessions held at Duché's. That eclectic joiner, General Charles Rainsford belonged to no less than ten masonic lodges, maintaining contacts with masons in London, Paris, Strasbourg, Lyon, and Narbonne, as well as at Avignon. A member of the Royal Society, Rainsford also belonged to the Exegetic and Philanthropic Society of Stockholm. It was in large measure through the efforts of men like Chastanier and Rainsford, given to peripatetic wanderings and maintaining a wide correspondence and extensive Masonic connections, that Swedenborgian and mesmeric ideas were spread across Europe. Writing to Gabrianka in 1788, Rainford asked for his opinion on Swedenborg's doctrines, whether they were a "key"; he mentioned his own interest in freemasonry, kabbala, and animal magnetism which, he added parenthetically, "is at present the subject of admiration and Research for everyone here in our Country" (Garrett 1984, 75–76). Rainsford may have first learned of Swedenborg from his fraternal colleague Benedict Chastanier at Avignon. It was also in the early 1780s that Chastanier became disenchanted with the Avignon Society over their interpretation of Swedenborg. Rainsford joined Grabianka's enterprise, and added the Avignon Society to his numerous other commitments.

Recent scholarship has revealed even closer connections between the quasi-Masonic groups and the Swedenborgians. In 1776, Dr. Benedict Chastanier founded the London Universal Society, a Masonic order that was instrumental in attracting international Masons to London, where some attended Duché's Sunday meetings. By the early 1780s, Avignon member Chastanier had grown increasingly critical of Pernety, believing

---

5. Hindmarsh 1861, 44, states that Grabianka's great secret was evidently that there are four divine persons in the Godhead, including the Virgin Mary; but Hindmarsh might have just been mischievous or perhaps uninformed.

that his translations and his interpretation of Swedenborg's writings were "as far from the principles of Swedenborg as the Orient is from the Occident" (Garrett 1984, 75). And as the Avignon Society took a more apocalyptic, premillennial direction with the arrival of Count Grabianka, Chastanier, along with William Bousie and others, resigned and turned his attention exclusively to the New Church. The result was first the organization of the Theosophical Society in 1783, then of the first New Church chapel at Great Eastcheap in 1787 (Rix 2003, 103–104).

There was a further link extending from Avignon to Stockholm via Lyon and London. Claude de Saint-Martin, spiritual advisor to Willermoz and his mystical Masons at Lyon, was also an Avignon member and nominally also a member of the Exegetic and Philanthropic Society in Stockholm, as were Grabianka, Rainsford, and a host of other peripatetic Mason Templars. Of particular interest is Saint-Martin's joint authorship in 1792 with Baron Silverhjelm of the Swedenborgian tract *Le Nouvel Homme*, only a year after the collapse of the Swedish society (Rix 2003, 106), though the purpose and broader implications of this complex underground traffic in *fin-de-siècle* Europe is not clear. The revolutionary events in France probably put an indefinite hiatus to these connections, as they also would effectively finish the Avignon Society.

Duché kept in contact with the society at Avignon, especially Gabrianka and his "network of pious occultists," although his own belief, derived from Swedenborg, was in the prior advent of an "Internal Millennium." In this he differed vastly over the projected apocalypse, with Grabianka awaiting a transformation in the outer world prior to the Lord's coming, to be heralded by the conquest of Palestine and the conversion of the Jews. Avignon Society members reflect this admixture of influences. Around 1781, William Bousie and the Marquis de Thomé made an intensive study of Swedenborg, from which Thomé evolved his Masonic Rite of Swedenborg. It was also upon studying this rite that Borrée de Corberon was persuaded to abandon Deism for Christianity. We have seen that, before arriving at Avignon in 1790, Corberon had joined the Templars and had imbibed mesmerism; and through Bousie and Thomé, he now plumbed deeply into Swedenborg's writings. The alchemist Peter Woulfe also joined and, like William Sharp and Loutherbourg, he was an avid student of Swedenborg. In the mid-1790s, all three would be converted to the apocalyptic millenarianism of Richard Brothers (Garrett 1975, 106–107, 186). William Sharp, the famous engraver, was also a political radical, being an original member in 1792 of Thomas Hardy's Society for Constitutional Information (Garrett 1975, 191; Webb 1989, 95–96). He came to millenarianism by way of Swedenborg and Duché's circle. Later he tried without success to interest his colleague and fellow eccentric William Blake in Brothers, then in Joanna Southcott (1750–1814), to whose ravings he turned his loyalty finally after the new century.

Two English adventuring truth seekers, William Bryan (b. 1764?) and John Wright, were also welcomed into the Avignon Society in 1789. They too underwent an elaborate ritual of initiation, including ascending Tabor, there to recite prayers and burn incense on each of nine days (Harrison 1979, 69; Garrett 1975, 114). At certain seasons, members claimed immediate communication with heaven; they would assemble on Tabor where an angel, possibly *Sainte-Parole*, would converse with them. Every night at 7 o'clock, they celebrated the Resurrection by eating bread and drinking wine. Often at these sessions, the furniture shook, announcing the presence of angels (Hindmarsh 1861, 48; Garrett 1975, 112; Harrison 1979, 71). It is likely that these effects were produced through the use of *somnambules*, a foretaste of the infamous "physical phenomena" séances of the following century. The Avignon Society was on the periphery of the occult world, but it was of some importance as one of the conduits for a perceived urgent sense of spiritual regeneration during these last decades of the eighteenth century (Garrett 1975, 120).

Mesmeric Theories in the Romantic Era

On the Continent, heterodox religion in the early nineteenth century made a recovery, but they were now less close to the occult world of freemasonry, which went its own way. With the demise of Napoleon (1769–1821) after Waterloo, romanticism began to make headway. The Society of Universal Harmony, which had collapsed with most of its provincial affiliates after 1789, was revived in 1815 by Puységur as the *Société du Magnétisme*. Joseph de Maistre had spent time in St. Petersburg and other European cities assimilating the ideas of Saint-Martin, Swedenborg, Willermoz, and other mesmerists. Like Balzac in a later era, he found the theory of mesmerism already formulated in Swedenborg. A fillip was given also by the Baroness Juliane de Krüdener (1764–1824), a mystic who arrived in Paris in 1815 and gathered around her Bergasse and Puységur (Darnton 1970, 139, 141).

With the return of interest in animal magnetism in the romantic era, the legacy of Mesmer and Swedenborg developed a new and less physicalist outlook. At the turn of the nineteenth century, there were widely differing opinions about animal magnetism. Sceptics denied its existence or believed that it was at most a kind of autosuggestion. Madame de Krüdener regarded hypnosis as a link between the natural and the supernatural worlds, the means through which the individual human soul might gain access to the "world soul." Between these two extremes, there were all manner of intermediate opinions (Ellenberger 1970, 119). Mesmer held fast to the view of hypnosis as a physical fluid that circulated in the body of the magnetized or between the subject and the magnetizer. By now "an active and very sociable old gentleman," Mesmer had retired to Lake Constance in comfortable circumstances. He no longer practiced but would magnetize friends or deserving cases free of charge. He possessed a great love of animals, and he exercised a strange power over them. He liked to talk, retaining an obstinate conviction that his system was a boon to humankind and dwelling upon the bigotry and short-sightedness of governments and faculties of medicine (Gauld 1995, 88).

After 1815, the German romantics were in the ascendant in esoteric circles throughout the Continent, and as part of the reaction against an arid rationalism, all manner of ideas about transcendence and related subjects were in the air. Many like Krüdener spoke of a world soul and held to the most formidable spiritistic ideas. As with their counterparts in England, they believed

> that the contemplation of nature could reveal a spiritual reality coterminous with the physical world, that this reality might be particularly evident in the rustic and the primitive, that the earth, man, and the universe are part of and influenced by great cosmic

forces, and that human beings possess non-discursive mental faculties which permit them to transcend the world of their senses. (Turner 1974, 118)

The most important of the German romantics was Baroness Anne-Louise-Germaine de Staël (1766–1817), whose husband was a Swedenborgian, and a close friend of Johann Caspar Lavater (1741–1801) and Saint-Martin. Dr. D. F. Koreff (1783–1851), a German mesmerist doctor, described as a kind of mesmerist literary agent, knew most of the important romantic writers of France and Germany, many of whom he mesmerized. Around this time, eminent romantic philosophers like J. G. Fichte (1762–1814) and Friedrich Schleirmacher (1768–1854) were availing themselves of the revived *bacquet* sessions, organized by Dr. Karl Christian Wolfart (1778–1832) for famous visitors (Darnton 1970, 149; Gauld 1995, 89). Another trend was toward magnetic magic. Among the German romantics, the best known was Carl August Eschenmayer (1768–1852), who followed Paracelsus in positing the existence of an "Adamish" and a "sidereal" body in humans. He wrote, "The individual soul is also a universal soul . . . [I]n the sideral body . . . it gives itself up to ideas and speculation." The Adamish body is preoccupied "with a finite cycle," while the sidereal body "strives for the unending and eternal." Unlike Eschenmayer, his colleague Joseph Ennemoser (1787–1854) accepted that spiritual agency intervenes in the lives of humans (Crabtree 1985, 192–193).

Magnetic somnambulism developed in Germany upon a more mystical basis and reworked the potent influence of the early magnetists in a new way. The most important figures were J. H. Jung-Stilling (1740–1817) and Justinus Kerner (1786–1862). Born in 1740, Jung-Stilling took a medical degree, then became professor of Political Economy at the Universities of Marburg and Heidelberg. In 1808 he published *Theorie der Geister-Kunde*, expounding a doctrine of the psychic body that he associated with a luminiferous ether, explained by illustrations drawn from the observed phenomena of somnambulism. Following Swedenborg after a manner, he believed it could be shown through such empirical evidence as somnambulists' ecstatic visions that human beings simultaneously dwell in two worlds, the material world and the world of spirits (Podmore 1963, 1:95; Crabtree 1985, 119).

Justinus Kerner from Weinsberg was also a physician and a poet, who became deeply interested in the therapeutic value of the trance state. Although ridiculed by the professors at Heidelberg University, he worked with *somnambules* and crystal-gazers, and wrote on guardian spirits, demons, and angels (Watts 1883, 216). In 1826, Kerner began experiments on his most promising subject, Frederica Hauffe (1801–1829), the famous "Seeress of Prevorst," who died three years later. In his view, Hauffe differed greatly from other *somnambules* in the numerous proofs she presented of abnormal powers of vision, both distant and pre-voyant; of conversing with ghosts; in the "physical phenomena" that occurred in her presence; and most of all, in her extraordinary revelations of things spiritual. In particular, the seeress taught that the human organism consists of body, soul, and spirit. After leaving the body, the soul is clothed for a time by an ethereal body, which she called *Nervengeist*, that also carries on the vital processes when the soul leaves the body temporarily, as in magnetic trance (Podmore 1963, 1:99–100, 107).

The importance of these early German magnetists was in their influence on the later theories of spiritualism, especially in England, where they laid the early foundations of the movement. It was from this source, after Swedenborg, that the Howitts, Thomas Shorter (b. 1823) (also latinized as Brevior), Mrs. Sophia De Morgan (1809–1892) and others among the prominent early English spiritualists derived most of their philosophical opinions (Podmore 1963, 1:109).

First Revival of Magnetism in France

In France, the revival of magnetism occurred after the downfall of the First Republic and was more closely related to their scientific efficacy than to any transcendent interest. This generation of French magnetizers was interested in its use as a healing power and as illustrating the workings of a new physical force (Podmore 1963, 1:78). There were those like the Abbé José Custodio de Faria (1756–1819), a Portuguese Jesuit who had traveled extensively in India and gave public demonstrations of magnetism in Paris from 1813, wearing eastern robes. He departed entirely from Mesmer's methods, relying on the force of will, and he commanded his subjects in a loud voice to be "healed," or sometimes in a quiet voice he would say "*Dormez*" (sleep). Though principally a showman, Faria was among the first to draw the scientific conclusion that magnetic cures were brought about not by an external fluid but by the receptive attitude of the subject. This established a rapport, based on the patient's susceptibility to the magnetizer's influence. Thus, he presaged the methods of Alexandre Bertrand (1795–1831) and, later still, of the suggestion school of hypnotism at Nancy. It was said that the Abbé Faria could make water taste like champagne. Popular also were the performances of Alinea d'Elder, the beautiful Indian somnambulist (Owen 1971, 177; Darnton 1970, 140; Goldsmith 1934, 180).

Dr. Guillaume Pascal Billot's (1768–1841?) experiments in France during the 1820s were given a spirit interpretation, where guardian angels spoke through *somnambules* along with manifestations like the "apports" of flowers, allegedly transported through solid walls. However, a more long-lasting legacy came from the work of the new wave of interested scientists. Foremost among these were the physicians Joseph Philippe François Deleuze (1753–1835) and Alexandre Bertrand. Deleuze, Puységur's best known student, in 1813 expressed his belief in a magnetic fluid, but unlike Mesmer he argued that if a *somnambule* could see without eyes, it was because impressions from without were conveyed directly to the brain through the magnetic fluid, without the intervention of organs or nerves. This for him also explained the influence of the operator on the magnetic subject, what was now being called "community of sensation" (Nelson 1969, 50; Podmore 1963, 1:64).

In France magnetic practitioners were pursuing empirical facts, as after the disastrous 1784 commission, mesmerism had acquired a poor reputation there. With the easing of repression after the Revolution, work in France proceeded again. From this time, with the publication in 1813 of Deleuze's *Histoire du Magnétisme Animal* and up to the mid-century, many investigators turned their attention to lucid or artificial somnambulism, among them Jules Charpignon (1815–?), A.S. Morin (1807–1888), Baron Jules Du Potet de Sennevoy (1796–1881), Lafontaine, Charles Despine (1775–1852), and a Dr. Perrier. Baron Du

Potet, in particular, was influential both in Europe and in Great Britain. In his chambers, above his officiating throne there was a plaster bust of Mesmer crowned with laurel leaves (Owen 1971, 175; McIntosh 1975, 57). Du Potet toured England where he demonstrated magnetic therapy, and he was instrumental also in establishing the second commission in 1826 to investigate magnetic phenomena. In the 1820s, he was among the first to raise the psychological problems of dual personality and abreaction and to demonstrate the therapeutic benefits of physical insensibility induced by a magnetic state, when he assisted in two surgical procedures at the Hôtel-Dieu in Paris, one to relieve a buildup of fluid in the abdomen of a young woman, the other to treat sciatica in the thigh of a man. Although the surgeon, Joseph Récamier (1774–1852) found these exhibitions successful, he did not consider magnetism suitable for general use by physicians (Goldsmith 1934, 185; Crabtree 1993, 136).

A new era dawned with Alexandre Bertrand, a young Paris physician. He was the true originator of the theory of suggestion and, among scientists, almost the first of the "animists" as opposed to the fluidists. Though he died young, Bertrand remains an important figure. After graduating in medicine in 1818, he became interested in animal magnetism when he witnessed a demonstration in his birthplace near Nantes. He brought one of his intractable cases to a *somnambule*, who diagnosed the patient's disease correctly; and he was further astonished when, having no means of knowing the facts, she correctly diagnosed another visitor as "*un jeune homme blessé par une balle dans la tête!*" This was a young man unexpectedly brought to Bertrand by a friend. He had been involved in a duel and had suffered a bullet wound that entered through his mouth and lodged at the base of the neck. Amazingly, he had survived and now came for a consultation. Bertrand used the unexpected visit to test the *somnambule* he was then working with, putting her *en rapport* and asking if she could tell him the nature of the young man's problem. What impressed him was the fact that the sensitive doubted her own determination, saying as if to herself, "*Non, non, ce n'est pas possible; si un homme avait eu une balle dans la tête, il serait mort*" (No, no, this is not possible; if a person received a bullet in the head, he would be dead). She was assured that her surmise was correct, and she went on to trace the exact path of the wound (Podmore 1963, 1:70).

At this period, it seems, Bertrand believed in the theory of animal magnetism, but he soon changed his mind. Between 1823 and 1826, he came to deny the fluidic theory, now believing the phenomena were due to the command, expressed overtly or subtly, that the magnetizer conveys to the subject. Bertrand based many of his own deductions on Abbé José Custodio de Faria's hypothesis. With *Traité du Somnambulisme*, penned in 1823, he was among the first to realize the power of suggestion as a therapeutic agency, and to wonder vaguely about the subconscious mind as a vital factor in the cure of nervous disorders, what he called *transmission des pensées*. A brilliant career was cut short by his untimely death at the age of 36 (Owen 1971, 177; Gauld 1996, 128, 132; Crabtree 1993, 126; Goldsmith 1934, 182).

There was a second revival of interest in animal magnetism or, as it was increasingly termed, mesmerism, in France. In 1825, the magnetizer Dr. Pierre Foissac (1801–1886), a follower of Puységur and a fluidist, persuaded the medical section of the academy to appoint a commission. The resultant second commission was organized in 1826 by Du Potet, with H. M. Husson (1772–1853), physician-in-chief at the Hôtel Dieu, serving as chairman. They conducted investigations over five years, which led to their 1831 report vindicating magnetic sommanbulism: the alleged phenomena were genuine, and in particular "the peculiar state called somnambulism, though of comparatively rare occurrence, was well authenticated." This 1831 commission under Husson was ignored by the medical establishment, as it stressed the marvelous and preternormal aspects of somnambulism (Goldsmith 1934, 87; Crabtree 1993, 185; Podmore 1963, 1:73; Owen 1971, 178). Hence, the 1831 commission conceded some therapeutic value to mesmerism, but the academy returned to the attack in 1837 with a commission heavily weighted against animal magnetism and strongly opposed by Charles Burdin (ca. 1778–1856) and Husson. Burdin offered a 3000-francs prize for proof of eyeless vision, but the prize was never claimed (Darnton 1970, 142; Crabtree 1993, 188).

An increasing transcendental focus is evident later, as in the occupations of Louis Alphonse Cahagnet (1809–1885), a cabinetmaker by trade who spent much of his time communicating with ghosts. Cahagnet was also deeply interested in Swedenborg. Around 1845, he became interested in the phenomena of somnambulism. Three years later, he published the first volume of *Arcanes de la Vie Future Dévoilés*, which gave accounts of communications received especially through the *somnambule* Adèle Maginot. At this time, there was a great interest in magnetism in Germany and France, but not in England. In 1820, Möet translated some of Swedenborg's works into French, and Honoré de Balzac (1799–1850) helped the Swedenborgian trend further with his novel *Séraphita*, the third chapter of which expresses Balzac's belief that Swedenborg preceded Mesmer in the discovery of animal magnetism, as de Maistre had speculated a generation before (Darnton 1970, 141, 154–155; McIntosh 1975, 195).

The third revival, initiated by Dr. Charles Richet (1850–1935) in the 1870s and anointed by the support of the doyen of French neurology, J. M. Charcot, would lead almost directly to an increased British attention to the subject and thus to the formation of the Society for Psychical Research. Both spiritualism and the S. P. R. in England were further influenced by the medical rediscovery of hypnosis in the 1870s. This revival arose from the older streams of mesmeric beliefs and increasingly from the medical connections with Germany. These exercised a deep influence on the more progressive thinkers among spiritualists such as William Howitt (1792–1879) and Professor Augustus de Morgan (1806–1871), and latterly on the French medical writers, especially on Richet and Charcot.

Charles Richet, while serving his internship at the Beaujon Hospital in Paris and after seeing demonstrations by a local magnetizer, gave serious attention to hypnotism. He published his results in 1875 in the *Journal de l'anatomie et de physiologie*, being particularly insistent on the genuineness of hypnotism. He wrote later that, although they were then held to be occult sciences unworthy of the attention of scientific men, "in 1875, while still a student, I was able to show that hypnotism is ... a physiological and psychological fact" (Richet 1923, 99). These courageous experiments occurred two years before Charcot and Heidenhain opened the subject to scientific investigation (Owen 1971, 184).

It was no secret that, in the period 1878–1882, Jean-Martin Charcot was deeply interested in hypnotism and that intensive work was being done at the Salpêtrière hospital in Paris. A pioneer neurologist who named "multiple sclerosis" and holder of the chair of Diseases of the Nervous System with a high standing in the scientific world, Charcot's use of hypnosis in treating hysterical and epileptic patients brought it within the charmed circle of academically respectable subjects, after he published a famous supportive paper in 1882.[6] He assumed that the hypnotic state is a kind of neurosis. His method "avoided the pursuit of the unexpected and the mystic" and attempted "to analyze the meaning of the clinical signs and physiological characteristics that can be identified among various conditions and phenomena caused by nervous reactions" (Owen 1971, 198-199). Charcot was the first to demonstrate that hysterical paralysis is of a psychic rather than a physical origin. Like Janet, but taking a different route, he arrived at the conclusion that there is a mental etiology for hysterias. In the course of his work with patients at the Salpêtrière, Charcot noticed that hysterical cases would mimic the seizures of epileptics when the two kinds of disorders were confined in the same ward. No organic lesions or other causes could be found in his hysteric patients. Charcot then demonstrated with hypnotized subjects that each symptom of hysteria is the result of a subconscious fixed idea that could be traced back to its original cause, usually the memory of some traumatic experience (Taylor 1983, 56). The conception of a "fixed idea" found its psychiatric application in the work of Charcot's student, Pierre Janet.

At the end of the nineteenth century, this also generated a rival "suggestion" school at Nancy through the efforts of Ambroise Liébault (1823–1904) and Hyppolite Bernheim (1840–1919), which confirmed the wealth of psychological questions that could be explored through the use of hypnotism. Having found Liébault able to derive therapy rather than hysteria from the trance state, Bernheim introduced hypnotherapy into his own hospital and concluded that Charcot was mistaken in his analysis of the physiological mechanisms by which hypnosis worked (Owen 1971, 185, 199; Oppenheim 1991, 299–300).

By the 1850s, when spiritualism began to make its mark, along with hypnosis now being studied and applied by medical men like James Esdaile

---

6. Collected as J. M. Charcot, *Lectures on Diseases of the Nervous System* (London: New Sydenham Society, 1889), especially lecture III.

(1808–1859) and James Braid, a term coined by the latter from the Greek word for sleep, new approaches to the mind were also opening; and in this sense, spiritualism's advent was an event of major importance to the budding discipline of psychology. This was a long process that met with much medical opposition along the way. However, by the third quarter of the century, automatic writing, one of the procedures introduced by the spiritists, was taken over by scientists like Janet as a method of exploring the unconscious. A new subject, the medium, became available for psychological experimentation, out of which evolved a new model of the human mind, based on a conscious and an unconscious arena of mental processing (Podmore 1963, 1:125; Owen 1971, 179–180; Ellenberger 1970, 85).

4

THE END OF
THE COVERT ENLIGHTENMENT

Occurrences which, according to received opinions, ought not to happen, are the facts which serve as clues to new discoveries.

Sir John Herschel

The European Enlightenment—and its lengthy aftermath in secularism and twentieth-century humanism—is perhaps unique in the world's history, in its tendency to reject not only formal religion and its attendant values, but also the mystical and occult aspects common within many other societies. In a sense, the revival of occult and millenarian modes in the late eighteenth century and their revivification in a more secular order at the mid-nineteenth century in movements like spiritualism and theosophy can be perceived in the longer term as the minority reaction to an impending hegemonic secular order. The 1789 revolution in France was an important watershed in this complex process. The destruction of the monarchy and the events that saw *citoyen* Napoleon raised first to consul, then to emperor, and the long period of war in Europe from the 1790s brought the urgency of millenarian movements like those of Richard Brothers and Joanna Southcott to the fore in England, while they virtually ended contacts on an intellectual level between and among the European nations. This would help to change the focus of the trends we have observed through the last decades of the eighteenth century to the

New World, where Swedenborgianism would have an impressive revival and where mesmerism would be relegated for a time to the world of the carnival and the stage performer, until it was gradually taken up again in earnest in the West by the medical fraternity. By the mid-nineteenth century, now amalgamated with certain key Swedenborgian concepts, this would form the basis of the popular religion of spiritualism.

Unlike the eclectics and syncretists at Strasbourg, Lyon, and Avignon, some of Swedenborg's followers in his native Sweden had serious reservations about the uses to which his works were now being applied. Because of Swedenborg's exclusive claims to revelation and the dangers he warned of from unwanted spirit influences, the majority of the New Church faithful were enamored neither to mesmerism nor later to spiritualism. To be sure some adherents, among them the Reverend John Clowes himself, failed to heed this advice. Although an enthusiastic follower, Clowes readily departed from some of Swedenborg's prime injunctions. In a 1799 letter to Robert Hindmarsh, Clowes admitted having received some of his sermons through spirit dictation (Hindmarsh 1832, 123–124; Brotherton 1860, 41).[1]

There would also be minor schisms at the mid-nineteenth century, when a succession of New Church clergy like the Reverend Samuel Worcester (1793–1844) and the "New Era" movement, and the Reverend Thomas Lake Harris (1823–1906) advanced the notion of the need for a supplementary revelation, including spirit intercourse, so as to reinforce Swedenborg's message of regeneration.

When Swedenborg had proclaimed a revelation in 1745, it was on the basis of a new understanding of the Word and the demands of the religious life, the growth of an inward morality leading to spiritual regeneration. Somewhat later, Mesmer, working through a steadfastly empirical and physicalist theory, advanced a therapeutic system he believed to be based upon physical laws underlying previously untapped powers, and now directed to the healing of disease. Though Mesmer never worked out their broader implications, his ideas concerning "rapport" or, as it was later also known, "community of sensation" between magnetizer and subject and

---

1. See also the Reverend John Clowes letter of September 11, 1820, on deceiving spirits, cited in *New Jerusalem Magazine* XIX (Nov. 1845): 96–97.

The End of the Covert Enlightenment

the induced "crises," held stupendous consequences for psychology and for theories of the soul alike, especially as developed further by Puységur. In a sense, both Swedenborg and Puységur were concerned with unusual states of awareness; Swedenborg claimed direct experience of another reality, while a generation later Puységur was examining another level or other levels of consciousness within this mundane reality, which many investigators believed was the portal to a deep magnetized state that ultimately facilitated contact with the soul.

Hence Puységur, influenced by Saint-Martin, was convinced that his technique of magnetic sleep had uncovered the pathway to the soul. With the advent of his "psychological" techniques, together with T. D. M. (Tardy de Montravel), Barberin, and others, and the discovery of magnetic sleep or artificial somnambulism, the door was apparently opened to both realms. First, there was a more direct use made of the dissociated state in a mode of psychological healing that now abandoned the *bacquet* and the crises, and even the fluid, for the control of the subject's will. Through these means, diagnoses and prescriptions were frequently procured, allegedly through some deeper level of the magnetized subject's own consciousness. It was but a short step from the accession of more sublime levels of the human mind to the merging of its consciousness in the dissociated state with higher consciousnesses. It was here also that the assistance of spiritual beings was mooted, giving rise to a mode of spiritual healing in a trance state that has survived to modern times, the most famous exponents being Andrew Jackson Davis in the 1850s and Edgar Cayce (1877–1945), the "sleeping prophet" of Virginia Beach, in the 1920s.

Some Swedenborgians evidently recognized early on a possible relation between mesmeric practices circulating throughout Europe at this time and their special insights into the nature and cure of disease, which they owed to Swedenborg's teachings. In June 1787, some fifteen years after Swedenborg's death, Baron Karl Göran Silfverhjelm (b. 1762) on behalf of the Stockholm Exegetic and Philanthropic Society, wrote to the Strasbourg Harmonial Society. Copies were sent to other harmonial societies and to learned journals throughout Europe. This letter is an important document, a striking instance of an attempted *rapprochement* between two modalities, theology and science, that breaches the chasm generally associated with them during the high Enlightenment. The letter is important also as perhaps the first documented account of what would later be called trance mediumship in European intellectual life.

In this letter dated June 19, 1787, a date of fundamental significance to the New Church, marking the seventeenth anniversary of the era of the New Jerusalem, the Stockholm Swedenborgians offered the fruits of their mesmeric investigations according to their understanding of the Word based on Swedenborg's teachings; moreover, they believed these assumptions to be vindicated by the methods of experimental science. Baron Silfverhjelm, the author and a nephew of Swedenborg who later served as Swedish ambassador to London, was engrossed in the study of hermetic wisdom and animal magnetism. This had not been the original aim of the society, but it does underscore the historical judgment that "mystical enlightenment was a preoccupation of the Swedish intelligentsia throughout the eighteenth century" (Garrett 1975, 155, 114).

The history of the Exegetic and Philanthropic Society is intimately related both to court politics in Stockholm and to attempts by Swedenborg's followers to gain general acceptance for his revelation in his native country. It also highlights a regular refrain in the early New Church, a tension between those adherents who considered Swedenborg's revelation as complete and those who believed that it could or should be augmented, especially through spirit contact. Thus magical spiritism plays an important part in both the society's inception and in its demise.

King Gustavus III of Sweden (1746–1792) experienced a transformation during the 1770s. From an early enthusiasm for the "free thought" of Voltaire and the French rationalists, along with a somewhat dissolute private life, the king acquired a strong interest in freemasonry into which, together with his brother Crown Prince Charles (later King Charles XIII, 1748–1818), he was initiated in 1772. Through these Masonic channels, he gradually became more deeply involved in magic and spiritism. One apocryphal story has the king traveling to Italy in 1783 to be anointed into the highest Masonic degree by the Stuart Pretender, who held the highest Masonic dignity and was empowered to transfer it to another monarch (Odhner 1897, 73).[2]

2. For interesting speculations on possible connections between Swedenborg, Rosicrucians, and freemasonry, see also Schuchard 1988, 359–379.

The End of the Covert Enlightenment

During the early 1780s, Gustavus came increasingly under the thrall of courtiers involved in occultism. A Captain Uilvenklon, a master of "astrology, chiromancy, geomancy and hydromancy" was gaining influence at court; he claimed "communication with all possible spirits" and gave Prince Charles a "consecrated hazel-stick" and a "pentacle" that would enable him to command the spirits (Odhner 1897, 75). Johan Gustav Halldin (1737–1825), another adventurer who had narrowly escaped execution for criticizing the king's ownership of whisky distilleries, was reprieved and came into royal favor. Widely traveled, Halldin had been impressed by Cagliostro and by Mesmer, whom he had met in Paris. Halldin seems to have been the principal channel for the entry of spiritism into royal circles, mixed with some Swedenborgian doctrines. He was also a freemason; and at a meeting of the Templars, he flattered the king in explaining, through the science of correspondences, a passage from Swedenborg's writings that implied that each of the members present represented disciples and that the king himself represented the Master Jesus. Halldin's chief patron was the Crown Prince, who was now head of the Templars and had become a bitter enemy of his brother the king (Odhner 1897, 74, 91).

In 1786, Carl F. Nordenskjöld (1754–1828) and Carl B. Wadström (1746–1799) organized the Exegetic and Philanthropic Society, together with Silfverhjelm and about two hundred others; its stated purpose was to publish Swedenborg's works in Swedish, Latin, French, and other languages (Block 1984, 52). In Swedenborg's own country, the Lutheran clergy was powerful and largely hostile opponents of Swedenborg, whose teachings they regarded as heresy. This was despite the patronage of Gustavus III; and as with its ascendancy, the Exegetic and Philanthropic Society's decline was again related to court politics. The king shortly withdrew his protection when his hated brother, Crown Prince Charles, was made a regular member of the society. Among its patrons were a majority of clergymen, various officers of state, and, as its circular proclaimed, "two of the first Princes of Europe." In addition to their publishing program, they formed perhaps the first antislavery movement, based upon Swedenborg's views about the purity of the African races. In that same year, the king sent Wadström, author of *An Essay on*

Colonization, to head a scientific expedition to explore the west coast of Africa in preparation for a Swedish colony that would operate against the slave trade, a venture that unfortunately never came to fruition (Odhner 1904, I:133; Hindmarsh 1861, 40).

The Exegetic and Philanthropic Society was founded with the ostensible aim of disseminating Swedenborg's writings and producing a new translation of the Bible. However, probably through Halldin, the society was soon dominated by members favorable to mesmerism "as affording positive proofs of the verity of Swedenborg's revelation regarding the spiritual world" (Odhner 1897, 113). As one commentator puts it, "The cunning serpent of magical spiritism had established himself in the society" (Odhner 1897, 113). The phenomena of animal magnetism were creating a perfect furor all over Europe and were then fashionable at most of the European courts (Block 1984, 53; Odhner 1904, I:134).

In May 1787, the society began conducting experiments in which it was claimed that the spirits of the dead communicated through a *somnambule*. The 1788 journal of the *Societé Exegetique et Philantropique*, probably the only issue printed, explains that the wife of a gardener named Lindquist had been placed in a state of magnetic sleep or trance, along with the spirits of two children, who had also been controlled (Podmore 1963, 1:76). They believed that they had found a "rational and favourable" explanation for these phenomena in Swedenborg. This was among the first interpretations for these new abnormal phenomena as being the results of supernatural influence, and like the Society's pioneering opposition to slavery, it was based on a particular interpretation of Swedenborg's writings (Nelson 1969, 50).

There were many among the inaugural membership, like Nordenskjöld and Wadström, who were interested mainly in the exegesis and dissemination of Swedenborgian thought, but they soon became resigned to the new emphasis on spiritism. The society was supported by powerful magnates at court like Count Anders von Höpken (1712–1789) and its first president Baron Sven Liljencrantz (d. 1796), and Swedenborg's nephew Baron Silfverhjelm rapidly became the leader of the magnetists and spiritists. Besides others like Halldin and Captain Uilvenklon, this trend was reinforced by foreign members. Among these were Avignon members the Marquis de Thomé, General Rainsford, and their leader the Abbé Pernety (Odhner 1897, 93).

By June 1787, the society had some 150 members and was about to open a printing office in conjunction with the Masonic Templars (Odhner 1904, I:134). But things went badly from this point. Their greatest heights and also the seeds of their dissolution came within two years, when Crown Prince Charles was accepted into the society in August 1787. Gustavus III, already disposed against it because of the hostility of the Lutheran high clergy, had withdrawn from the society his permission to publish; and when enemies of the Swedenborgians like the poet Johan Henrik Kellgren (1751–1795) set to work building upon the suspicion of his brother's motives, he withdrew his protection altogether. Subsequently, their tracts had to be printed in Denmark and smuggled into the country.

Meanwhile Halldin, Silfverhjelm, and other magnetic spiritists had gained control of the society, which now focused almost exclusively on animal magnetism. They began experiments. Silfverhjelm, the main proponent of the society's new thrust, "praised God, who had given this boon to men as a means of again gaining communication with the spiritual world." As we have seen, Silfverhjelm was the principal author of the letter of June 19, 1787; and as noted by C. T. Ohdner, together with the problems exacerbated by Prince Charles joining the society and his leadership of the Templars, this did "incalculable harm in the learned world by presenting Swedenborg and the Writings in a false light. By the publication of this letter, the Society had signed its own death warrant" (Odhner 1897, 113). Against this background, we may now examine the contents of this letter, for what it can reveal about the assumptions and beliefs of the now dominant magnetic spiritists and the relation of this group with other societies in France and elsewhere.

The Infamous Letter of June 19, 1787

The letter dated June 19, 1787, was sent from Stockholm, in Swedish and in French, addressed to the *Societé des Amis Réunis* at Strasbourg, with an attached brochure arguing for the spiritual origins of the phenomena associated with animal magnetism. It appears that the Swedenborgians were concerned about the undisciplined nature of the communications made at Strasbourg and elsewhere. The letter explains that "members' experiments have contributed much to direct our attention to the true principles of Magnetism and Somnambulism, and consequently to a solution of the phenomena which they exhibit" (Bush 1847, 261; Darnton 1970, 67).[3]

The distinction in the terms employed suggests that, by 1787, Puységur's work was recognized as growing out of, yet being distinct from, Mesmer's own system. The author recounts that angels had possessed the inner beings of somnambulists in Stockholm, whereupon they had communicated "an adumbration, though feeble, of the first immediate correspondence with the invisible world," by which he means Swedenborg's own intromissions. He maintains that mesmerism and Swedenborgianism complement one another perfectly and urges that the two societies cooperate in the business of regenerating humankind, by disseminating one another's works. A solution was then offered for these puzzling phenomena:

> [I]t seems to be impossible fully and rationally to explain them, unless we once for all, and without shrinking from the shafts of ridicule, take it for granted that spiritual beings exert an influence upon the organs of the invalid during the time that the power of Magnetism has produced a partial cessation of the functions of the soul, and that these spiritual agents, in virtue of the higher degrees of knowledge which they possess, originate these wonderful and otherwise inexplicable phenomena. (Bush 1847, 262)

The soul, the writer goes on to explain, "in essence consists in the will and the understanding; properties which can never exist, except man possesses self-consciousness (*conscientia sui*), which somnambulists generally do not."

As we have seen, the Lyon Masonic and mesmeric school, *la psychologie sacrée*, was directly influenced by the events at Strasbourg under Puységur's

---

3. The letter is reproduced in its entirety in Bush 1847, 261–269.

leadership. Magnetism in this case was regarded as a method for inducing a "partial cessation" of perception, discrimination, and other normal functions of the intellect, thus affording the benign spiritual beings a chance to do their work. The Swedenborgian notion of spiritual "exhalations" informs this view that the soul can be operated upon by spiritual agents, just as disease itself is sometimes produced by evil influences. The will and understanding were for Swedenborg, as for Kant, the essence of the individual, and of fundamental importance to the exercise of free choice. It is maintained that the "spirit sleep-talker" in these operations was a being completely independent of the magnetized patient. As a result of their experiments they had found that "a Magnetizer speaking only to the spirit as to another person, and not to the sleeper, can, by rational, directed, and well-digested questions, render it practicable for the spirit to make itself known as a being different from him whose tongue it makes use of" (Bush 1847, 263). This suggests that disease is caused by malevolent spiritual beings and that a cure depends upon their dislodgment, which in turn relies upon the dissociation of the magnetized subject's intellect, in effect a form of exorcism carried out with the help of benign spirits.

The letter is of general interest also for what appears to be a veiled attack on Mesmer himself. It rails against the *philosophes*, "those ignorant and self-worshipping people . . . eager to assail . . . anything . . . which bears any reference to a future life, the solemn thought of which they hoot at with impious temerity . . . and impudently assume the name of philosophers, [basing] their false conclusions upon an imaginary foundation which they call Nature" (Bush 1847, 264).

The crux of the argument is then presented: magnetism and somnambulism, if rightly understood and applied, are intimately connected with the advancement of divine truth; they corroborate this truth by means of a "speaking illustration" discussed by Swedenborg in *Secrets of Heaven*, which had led some like de Maistre to claim that the principles of mesmerism had first been discovered by Swedenborg. Thus, if the magnetism be directed "not to the natural and physical alone, but especially to the spiritual good of the soul" and if the magnetizer is convinced that all diseases are the results of moral evil, the direct influence of the hell spheres, then "the act of magnetizing is chiefly a moral act. . . . [T]he operative cause is the magnetizer's strong desire to benefit his neighbour; and the effect is that of removing or expelling the influence of the disease" (Bush 1847, 265–267).

Hence, the moral condition of the magnetizer, together with the dissociated state of the magnetized subject, creates the conditions for the expulsion of unwanted influences that manifest in disease. As the writer puts it, "the state of the Somnambulist . . . may be called ecstatic. . . . [W]hat is said and done through the sleeper's organs is not the act of his soul, but of some other being, who has taken possession of his organs, and operates through them" (Bush 1847, 268). Paroxysms and the like denote that the spirit of disease is still present; but when the subject begins to talk in his "sleep," that is, under magnetic influence, this is regarded as a sign of the presence of a friendly spiritual being, his guardian-angel or good genius, who possesses the same measure of goodness and wisdom as the patient. It is not explained how, in this circumstance, the disease takes hold of the patient in the first place, but only that the guardian angel speaks through the *somnambule*, once the spirit of disease is dislodged (Bush 1847, 268–269)

Swedenborg's theology is marshaled for support. Not only was the "speaking illustration" one means whereby the reality of the spiritual realms could be made known, but the arrival of somnambulism itself is seen as confirming the trend of the new revelation, whose embodiment was the Church of the New Jerusalem. It is explained that, from the time of the councils of the early Church, the gift for healing had ceased because the Christian world had perverted pure religion by "the spurious glosses and additions" of later ages. Thus, by Swedenborg's era, the divine influx was being obstructed by the multitudes now existing in the intermediate spheres that he termed "the world of spirits." However, since the Second Coming that Swedenborg witnessed in the heavens in 1757, great progress had occurred, along with an unprecedented revolution in habits of thought and action. The writer is leading to the point that the new phenomena then bursting forth throughout Europe held a far deeper, a cosmic, significance:

The End of the Covert Enlightenment

> The transition which the natural world is undergoing . . . renders it probable, as our sleep-talkers have declared: that supernatural gifts and powers will be bestowed upon such, who abstain from all known and deliberate sinning, and in their hearts sincerely and humbly desire and pray, that the Lord's will may be done in everything, and theirs only in as far as it shall be perfectly conformable to His. (Bush 1847, 268)

In sending this letter to magnetic societies and learned institutions, the Stockholm society had taken a courageous stand in favor of a spiritistic interpretation of the magnetic phenomena. This was a new explanation, deriving from a broader Swedenborgian framework that comprehended the human experience as a battleground between good and evil; all beneficial effects were attributed to the work of wise and helpful spirits who, upon the induction of magnetic sleep, were given the opportunity to act. Disease resulted, in their view, from the action of an evil spirit adventitiously lodged within the body of the patient, while healing was brought about by good spirits acting through the mechanism of induced somnambulism, which resulted in the ejection of the evil influence (Crabtree 1993, 71).

Marguerite Block (1984, 53), in her study of the New Church, concluded that the Strasbourg society rejected the hypothesis of the Exegetic and Philanthropic Society concerning the phenomena of animal magnetism because they "insisted on a naturalistic interpretation of the phenomena, and ridiculed the Stockholm society's spiritualistic theories." This judgment does not sit well with other accounts, and the term "naturalistic" is not a true description of Strasbourg's views. It is true that, on a psychological and functionalist level, as a therapeutic tool, they rejected the Swedenborgians' opinions as to the true causes of disease; to them, this view, whereby disease originates from the influences of exhalations from spiritual realms, was tantamount to exorcism. They rejected also the notion that guardian spirits were necessary to effect cures, for this would have eclipsed their evolving psychological theory, where the magnetizer's will becomes the most important factor in the establishment of rapport with the patient, and in the mingling of fluids. But they did not in principle reject supernatural action; on the contrary, they were at one with their *confrères* at Lyon in regarding the new phenomena as "the final rejection of materialism." Adam Crabtree focuses on the real dilemma for the Strasbourg society: if they rejected some species of "intrusion" as an explanation for therapeutic efficacy, then they must account for the observed phenomena according to a differing paradigm (Crabtree 1993, 71–72). This they did in positing a second consciousness, largely independent of the waking consciousness, which, according to their Catholic cultural understanding, was none other than the soul. Thus did Puységur and the early magnetizers break new ground in the study of the human unconscious. By the next century, with the advent of Janet, Freud and others, this would lead to a radically different view of the human mind, bearing enormous implications for the cure of mental disease.

The letter of June 19 was sent broadcast throughout Europe to men and institutions of learning, exciting much opposition and some ridicule. Along with its rejection by Puységur's society at Strasbourg, it was attacked in the learned journals of the German universities, like those at Weimar and Jena. A combination of attacks from outside and internal dissensions resulted in the complete collapse of the society in 1791 (Block 1984, 53, 56).

Seen from the psychotherapeutic vista of its author, Crabtree attributes Strasbourg's rejection of the Swedenborgian explanation to its unsatisfactory account of the somnambulistic state. While they could agree that some sort of spiritual forces were at work in somnambulism, they disagreed over their nature. Although the evidence allows no firmer conclusions to be made, their disagreement with the spiritistic Swedenborgians led by Silfverhjelm seems to have been based on the alleged operation of spirits and angels. To the Strasbourg mesmerists, searching for the hypnotic stratum, the arena of mental processing was neither the mind of an external entity (spirit) nor the conscious mind of the somnambulist. The positing of mental acts that occur "within human beings but outside of and unavailable to consciousness" was, for the magnetists at Strasbourg and Lyon a result of direct gnosis, the operation of a deeper state of consciousness coeval with the soul.[4] While this interpretation of the grounds for their disagreement is necessarily speculative, it seems consistent with the psychological insights indicated by the work of Puységur and his followers since 1784.

The End of the Avignon Society

In this same period of the late 1780s, we can see the final connections within the covert Enlightenment between the occult revival in England and France, just prior to the storming of the Bastille in July 1789. It is instructive to follow some of these connections among the various societies we have been considering, to observe how quickly the world of freemasons, mystics, and occultists receded before the maelstrom of revolution and repression, and what ramifications these events would hold for the further elaboration of Swedenborg and Mesmer in the new milieu of the New World.

With the eager recruitment by Grabianka preparatory to the arrival of the millennium, the Avignon Society was attracting adherents from all over Europe. In England these close links were exemplified in the careers of two intrepid millenarians, John Wright and William Bryan, who are representative of the trend among English millenarians during the 1790s and beyond. Their attraction was firstly to the quasi-Masonic organizations, their interest having been sparked by Swedenborg's writings and by the numerous contacts established through Duché's Lambeth circle. Like many English millenarians, they went on to become followers of Brothers and later of Southcott (Garrett 1975, 96).

John Wright, a carpenter from Leeds, heard the Swedenborgian preachers Ralph Mather and Joseph Salmon during their tour of northern England. After the formation of the New Church, these former Methodists endeavored to apply that sect's mode of field preaching to obtain converts. John Wesley remembered Mather as "a devoted young

---

4. Crabtree writes, "Needless to say, thinking about magnetic sleep had not yet developed to such a sophisticated stage. It would be much later, when a new form of spiritism (American spiritualism with its table-turning phenomena) met with a more advanced form of animal magnetism (magnetic and hypnotic experiments with double consciousness), that this mystery at the heart of magnetic sleep could be solved" (1993, 72).

man, but almost driven out of his senses by Mystic Divinity" (Garrett 1975, 159). After hearing Salmon and Mather preach at Leeds in early 1788, Wright, leaving wife and children behind, set off for London. Unfortunately, he was disappointed by the Swedenborgians. At Great East Cheap he found only "old *forms* of worship established by man's will and not according to the will of God" (Harrison 1979, 69; Garrett 1975, 159–160). In October of that year, Wright met William Bryan who had left his native Shrewsbury for London at age 16, where he became a copperplate printer under the tutelage of the radical millenarian William Sharp. They were probably introduced by Duché, at whose Sunday evening circle Sharp was a regular participant (Garrett 1975, 175).

Bryan had grown up in Shrewsbury, where his family worshipped in the established Church. In London working with William Sharp, he fell into bad company, associating with several young men from his town by whom he was led to spend Sundays "at some public gardens or place of amusement, drinking, &c" (Bryan 1795, 16–17). Then he met some Quakers; and at one of their silent meetings, "my mind was reached by the great, good and merciful Lord." For a time, Bryan went to the excess of altering his dress to the somber Quaker style and cutting off his hair. His restless intelligence was not fulfilled, and he began attending Duché's circle with his employer.

Through this new milieu of urbane Swedenborgians like Duché, Chastanier, and William Bousie and freemasons like Major Tienman von Berend, known in Masonic circles as Tieman and General Rainsford, Wright and Bryan learned of the Avignon Society and sought to establish contact. Bryan received "confirmation of the Spirit that I should be required to go to Avignon" (Harrison 1979, 72; Block 1984, 62; Bryan 1795, 20). It promised more of the miraculous they were seeking, and the following year they set out for Avignon, stopping first at the Paris home of Bousie. After many trials, including abandoning their wives and families, they reached Avignon in January 1789, where they remained for seven months, receiving "revealed knowledge" through a divine spirit, presumably in French. These two English tradesmen, who unlike most of the membership were neither nobles nor clerics nor wealthy bourgeois, were received kindly by the brethren. Soon they were "favoured with divine communications"; and although it is not stated what form these communications took, they almost certainly involved somnambulistic subjects (Garrett 1975, 111–112; Harrison 1979, 69). Bryan (1795, 28) recounts that "we were employed in reading, and making extracts from the journals of the society, by which we were informed of the many changes taking place, and to take place, in the nations of the earth, to prepare the way of the Lord's second coming, and the restoration of his people, the whole house of Israel, according to the prophecies in the Scriptures."

European religious heterodoxy began to breathe somewhat the same air of mystery and magic that could be found within freemasonry and at harmonial lodges, but now with a different and millenarian intent. With the diminished therapeutic concerns and an increasing metaphysical curiosity over large questions such as the continuance of life after death and the alleged communications with higher intelligences, came also a *fin de siècle* wave of millenarian movements, especially in Britain. This trend was particularly strong during the war years of the 1790s, which witnessed the rapid spread of the enthusiastic ravings of Richard Brothers and his "Israelites." Later still Joanna Southcott, the prophetess of Exeter, a washerwoman turned seer, gained extreme popularity in the early nineteenth century, claiming to be the "Woman clothed with the Sun" proclaimed in Revelations. Southcott's utterances were produced by a kind of automatic writing, usually directed by God, and often in the form of inelegant but rather charming doggerel verse. Southcott was the best known among the plethora of contemporary female saviors like Elspeth Buchan (1738–1791); Jemima Wilkinson (1752–1819), the "Publick Universal Friend"; and the Shaker leader Mother Ann Lee (1736–1784). When she died in 1814, Southcott had gathered one hundred thousand supporters in London and thousands more in the Midlands, Lancashire, and Yorkshire. Southcottian numbers were especially strong in Nottingham (Garrett 1975, 216; Owen 1989, 13; Barrow 1986, 32). Also like Buchan, her followers expected her resurrection; but after a few days, and with little fanfare, her physical remains were buried quietly.

Returning to England as the French Revolution spread, Bryan and Wright joined the millenarian movement of Richard Brothers. For a brief period of three years in England between 1792 and 1795, Richard

Brothers was hugely popular. He was regarded by scores of thousands as the prophet of the end days, and he even had a champion in the Parliament in Nathaniel Brassey Halhed (1751–1830), M.P. A former naval officer, Brothers was the principal English proponent of Isrealitism. Philosemitism was one outgrowth of the current millennial fervor. In 1751, the poet Christopher Smart (1722–1771) had declared in *Jubilate Agno* that "the ENGLISH are the seed of Abraham"; Smart believed himself to be descended from David, that Christ would come in 1760, and that the New Jerusalem would be manifest in England (Harrison 1979, 58; Garrett 1975, 185).[5]

Before he slipped inexorably into madness, Brothers' claims to be the "Prince of the Jews and nephew of the Almighty" had a tremendous effect on many earnest inquirers, such as Sarah Flaxmer, William Sharp, Philippe-Jacques de Loutherbourg, as well as on the dependable Wright and Bryan. Brothers believed he was destined to lead those whom he called the "invisible Hebrews," English descendants of the ten lost tribes, to Jerusalem, when the millennium would commence on a date he fixed at November 19, 1795. After this, he foresaw the time of the end as foretold in the Book of Daniel, the toppling of European thrones and empires, and the binding of Antichrist. Bryan and Wright abandoned their Avignon practices to join his movement. The Swedenborgians were hostile, the printer Robert Hindmarsh refusing to print Brothers's manifesto, *A Revealed Knowledge* (Harrison 1979, 61, 67–68).

One may speculate that Bryan and Wright might have been lured away from Avignon by acolytes of Brothers or that they turned against the Avignon Society after their new conversion. In 1795, the year when the final conflagration ought to have occurred, Sarah Flaxmer, a devotee of Brothers, wrote a long and rambling defense, where she warns regarding Avignon: "Satan knowing that the kingdom of Christ was now at hand, he has established a synagogue at Avignon. Now the members of this synagogue are his angels; some of these are dispersed into all nations, and go about as angels of light, to deceive the elect of God" (Flaxmer 1795, 9). Although the facts are too sketchy to come to any definite conclusions, it

---

5. See also Nathaniel Brassey Halhed, MP, *Testimony of the authenticity of the Prophecies of Richard Brothers and of his Mission to Recall the Jews* (London: H. D. Symonds, 1795).

is noteworthy that the Avignon brethren were being demonized just then by this English sect. Perhaps it was the malodor of all things French in this period of war.

Brothers was regarded as the Elijah mentioned by the prophet Malachi, who is to precede the Lord's Second Coming, as John the Baptist did his first (Bryan 1795, 2). It had been communicated to Brothers that most of the inhabitants of Great Britain were Isrealites, mainly of the tribe of Benjamin, but some were of Judah, and others like Wright were of Levi; Bryan, apparently descended from Judah, was told that he should recognize all of that tribe "by a peculiar mark in the right eye" and also by a distinguishing mark on his beard, for "the beard of each different tribe has a different form" (1795, 8). The movement collapsed when the millennium failed to arrive on November 19, 1795, as predicted and as Brothers descended into madness. Like William Miller (1782–1849) at a later era the passing of the appointed date, the "stubborn continuation of time" discredited the prophet along with his prophecies. The "nephew of the Almighty" ended his days in a lunatic asylum. The desperately seeking pair of Wright and Bryan then turned their allegiance to a new prophet, Joanna Southcott, who also failed as prophet and seer when the millennium once again failed to arrive, and likewise neither did her expected resurrection thereafter from the dead eventuate.

John Wright became a bookseller, specializing in books by or about Brothers. For his part, after moving through these movements, Bryan did find contentment later as a magnetic healer, herbalist, and apothecary; and like Barberin some decades earlier, he practiced a form of sympathetic healing. He believed that by the power of the Holy Spirit, "I have at times been favoured to feel so much of that love as to enter into a sympathy of feeling with my patient, so that I could describe every symptom of their disease from feeling it in my own body" (Bryan 1795, 30; Garrett 1975, 199; Harrison 1979, 71). Then living in Bristol, Bryan was described as a prophet by Robert Southey (1774–1843), who paid him a visit. With his considerable charm and intelligence, Bryan impressed the poet laureate, who remarked that his resemblance to pictures of Jesus Christ was "so striking as to astonish." Robert Hindmarsh, also a printer, knew Bryan and considered him a crackpot (Garrett 1975, 175–176). At the turn of the century, when they became devotees of Joanna Southcott, Bryan and Wright disappear from historical view.

During its brief existence in France, the Avignon Society had many visitors from other like-minded organizations. At the end of 1789, Count Gustav Reutherholm and Baron Silfverhjelm made a grand tour of various French societies. Like Grabianka, they were Masonic Templars, the order headed by the Prince Charles of Sudermania, hated brother of King Gustavus III. After a brief stay in Paris, they proceeded to Lyon to visit Jean-Baptiste Willermoz, then on to Avignon. Significantly, they did not visit Strasbourg or London. Reutherholm was initiated into the Avignon Society, ascending the hill Tabor for each of nine days in the prescribed manner, reciting prayers and burning incense at the top (Garrett 1975, 113–114). It is not clear if their visit was intended to round up support for their society, in order to buttress its position since the almost fatal withdrawal of royal protection. From this significant omission, a strong inference can be made that the June 1787 letter had soured relations with the less millenarian-inclined harmonial societies. It is not known whether Silfverhjelm and Reutherholm visited Lyon and Avignon at the invitation of Willermoz, Pernety, or Grabianka. The odium heaped on the Exegetic and Philanthropic Society by the German university journals had created disharmony within the society itself. But it seems that presently there was a split at Stockholm between the orthodox Swedenborgians and the magnetic spiritists led by Silfverhjelm.

In May 1790, Baron Silfverhjelm became president of the Exegetic and Philanthropic Society. The most zealous of the magnetizers, he produced much disharmony within the group and at court, which led to the dissolution of the society in 1791 (Odhner 1904, 1:162). Hence the introduction of magnetic and spiritistic practices, mingled by Halldin, Silfverhjelm, and others into an eclectic set of beliefs to which they attempted to lend the authority of Swedenborg's doctrines, resulted in the strengthening at court of the opponents to the seer's teachings, like the acerbic poet Kellgren, whose ideals were those of the *philosophes*, and now he had the king's ear (Odhner 1897, 113). It also exposed the society to ridicule in France and Germany. More needs to be learned about the various appropriations of Swedenborg's doctrines in the diverse European societies that together embodied the covert Enlightenment, but it seems that Strasbourg was least enthusiastic, probably because of Puységur's psychological interests and his Catholic associations at *La Candeur* and elsewhere. The Strasbourgians were clearly not convinced by the explanations proferred in Silfverhjelm's 1787 letter.

Grabianka's desire for kingship seems to have been a major preoccupation of the Avignon Society from this time; and amazingly, it seems that the society was even contemplating a military exercise against the Turks to reconquer Palestine, presumably as precondition to the arrival of the millennium and perhaps to enthrone Grabianka as king of Israel (Garrett 1975, 116). At any rate, the plan came to nought, as in 1791 the revolutionary government annexed Avignon from papal authority to that of France. This brought the activities of the Avignon Society effectively to an end. Although they now abandoned occultism for demonstrations of civic patriotism, the society remained suspect in official eyes. Vice-légat Casoni moved against the society, and a rare Vatican report of 1791 outlines other complaints against these "new people of God": it recounts that they pretended to be Catholics but were consecrated with a superstitious rite and that they purported to be assisted by angels and were inspired with "new" interpretations of the Bible, meaning Swedenborg's. They were distinguished not by names, but by numbers, and had both a king and a pontiff. More horrifying yet were the mesmeric phenomena they claimed to manifest. One Ottavio Cappelli (d. 1798), according to a papal report a gardener by trade, but actually an Italian mystic, claimed to be in communication with the archangel Raphael and had composed a rite of initiation. He spent two years at Avignon from 1787 (Garrett 1975, 105). For his troubles, Cappeli was condemned by the Inquisition and imprisoned for seven years. Later the unfortunate Cappelli was put to death as a Russian spy by the papal authorities. Their heresy brought the same sentence on other Avignon members, but this condemnatory report was never put into effect, being overtaken by the more secular events stemming from the French Revolution, as many of the Avignon brothers were jailed by the government (Garrett 1975, 105; Bricaud 1927, 94).

During 1793 and 1794, Pernety, Gabrianka, Corberon, and Bousie were arrested. Others fled in the face of Jacobin repression, so that by 1800 only fifteen members remained at Avignon. Pernety died in 1796, and Gabrianka fled to St. Petersburg, where he was imprisoned in 1807 on suspicion of plotting against the czar. Thus, the organization that reflected more than any other the complex synthesis of the main currents in the covert Enlightenment came to an ignominious end. The Avignon Society membership dispersed, some adopting the other-worldly mysticism of Saint-Martin, and others like William Bousie joining the New Church (Garrett 1975, 117–119). At Strasbourg, the suspect *Societé des Amis Réunis* was also disbanded because of its aristocratic connections. Puységur published three volumes of the Proceedings of the Strasbourg Society before being imprisoned by Napoleon. He served two years and, after recovering his estate which had been confiscated, Puységur returned to his work with Race and other sensitives. In 1807, he published *Du Magnétisme Animal*, which instituted a new era in the history of magnetic phenomena and a brief renaissance in their therapeutic application (Podmore 1963, 1:59–60). Even the Lodge of the Nine Sisters in Paris came under suspicion by the Jacobins and was disbanded in 1792 (Weisberger 1993, 106). With the restoration, the era of the romantics brought a new life also to the spiritistic style of mesmerism. P. S. Dupont de Nemours (1739–1817) wrote lyrically of "a chain of invisible spirits [that] stretches between us and God; the spirits communicate with our sixth sense by means of an invisible fluid; our souls migrate through the mineral, vegetable, and animal worlds. . . ." (quoted in Darnton 1970, 136).

Several significant patterns are discerned during the relatively brief period of the covert Enlightenment. At the Exegetic and Philanthropic Society in Stockholm, as at the *Amis Réunis* in Strasbourg, at Avignon and among the mystical Masons of Lyon at *La Concorde*, there was a common though fluid membership. A degree of cooperation and cross-pollination of ideas existed between these quasi-Masonic societies and the reformed freemasonries like the Templars, *La Candeur*, and the *Loge Élue et Chérie*. These societies became clearing houses for a wide variety of heterodox perspectives, ranging from mystical Catholicism, Talmudic and Kabbalistic magic to somnambulism and Swedenborgianism. Their activities were adapted into a syncretic belief system that exemplifies the most durable aspects of Enlightenment thinking: an extreme curiosity about the world and a propensity for constructing systems.

By the close of the eighteenth century the quasi-Masonic, Swedenborgian and mesmerist currents of the covert Enlightenment had largely dissipated. Mesmer's theories were rejected, his harmonial lodges were moribund, and his therapeutic techniques were being modified and even abandoned by his disciples (Ellenberger 1970, 53). There was a second wave of support for magnetism inspired by the work of du Potet and Husson, resulting in a second commission. With numerous advocates and detractors, this wave also ended when a third commission in 1837, heavily weighted with medical men, turned up negative conclusions. Half a century would elapse before Braid and others in the medical world would put Mesmer's ideas into practice, providing the decisive impulse toward the elaboration of dynamic psychiatry, in England through the S. P. R.'s work and in France principally through the medical application of hypnosis by Charles Richet and J. M. Charcot. The millenarian sects did not fare well in France, and with the exception of Edward Irving's (1792–1834) brief ministry in the early 1830s, neither did they find a wide appeal in Britain after Brothers and Southcott. There was, however, considerable appeal for all sorts of reform, radical movements, and sects across the Atlantic, where, from the early nineteenth century, both magnetism and the New Church found increasing numbers of adherents. It is to America that this narrative now shifts, where the final transformation of the ontological and alternate-consciousness paradigms can be traced, together with its cultural product, the synthesis that yielded the mediumistic séance.

5

MILLENARIAN PROPHETS IN AMERICA: HEAVEN ON EARTH

"In the last days it will be, God declares,
that I will pour out my Spirit upon all flesh,
and your sons and your daughters shall prophesy,
and your young men shall see visions,
and your old men shall dream dreams.
Even upon my slaves, both men and women,
In those days I will pour out my Spirit;
And they shall prophesy."

Acts 2: 17-18

The concluding chapters of this study focus principally on the American experience. This chapter deals with the transformation of an older millenarian tradition, while the remaining chapters regard a newer "scientific" trend in the magnetic movement, set in counterpoint to the concerns in the New Church over its "disorderly" uses. Both of these trends form part of the aftermath of the covert Enlightenment, in the changing views relating to the human mind and consciousness and to the accessibility of higher states of being. Robert Fuller locates this new direction as a combined outcome of the revivals and Protestant evangelism (Fuller 1982, 73, 79, and passim). I endeavor to sketch the contextual overview stemming from the insights of the eighteenth-century savants Swedenborg and Mesmer. In the final chapter, these in turn are shown to form a new synthesis, which employs the mechanism of hypnotic entrancement derived from Mesmer, Puységur *et al*, combined with a positive outlook on the accessibility of a higher reality or realities, which yields the mediumistic séance.

It is instructive at this point to introduce the varied movements that formed the center of gravity for these developing transformations. The paradigms of mind now centered in the New World but imbued still with Old World concerns of the coming millennium and the means of meeting it were, in the wider America, channeled into evangelical ventures. In the heterodox assemblies we are concerned with in this study, a strong messianic temper along with an absolute faith in the Bible as verbal inspiration produced a small but intensive trend toward millenarian organization, which often took the form of communitarian societies. This was as true of the German Pietists as of the Shakers and the Brook Farmers. Communitarianism formed the principle of family organization in the secular Owenite and Fourierist ventures also, in their attempts to forge a "new kind of family." Another and related tendency was the abiding interest among these communities in what we would call the hypnotic substratum, but which to groups like the pious Rappites and the Amana community manifested as guiding wisdom directly from God or through an angelic spirit, or simply arose out of a deep faith in the Second Advent. Often, though not always, these interests took the particular form of the induction of trance conditions in selected mediums, and they were frequently related to an interest in methods of alternative healing.

One significant trend at the turn of the nineteenth century was the millennial imperative based on biblical prophecies, with a corresponding gradual shift in focus among sects from these prophecies to the teachings and other pronouncements of a charismatic leader. A simple faith in the Lord's Second Coming was augmented by faith in an agent of the Lord, who would guide the faithful to that blessed event and to salvation. Religious optimism for many took the form of belief in an early millennium (Cross 1965, 79). R.A. Knox writes in *Enthusiasm* that "we ought not to judge the religious temper of the 18th century by the religious temper of its political idols or of its literary interpreters. There were deeper currents below the surface; the age of enlightenment was also an age of fanaticisms" (Knox 1950, 388). For millenarian and extreme perfectionist sects like the Shakers, the Shadrach Irelands, the Jemimakins (as Jemima Wilkinson's followers were known), and the Buchanites, a recurring theme of their quest was the biblical image given in Revelations 12, wherein are described the great red dragon, the beast that persecuted the church, and the woman clothed with the sun who fled into the wilderness

(McLoughlin 1978, 70). In general, according to Newton (1900, 39), there were two sources of biblical prophecies: Daniel 8:14, relating to the cleansing of the sanctuary, and the 1,260 days in Revelations 12:3–6, where days signify years:

> Then another portent appeared in heaven: a great red dragon, with seven heads and ten horns, and seven diadems on his heads. His tail swept down a third of the stars of heaven and threw them to the earth. Then the dragon stood before the woman who was about to bear a child, so that he might devour her child as soon as it was born. And she gave birth to a son, a male child, who is to rule all the nations with a rod of iron. But her child was snatched away and taken to God and to this throne; and the woman fled into the wilderness, where she has a place prepared by God, so that there she can be nourished for one thousand two hundred sixty days.[1]

And in 12:14–15: "But the woman was given the two wings of the great eagle, so that she could fly from the serpent into the wilderness, to her place where she is nourished for a time, and times, and half a time. Then from his mouth the serpent poured water like a river after the woman, to sweep her away with the flood." The doctrines of these prophets and of the plethora of other apocalyptic sects led by a charismatic leader mirror varying interpretations to these famous passages in the Apocalypse of John; for our purposes, they illuminate two current trends in American reform germane to the transformation of the core paradigms that have been presented: millenarianism and communitarianism.

We have seen that, until the *terreur* of the French Revolution and the almost constant state of war in Europe for another generation, the occult revival had survived in quasi-Masonic associations like *Les Amis Réunis*, the Avignon Society, and the Exegetic and Philanthropic Society in Stockholm. The concepts and doctrines of Mesmer and Swedenborg

---

1. The Scripture quotations contained herein are from the New Revised Standard Version Bible, copyright © 1989 by the Division of Christian Education of the National Council of the Churches of Christ in the U.S.A., and are used by permission. All rights reserved.

found their way into the same educated elite through the harmonial societies and other mystically inclined groups; and during the early 1780s, both systems were carried to the United States. In 1784, the same year that the merchant James Glen lectured on Swedenborg in Philadelphia and Boston, the Marquis de Lafayette was attempting to interest the revolutionary elite in Mesmer's ideas, but meeting with little success; Washington was equivocal, while Jefferson and Franklin were hostile to the new sensation, the latter giving practical effect to his opposition through the 1784 commission (Darnton 1970, 88). From the 1780s, there was another wave of influence, drawing more firmly on working-class culture and bearing a more eschatological emphasis; this trend was evident among the migrant adherents of the Shakers, the Buchanites, and other small groups that carried the legacy of European religious heterodoxy into the New World.

The Spiritualist Movement: Antecedents in England and America

J. F. C. Harrison (1979, xvi) has called millenarianism "an ideology to take account of radical social change." We have seen that the close fraternal and looser institutional links between the Swedenborgians of Jacob Duché's circle, the harmonial freemasons at Strasbourg and Lyon, and the mystical millenarians at Avignon were abruptly severed by war and revolution. Kingship was brutally rejected in France, while in England, at war and trying to adjust to the burgeoning Industrial Revolution, many people were seeking satisfaction through new forms of belief. From a strong millenarian inheritance, there existed in the 1780s and 1790s an intellectual milieu favorable to the eschatological interpretation of events. Moreover, sects like the Quakers, the Muggletonians, and even a few Ranters, remained as visible links to older forms of enthusiasm. The Swedenborgian Robert Hindmarsh met an elderly Ranter in the 1780s at Shoreditch, who claimed "there was no God in the universe but man" and that "he himself was a God" (Harrison 1979, 14). The legacy of the Camisards and the English Prophets flowed into the Shaker movement in the Midlands, where William Law's translations of Boëhme, and latterly the Swedenborgian influence, further enriched working class heterodox religious culture.

Reaching back to the seventeenth-century sectaries, this millenarian tradition constituted an alternative to the dominant rationalism of the Enlightenment. It surfaces again in the radicalism of William Sharp in his adherence to fringe movements like those of Richard Brothers and Joanna Southcott, and of his radical colleague William Blake, perhaps the archetype of those who rejected the "Dark satanic mills" of the new industrialism (Harrison 1979, 84). While the Avigon *Illuminés* were being hounded as dangerous counterrevolutionaries and as the Exegetic and Philanthropic Society was disintegrating in acrimony over "spiritistic" interpretations of Swedenborg's doctrine, apocalyptic movements were attracting increasing attention among the English public and in the press. Forged in the urban maelstrom of the industrial era, these sects were less elitist than the genteel societies of the high Enlightenment. They appealed to a wider public, a surprising number of whom, in Southcott's period of prominence in the opening decades of the nineteenth century, were "sealed" in various ways into her doctrines and aims.

On the eve of the 1789 revolution, John Wright and William Bryan had made a pilgrimage to Avignon after tasting disappointment with the London Swedenborgians. Over the next decade, they first joined Brothers, then converted to Southcott's movement in their continuing quest for mystical certitude. Bryan represents a trend in the medical application of mesmerism, taken up by others like Andrew Jackson Davis some decades later, the ideal type of what might be called the "mystical reformer," an exemplar of the contiguity of the alternate paradigms; confined now to a few individuals, this aspect would later comprehend numerous others with the rise of popular spiritualism. At that time, this class of reformer varied along a continuum ranging from the conservative Christianity of Swedenborg's New Church, to the chiliastic cults like Brothers' New Israelites and the Southcottians, and the radical communitarianism of the Buchanites and the Shakers.

The ready acceptance of Wright and Bryan was unusual in France, but less so among an English working class alienated by the effects of enclosures, by the Industrial Revolution and its attendant massive urbanization, and by an Established Church that no longer spoke to their spiritual concerns. Methodism and a host of dissenting sects flourished, especially in the industrial north. It was here also that artisans drew on William Law's translations of Boëhme, and where the Swedenborgians had moderate success in their missionary efforts (Garrett 1984, 78). While the Swedenborgians achieved some degree of respectability, other imports to the New World had a more radical edge. For Swedenborg and his postmillennial followers, the Second Coming had commenced in 1757. Other movements for the most part taught a premillennial vision, wherein the revelator was the harbinger of a coming millennium, often envisaged as a conflagration and drawing on biblical prophecies as to the Last Days. This English working-class millenarian culture, the cult of the mystical reformer, was to exercise a profound influence on the religious heterodoxy of the eastern United States over the next half century, and it is worthwhile examining the nature and assumptions of some of its more exotic exports to America.

Elspeth Buchan

A different perspective to Swedenborg's is presented on a rejuvenated Christianity by Elspeth Buchan. "Friend Mother," as she was known, was the leader of one of the chiliastic groups emanating from the British Isles at this time, whose members migrated to the United States. Unlike the Swedenborgians, they left little or no remnant of their organizations behind. Elspeth Buchan was born in the west of Scotland in 1738. She taught that a regenerate Christianity would be achieved via an imminent Second Coming, manifesting through an apocalyptic conflagration. The Buchanite beliefs bear close resemblance to the chiliasm of Jane Lead and the Camisard prophets a century earlier. They prepared assiduously for their expected ascension, holding a forty-day fast prior to the "Midnight Cry" (Harrison 1979, 34). Unlike other British millenarians, they lived in a communal setting, and their key ideas strongly influenced those of the Millerites a few decades later. According to one unsympathetic commentator, "Luckie" Buchan "gave herself out to be the Third Person in the Godhead, and pretended to confer immortality upon whomsoever she breathed" (Train 1846, 5). The poet Robert Burns (1759–1796) wrote to a friend in August 1784 about the new religious sensation, how "a Mrs Buchan from Glasgow . . . began to spread some fanatical notions of religion" among the Relief congregation at Irvine. He described how Buchan, "with posture and practices that are scandalously indecent pretended to give them the Holy Ghost by breathing on them." They held a community of goods and lived in a manner he characterized as "a great farce of pretended devotion in barns and woods, where they lie and lodge altogether, and hold likewise a community of women, as it is another of their tenets that *they can commit no moral sin. . . .*" (quoted in Train 1846, 57).

Like John Humphrey Noyes (1811–1886) at Oneida a century later, the Buchanites combined communalism and a trend of perfectionism, the antinomian doctrine that denies that the "saved" can commit sin. Their central tenets rejected marriage outright. Buchan claimed to personify the "Woman clothed with the sun and the moon" in Revelations, who had brought forth a man child who was to rule all nations with a rod of iron; this "man child" she averred was her principal acolyte, the Reverend Hugh White (d. 1827). The coming millennium was always in the forefront of their concerns. Citing John's apocalyptic vision at Patmos in chapter 20, White informed a fellow cleric "that there is to be a thousand years betwixt the resurrection of the righteous and the wicked, in which thousand years the righteous, now in their graves, after being raised at the second coming of Christ, shall . . . reign with Christ." At the close of the thousand years, the wicked would also be judged and "appointed their eternal abode" (Train 1846, 1; Denovan 1785, 7).

The Buchanites, never exceeding a hundred followers, fervently believed they were "commanded to hasten the second coming of Christ." They enjoined others to follow, as they would have there the "pleasure and satisfaction alive to meet the Lord in the air" and so to remain with him. Hugh White was the man-child to whom, in some mysterious way, Elspeth had given birth. He advised followers that in this world, "at best, you have nothing but fears, cares, wants, disappointments, sickness, and the cold grave—the conclusion of all." But

> In the new heaven, and new earth, before the general judgment of
> the wicked, there shall be health, glory, peace, for a thousand

years; at the end of which, an endless continuation of glory in heaven. O world! world! world! hear me: peruse this to the purpose, and my pen shall not be wanting to you while the world lasts. (White 1785, 43)

Early in 1785 they abandoned their homes at Irvine and set out, so they believed, to heaven, singing on the way to the New Jerusalem, according to Train (1846, 61), under the direction of a "hypocritical old woman and a wrong-headed priest." He also recounts that Mrs. Buchan was attired in a scarlet cloak and that Our Lady, so they called her, rode in front on a white pony and often halted to lecture them on the loveliness of the land (Train, 61–63). In all, forty-six persons traveled together: some rode in carts, some were on horseback, and many traveled on foot. They agreed to keep their faces east, where they supposed the Savior of the world would soon appear at his Second Coming. For subsistence, they had a piece of oat-cake, and a drink of water, but Friend Mother "lighted her pipe and took a smoke of tobacco." Finally they reached their destination, which they called Buchan Ha, in Dumfriesshire, about 100 miles north. All came to await the Second Coming of Christ. Train (95) cites *The Christian Journal* of January 1835, which stated:

> The Buchanites pay great attention to the Bible, having it always at hand. They spend a great deal of their time in singing hymns . . . and in conversing about religion. They believe that the last day is at hand—that none of their number shall die; but soon shall hear the sound of the last trumpet, when all the wicked shall be struck dead, and remain so for a thousand years, while they [the Buchanites] shall live and reign with Christ on the earth.

The forty-day fast. Their faith reached its apotheosis when in 1785 Friend Mother decided on a forty-day fast with Hugh White, preparatory to the final and imminent conflagration. A hymn written in this period waxes lyrically that "the more on living words we feed, the less of earthly food we need." At the conclusion of the fast, they proceeded before sunrise to the top of Templand Hill, at nearby New Cample. Struthers (1843, 343) relates that a Mr. James Hossack, as he was passing, was "very much surprised at the sound of many voices in full chorus." There he recognized several faces on the hill, particularly that of Luckie Buchan herself. "She was raised nearly her whole length above the crowd by whom she was surrounded, who stood with their faces towards the rising sun, and their arms extended upwards, as if about to clasp the great luminary as he rose above the horizon." For this momentous occasion, the Reverend Hugh White had dressed himself in full canonicals and put on his white gloves, and he "walked about scanning the heavens. Crowds of country people were looking on, and expecting every minute that the sound of the archangel's trump would break upon their ears." John M'Taggart was also there and recalled that when the glorious day arrived on which they were all to be taken to the sublime regions above:

> Platforms were erected for them to wait on til the wonderful hour arrived, and Mrs Buchan's platform was exalted above all the others. The hair of each head was cut short, all but a tuft on the top, for the angels to catch by when drawing them up. The momentous hour came; every station for ascension was occupied; thus they expected every moment to be wafted into the land of bliss. A gust of wind came, but, instead of wafting them upwards, it capsized Mrs Buchan, platform and all! (recounted in Train 1846, 127-128)

And so they waited in vain. Now in the late afternoon descending the hill to New Cample, that dispirited company, half-famished, deadly pale, and emaciated, resembled "living skeletons just eloped from the grave." This was with the exception of Luckie herself, who was compared to "one of those beauties who crowd the canvass of painters with hillocks of rosy flesh." Her hair was unbound and hung profusely over her back and shoulders. Although like everyone else, she was downcast and melancholy, in her case this was not due to the privations of the fast, which had no effect upon her personal appearance; Mrs. Buchan said that she had partaken of earthly sustenance during the fast ". . . merely to prevent her tabernacle becoming too transparent for human eyes to behold" (Train 1846, 127–128).

Alas, for them as for the later prophet of doom William Miller, the millennium did not arrive as planned, and when Buchan died in 1791, the Reverend White emigrated from Scotland to the United States with a small faction. This group of around thirty did not last long, as many refused to accept White as Elspeth's successor. He established academies at Richmond and Charlottesville, Virginia, and was ordained a Swedenborgian minister before 1812. The last that was heard of this former minister of the Church of Scotland is an 1817 tract *Cosmogenia* . . . , applying New Church principles to scientific subjects. The Reverend Hugh White, the man-child foretold, died in 1827. Of the fourteen followers left in Scotland, Buchan's last disciple was Andrew Innes, who died in 1846. After White's departure for America, Innes took possession of Friend Mother's bones and awaited in vain her return in the flesh (Block 1984, 83; Harrison 1979, 36–37; Train 1846, 187).

The Buchanites represent a significant chiliastic trend that continued over the following decade as numerous saviors, male and female, would claim powers of prophecy, especially as to the time of the End Days. Invariably, they were regarded as the manifestation of biblical personalities, or even as Christ reincarnated. Some were migrants, while others like Jemima Wilkinson, Shadrach Ireland (d. 1778) and Nathaniel Wood (1822–1876) were American born (Brooke 1994, 58; Cross 1965, 33; Roth 1933, 48–49 and passim). Nathaniel Wood, and more famously Joseph Smith (1805–1844), represent the American variants of Israelitism, another millennial trend of the 1790s.

The significance of these minor millenarian sects in popular transatlantic culture was threefold: they formed a continuity with previous chiliastic traditions like the Philadelphians and the Camisards; they were all carried in varying ways to the New World, where they mostly disappeared, but not without leaving traces in the popular imagination; and they drew, albeit indirectly, upon the millennial high culture tradition of Boëhme and Swedenborg and, through the mode they adopted to communicate with subtle realities, also upon the new mesmeric practices. Hence their significance to this study: as the vehicles of an emerging new cultural configuration, with a lengthy and troubled gestation, that a half century later would emerge as the ontological and doctrinal basis of the spiritualist movement, and later still, would provide the raw material for the investigations of the S. P. R.

The most important of these British millenarian imports were the Shakers, who brought together in a unique manner the main elements of the alternate-reality and alternate-consciousness paradigms. They drew on still earlier imports, the pietistic communities of German origin. Along with the potent influence of native movements, especially the Great Awakening and the Great Revival, new paradigms of religious gnosis were thus generated, in a new awareness of the divine reality, along with a new form of family organized along communal lines. Both of these trends would surface dramatically over the next half century, the former in the "ultraism" of the Finney revivals of the 1820s and beyond, the latter in the Owenite communities, then in the brief but intense spate of Fourierist communities during the 1840s.

European Imports to America

We have observed the transient popularity of Swedenborg and Mesmer in Europe through the early synthesis of their systems, relating to both cure and communication, up to the romantic era. For a brief period, to the Exegetic and Philanthropic Society, a *rapprochement* seemed possible between the insights of Swedenborg and the new science of animal magnetism, and as we shall see, so it would seem a half century later to the Reverend George Bush (1796–1859), when he put forward his arguments in *Mesmer and Swedenborg*.

It has been suggested that for many spiritual seekers an easy transition was made in the United States from orthodoxy to heterodoxy. Swedenborgians in the 1790s and mesmerists some decades later found there an environment amenable to their ideas, due in part to the absence of centralized authority structures and a freebooting frontier ethos. In France and England, the hostility of the religious and medical establishments meant that heterodox practices, along with unusual or unpopular beliefs, remained marginalized. By contrast in the early republic, new ways of thinking were melded into the cauldron of American society. To better understand the hospitality for these ideas and their consequences, we review some of the influences that loosened the hold of orthodox religion. This was especially so in the so-called "burned-over" district of western New York, the "psychic highway" that by the mid-nineteenth century became the matrix of spiritualism, Millerism, the Mormon religion, Christian Science, and a host of other religious heterodoxies that helped to shape American religious culture.

Religious revivalism has had a profound influence on the American psyche. Of especial importance were the Great Awakening of the 1740s and the Great Revival after 1799. These spontaneous waves of popular religious enthusiasm did much to build American individualism, and they lessened the influence of gentry-directed religion. The Great Awakening was a result of the split within the Congregational Church, the original church of the Puritan founders of the Massachusetts Bay colony. One branch had adopted the 1662 Half-way Covenant, whereby the children of church members could achieve full membership without having a conversion experience. Centered in Boston, this branch eventually coalesced into Unitarianism. The "New Lights," led by the Northampton preacher Jonathan Edwards (1703–1758) in the 1740s rejected the Half-way Covenant, maintaining that conversion remained the exclusive test of Church membership. The tour of George Whitefield (1714–1770) in 1740 also prompted fears among many seekers concerned for their salvation. The Great Revival of the early nineteenth century, also known as the Kentucky Revival, was centered on the then frontier regions of the republic; and within a few years, this prompted a revivalist fervor in other regions, like those of Charles Grandison Finney (1792–1875) in the western districts of New York State (Goen 1962, 34; Cross 1965, 7, 9).[2]

Robert Fuller has argued that between 1800 and 1850 Americans experienced what could only be described as "a congenital susceptibility to a wide assortment of religious sects and utopian social movements. Each competed for converts by promulgating simplistic moral and intellectual doctrines especially adapted to the exigencies of frontier life" (1982, 15). He asserts that mesmerism's early development in the United States owed a great deal to its apparent affinity with these enthusiastic sects.

---

2. According to some historians, the Great Revival endured until 1837, the terminal date being the Presbyterian split North and South occurring in 1837; see Walters 1978, 21.

Millenarian Prophets in America: Heaven on Earth

The Great Revival

As the Great Revival spread through Bourbon, Fayette, and other Kentucky counties from 1805, then further afield, the promiscuous exercises of prayer, exhortation, singing, shouting, and leaping for joy became increasingly more abandoned. One example of this fervor was in the performance of a boy about twelve years old during an early revival. William M'Nemar, the chronicler of the Kentucky Revival, related how the boy had mounted a log and, raising his voice in a very affecting manner, soon attracted the main body of the people. Many hundreds of families and individuals had camped in wagons and tents all along the open paddock where, after some days, the enthusiasm was reaching a crescendo. Held up by two men, the lad spoke for about an hour with a convincing, an almost preternatural eloquence. With tears streaming from his eyes, he cried aloud, warning them in a thin but clear voice of their imminent danger and denouncing their certain doom if they should persist in their sinful ways; he beseeched them to turn to the Lord and to be saved. Finally, with his strength quite exhausted, he raised a frail hand. A murmur went through the immense crowd as, dropping his handkerchief with great dramatic effect, and with sweat streaming over his little face, he cried out, "Thus, O sinner! shall you drop into hell, unless you forsake your sins and turn to the Lord." At that moment, some swooned and fell, like soldiers shot in battle; it was through the emotional appeal of such performances that the serious work of salvation spread even further (1807, 25–26). Most deeply affected in the following decades were New England and the frontier districts of New York.

Popular religion in this era, especially after the War of 1812, was characterized by a strenuous evangelism that transformed the frontier regions of New England and western New York State into the center of gravity for new spiritual stimuli. Over the next three decades, as new lands became available and in particular as the Erie Canal invigorated commerce deep into the hinterland, new settlers were exposed to a wide variety of religious influences. It was through this "psychic highway" that Charles Finney conducted his famous 1825 revival beginning at Western, in Oneida County (Cross 1965, 12, 13). It was here also that the Shakers, the

Jemimakins, the Mormons, and a host of other variants flourished, and later still, around Poughkeepsie and Buffalo, that A. J. Davis, the Davenport brothers (Ira Erastus, 1839–1911; and William Henry (1841–1877) and then the Fox sisters (Margaret, 1833?–1893; and Catherine (1839?–1892), would establish the new religion of spiritualism. But the waves of evangelical fervor from the 1740s onward were fed also by the already existing religious communities, mainly German and Protestant in their devotion. Although their closed communities did not contribute directly to evangelism, the Pietistic communities did exercise some influence on belief in the frontier districts. Characteristically, like the Shakers, they provided a refuge for those who sought a deeper spiritual life, after their devotion had been quickened by the revival experience.

The Religious Communities

From early colonial times, America had been a beacon of religious tolerance, providing a haven for Pilgrims and Puritans, Huguenots and other religious minorities. The Mennonites were the first German immigrants to arrive in America as a distinctive sect when, in October 1683, thirteen families reached Germantown, Pennsylvania. Next came Petrus Sluyter (1645–1722) leading the Labadists, a Dutch separatist sect, from Friesland in the autumn of 1684, who established an order practicing community of goods at Bohemia Manor in Maryland. Ten years later, Johann Kelpius (1673–1708) and his chapter of Pietists or true Rosicrucians landed in Philadelphia. Then came the Ephrata community in 1730, which was connected to Kelpius and his hermitage of the "Woman in the Wilderness," and lastly the Moravian Brethren, who arrived in 1742 (Sachse 1895, 4).

The pietistic communities arose from the deep dissatisfaction in central Europe with Lutheranism. Among the most important issues were those of infant baptism, leading to the Anabaptist and Dunker sects, and the continuing disagreements over the role of faith versus works in the religious life. These were issues of great moment to Protestants such as the Pilgrims and the Puritans who had settled Massachusetts Bay; and as with their English counterparts, the persecution suffered at home forced many Germans to migrate to the more religiously tolerant society in the New World.

Millenarian Prophets in America: Heaven on Earth

Just as the Shakers and other British millenarians entered the New World in the latter eighteenth century, so somewhat earlier considerable numbers of disaffected German religious had moved to America. The most enduring was the Ephrata cloister. Almost all of the Pietistic communities were of German origin, Bible-centered, and communitarian in organization. They served as the model for most of the mid-nineteenth century secular communities, and this was to be their principal legacy to heterodoxy in America. In one of history's strange encounters, they brushed briefly against a more modern trend, when Robert Owen (1771–1858) came into contact with the Rappites, from whom he purchased Harmony, the property that would become his ill-starred New Harmony experiment.

Ephrata

The best known communitarians until the Civil War were the Shakers. However, Pietistic communities like Ephrata, Harmony, Zoar, and Amana are of especial importance to this study, since in a variety of ways, they continued the counter-cultural trend of the covert Enlightenment, and in particular the direct access to alternate realities from which they believed they derived spiritual guidance and inspiration. More shadowy groups existed, like that of Henry Bernard Koster and the hermits, along with transient ventures like the Labadists. Many of these groups also practiced some form of magnetic or other healing and thus formed a link to the tradition of alternate-consciousness, serving also as conduit for a multitude of teachings and moral exhortation from the source of their faith. Apart from a penchant for biblical names, they were all German (Walters 1978, 41; Brooke 1994, 40; Andrews 1953, xi).

At around the same time in the Conestoga Valley of Pennsylvania, Johann Kelpius led his secretive German Rosicrucian sect. The Chapter of Perfection was founded in 1694 among Lutheran Pietists in Germany by Johann Zimmerman (d. 1694), who, through his calculations, had ascertained that the millennium would arrive in the autumn of that year (Sachse 1895, 180, 223). They expected the apocalypse, but that year Zimmerman died, and his disciple Johann Kelpius led members to Pennsylvania, where they formed the Society of the "Woman in the

Wilderness" near Germantown. In 1720, a young Conrad Beissel (1690–1768) migrated to Pennsylvania, seeking to join this community and to await yet another date for the imminent millennium, but by then Kelpius was dead and the community had dispersed. In 1732, Beissel founded his own community, eight miles from Lancaster. There in a dense forest, beside a fine spring on the banks of Mill Creek, Beissel built a log cabin and called it Ephrata, the original name for Bethlehem.

The Ephrata Brotherhood held esoteric interpretations of Scripture and indulged in unrestrained mysticism, believing that the image of the "Woman in the Wilderness" prefigured the great deliverance that would soon be displayed for Christ's Church. Among their practices was a sort of Pietistic mysticism, a celibate and monastic practice of gnostic "wooing" of the Virgin Sophia, which evidently derived from Boëhme's mystical tracts (Brooke 1994, 42). As described in Conyngham (1827, 2:135–153), she (the deliverer) was to come up from the wilderness leaning on the Beloved, and "the beloved [they] in the wilderness, laying aside all other engagements and trimming their lamps and adorning themselves with holiness," would observe "the signs and the times."[3]

Like Boëhme, the Ephrata Cloister practiced "automatic" utterance, believing that "the illuminated seer may at times become so permeated by the divine afflatus as to speak not out of his own consciousness but out of immediate inspiration." One German critic, Oswald Seidensticker (1825–1894), charged that, out of fragments of Revelations and the wisdom of Solomon, Conrad Beissel had prepared "a cabbalistic ragout in which fire-red dragons, serpents, the two tinctures, the one hundred forty-four thousand virgins, and other singular ingredients are minced into one indigestible mixture" (quoted in Jacoby 1931, 27, 35).[4]

Nevertheless, Ephrata was among the most enduring religious experiments in America. At one time, there were thousands of members, and even a century later a core of twelve or fifteen members remained (Walters 1978, 41–42; Noyes 1870, 133). Nor were these the only communities of a Dunker, Anabaptist, or Pietistic character. Personal links

---

3. As described in Rev. 12:14-17.
4. Jacoby takes the quote from Seidensticker's 1883 work *Ephrata, eine amerikanish Klostergschicht* (123).

among these varied outposts, and some missionary efforts, sowed the seeds for later developments further north. Of especial interest were the recurring instances of spirit contact and spiritual manifestations within these small communities. In the autumn of 1744, Ephrata pilgrims led by the Eckerlin brothers (Samuel, 1703–1781; Israel, b. 1705; and Gabriel) set off on a five-year pilgrimage. From Pennsylvania they crossed into New Jersey, spending some time at the existing Sabbatarian community at Barnegar Bay. In late 1745, they proceeded to Virginia, where they established a hermit village named Mahanaim on the New River. As early as the 1760s, there were instances of spirit contact in these isolated Shenandoah Valley communities. Elizabeth Beeler, and also Catherine Hummer, the daughter of a Dunker preacher, were experiencing spiritual visions that attracted great crowds of believers and were even drawing the Ephrata brothers. During one of Beissel's visits to the Antietam, Virginia, congregations, he came into personal contact with Catherine Hummer, who was said to have experienced visions over some three years, when they stopped inexplicably. These included the out-of-body voyages later observed among Mesmer's patients. During one experience in November 1762, her spirit "was taken from this visible creation, and out of her body up into invisible eternity" (Brooke 1994, 126; Sachse 1899, 381, 384). The significance of these events remains opaque, as does why they ended so abruptly, but no doubt they were based in their firm expectation of the millennium and were related in complex ways to the secret work in which the brotherhood was engaged.

Jemima Wilkinson

In New England, the portentous effects of the repeated waves of "awakenings" produced distinctive religious configurations, especially along the frontier. Jemima Wilkinson, born at Providence, Rhode Island, on November 29, 1752, was raised as a Quaker. As a young woman, she attended meetings of the New Lights and, though not a member, was greatly influenced by them, as she became henceforth more serious after attending these meetings. Soon after she became ill (Wilkinson 1844, 14).

A description of the 24-year-old Jemima Wilkinson's illness and vision was found tucked into her Bible. It begins with an account of "the

Columbus fever [after a ship then in Providence harbor] the Typhus, or malignant fever" that had broken out in the town in 1776. In October of that year Jemima was "seiz'd with this mortal disease and . . . until the fifth Day of the Weak [sic] about midnight, She appear'd to meet the Shock of Death." But then a startling vision ensued:

> Then the heavens were open'd And She saw two Archangels descending from the east, with golden crowns upon their heads, clothed in long white robes, down to the feet; Bringing a sealed Pardon from the living God; and putting their trumpets to their mouth, proclaimed saying, Room, Room, Room, in the many Mansions of eternal glory. . . . (Wiseby 1964, 11)

To her family gathered around her, it seemed that the typhus had claimed another victim. However, after some days of grave illness, as the clock struck twelve one evening, Jemima raised herself up in bed and appeared as if suddenly wakened from a refreshing sleep. She solemnly informed her startled auditors that "the body of Jemima Wilkinson had been dead, that her soul was then in heaven, and that this tabernacle, which Jemima had left behind, was re-animated by the power and spirit of Jesus Christ." She announced that this was to be the Second Coming of the Lord, who would remain on earth and reign a thousand years. As the eleventh hour had arrived, being "the last call of mercy that would ever be made to the human race," she had elected to reign on earth a thousand years, and the tabernacle she now inhabited, Jemima's old body, ". . . was immortal, that it would never die" (Wilkinson 1844, 22–24).

Jemima Wilkinson was unique in her assertions that she had been restored from the dead to preach her message. She claimed to have actually died and her soul gone to heaven, where it continued to exist. Then her body was reanimated with the spirit and power of Christ, after which she set up as a public teacher. Wilkinson declared she had an immediate revelation for all she delivered, being now in a state of absolute perfection (Wilkinson 1844, 263). Her power to move people was not in what she said, mostly "commonplaces from the Bible," nor even in the manner of her speaking, but in her absolute self-confidence and evident sincerity; one observer noted that "she preaches up Terror very alarming." Wilkinson contemptuously ignored the Revolutionary War going on around her. Ezra Stiles (1727–1795), who heard her preach in 1776 in Massachusetts, judged her "decent and graceful and grave" (Wiseby 1964, 16, 27–28). Wilkinson liked to attend executions and funerals, and she emphasized the transient nature of life and the need for repentance. Yet she never claimed to be Jesus Christ (Wiseby 1964, 19). She rejected with disdain all forms and ceremonies, all church government and discipline, and finally the sacraments too. An additional point of doctrine was her prohibition of matrimony among her followers as unlawful and "an abomination unto the Lord" (Wilkinson 1844, 30, 41).

The radical French aristocrat, the Duke François-Alexandre-Frédéric Rochefoucault-Laincourt (1747–1827), during his travels in the United States in 1796–1797 met with Jemima Wilkinson, whom he described as "a beautiful but artful woman" (Wilkinson 1844, 264). Her uncovered head and her practice of wearing masculine clothing gave a striking effect, and another variation was black robes with a man's white kerchief or cravat around her neck. Sometimes this garment was white or even purple, set incongruously against a white beaver hat, with a flat crown and broad brim like those worn by Quaker men (Wiseby 1964, 25).

Indeed Wilkinson's preaching was close to Quaker beliefs; like them, she rejected the Calvinist doctrines of predestination and election. Even her name was of Quaker origin, since "Public Friends," those who felt a calling to preach, had been traveling from meeting to meeting over many years (Wiseby 1964, 32–34). Her followers used "thee" and "thou" of the plain language, they rejected "heathen names" for days and months, and refused to practice sacraments like baptism or communion. They also stood steadfastly against war and violence and opposed Negro slavery. Men wore hats inside, and meetings ended with everyone shaking hands, as in Quaker meetings.

"Jerusalem": The Woman in the Wilderness. With her acolytes Wilkinson eventually settled in Genesee County, New York, opened up for settlement in the 1780s after Gen. John Sullivan confiscated the Iroquois' land for their support of the British in the Revolutionary War. "Jerusalem," comprising around 23,040 acres, was settled by some thirty families

(Wilkinson 1844, 265, 268; Wiseby 1964, 99, 119). Here Wilkinson revealed that she was the woman who "was given the two wings of the great eagle, so that she could fly from the serpent into the wilderness (Rev. 12:14). After attending a meeting in her house, Rochefoucault recalled her discourse as an eternal repetition of the same topics—death, sin and repentance—and also her hypocrisy. Whatever does not belong to her own sect "is with her an object of distaste and steadfast aversion." He concluded cynically that " . . . constantly engaged in personating the part she had assumed, she descanted in a sanctimonious, mystic tone, on death, and on the happiness of having been an useful instrument to others in the way of their salvation." She claimed to have prophesied the French Revolution, the decline and downfall of popery, and the impending end of the world (Wilkinson 1844, 270, 273).

The Friend was nothing if not bold. On a visit to Philadelphia, St. George's Episcopal Church was granted for her meetings, where she declared that she would, on a particular day, manifest her power and divinity by walking on a certain river. "Curiosity was upon tiptoe, to witness such a phenomenon in nature . . . thousands from every quarter repaired to the appointed place." At length, Jemima appeared and commenced with an address to the assembled multitude upon the important subject of faith. In the memory of an unsympathetic onlooker, she endeavored to persuade her hearers that, if she did not fulfill her promise, it would be owing to their unbelief. Then Jemima approached the margin of the river, "and lo! as she trod the water, it would not obey the sovereign command, to uphold her unhallowed and ponderous weight!" Whereupon she indignantly retreated, while reproving upon the multitude as being the cause of her failure: "This is an evil generation; they seek a sign, and there shall be no sign given it, for as Jonas was a sign unto the Ninevites, so shall Jemima be to this generation. . . ." (Wilkinson 1844, 278, 282–283). She then delivered a stirring sermon on faith and asked, "Do ye have faith? Do ye believe that I can do this thing?" to which in unison they responded, "We believe!" "It is good," declared the prophetess and added, as she departed with a flourish, "If ye have faith ye need no other evidence" (Wiseby 1964, 175).

Another widely circulated story, probably also by her enemies, was that when one of her favorite apostles died, Wilkinson said he would sleep only

122

four days in death, when she would raise him. Again an immense crowd gathered, and as Jemima and her family of solemn devotees walked in procession to the grave, she recited a sermon by rote (she was considered a perfect scriptorian) from the first verse of the eleventh chapter of John, until she came to the forty-first verse. Every spectator was "big with expectation, to witness the issue." Unfortunately, as the tale goes, an army officer who happened to be present commanded her, just as Jemima ended the fortieth verse preceding the prayer offered by the Lord before raising Lazarus

> ... to stop until he had run his sword through the coffin; and after that he would guarantee her beloved apostle would never rise again. [Meanwhile] the man in the coffin, having heard the conversation and the determination of the officer, forced off the cover of the coffin and walked out, to the no small terror of some, and the astonishment of all present! (Wilkinson 1844, 285–286)

How she escaped the vengeance of an indignant and insulted public was not recorded by the narrator; but he opined that being female and viewed as a fanatic, this was her passport to protection. Perhaps, as Dr. Johnson remarked, at this epoch the marvel about a woman preaching, like a dog walking on hind legs, was not that it was done well, but that it was done at all. Henry Barnes, the last Jemimakin, died in 1874; and until his death in 1863, James Brown was the last recognized leader. Jemima Wilkinson's body lay in a stone vault in the basement of her house, then was buried quietly by Brown several years later in an unmarked grave (Wiseby 1964, 168, 171).

Other Apocalyptic Movements in the United States

Among other apocalyptic American trends were the "New Israelites," founded in Vermont by Nathaniel Wood. As a movement it existed briefly in the 1790s, combining magical practice with biblical restorationism. Like their English contemporary Richard Brothers, they claimed to be descendants of the Lost Tribes of Israel, and began building a temple, expecting that a "Destroying Angel" would soon bring earthquakes and plagues upon the local "gentiles." This so alarmed the local village that, on the appointed night of the apocalypse, January 14, 1802, the militia under arms turned out; and when the end failed to arrive, Wood decamped to Ellisburg, New York (Brooke 1994, 58).

The best-known millenarians of this era were the Mormons, who emerged in Palmyra, in the heart of the "burned-over" district of western New York that followed the route of the Erie Canal. They represent one outcome in the patterns of awakenings occurring along that "psychic highway," as different denominations led the awakenings from time to time. The fundamental condition leading to the new Mormon faith was the credulity and spiritual yearning that made people anxious to follow a prophet, whoever he or she might be. Its popular appeal lay in their incorporation of literal interpretations of the Bible, a sacred history that was truly American, along with an expectation of the millennium coincident with the prophet's career on earth and the promise of a mode of fresh revelation direct from God. Above all, in the person of Joseph Smith, they found a living, intimately available embodiment of their entire faith (Cross 1965, 142–143, 146).

The Rappites

A later arrival was Father George Rapp (1757–1847). He came from Würtemburg, where his preaching on the imminent millennium led to his persecution and emigration to the United States with his followers in 1803. Two years later, they formed Harmony, a whole community transplanted on five thousand acres in Butler County, Pennsylvania. The Rappites "worked obsessively, lived hard, said their prayers, and made huge profits." They believed that the coming of the Lord was near, and they awaited him as his chosen ones separated from the world. Like the Shakers, they believed in the coming millennium and in a dual deity, for Adam had been created "in the likeness of God," a dual being containing within his own person both the sexual elements (Gen. 1:26, 27) (Lane 1972, 19; Nordhoff 1961, 72, 95). George Rapp expected to live to witness for himself the Second Coming of Christ, as described in Revelations 20:4, 5, when Christ and his saints would live on earth and reign a thousand years, and that he would have the honor of presenting his company of pious believers to the Savior whom they had endeavored to please with their lives.

They expected to be summoned to Palestine, to be joined there to the great crowd of the Elect (Hinds 1878, 19; Nordhoff 1961, 85).

Although Rapp did not condemn matrimony, in view of the imminence of the Messiah's Second Advent, he urged his people to the great work of purification and preparation. Thus might they be numbered among the 144,000 of the Elect who should "stand with the Lamb on Mt Zion," being "such as were not defiled with women, but were virgins." They sought to reestablish the ideals of the first Christian Church and believed that Rapp and his disciples were the Sun Woman, or the Woman in the Wilderness, of the Revelations (Williams 1866, 57; Arndt 1984, xvi).

In 1822, the Reverend Samuel Worcester of Boston, evidently writing for a group of Swedenborgians who were contemplating a similar community, asked Frederick Rapp, Father Rapp's adopted son and manager of the concern, about the underlying philosophy and basic economy of their Society. Rev. Worcester had heard of the society's successes through the enthusiastic traveler, John Melish (1771–1822). In October 1822, Rapp replied as follows: ". . . 18 years ago Harmonie laid the foundation to a new period—indeed, after the original pattern of the primitive church described in Acts of Apostles, chs. 2 & 4–. . . and now our Community stands proof firm & immovable upon its rock of truth. . . ." (Duss 1972, 54).

The Rappites differed from the Shakers in being all Germans and strict Bible-believers. In 1815, the community, now totaling some eight hundred members, moved to the Indiana territory, settling on the Wabash River, seventy miles above the junction with the Ohio River (Noyes 1870, 135, 32). In a development not without historical irony that heralds the end of Pietism and the brief but influential rise of socialism in the United States, Harmony was sold to Robert Owen in 1825, complete with its twenty thousand fertile acres, tenanted farms, and two hundred outbuildings. The Rappites built a steamboat, loaded their goods, and went down the Ohio River back to Pennsylvania. There, for the third time, they established a new community, Economy, in Beaver County. George Rapp died in 1847, aged ninety (Noyes 1870, 34; Walters 1978, 43). Economy, as described by Nordhoff (1961, 67) comprised in 1875,

120 houses, very regularly built, well-drained, and paved; it has water led from a reservoir in the hills, and flowing into troughs conveniently placed in every street; abundant shade-trees; a church, an assembly hall, a store . . . different factories . . . a pleasant pleasure-garden, . . . surrounded by fine, productive orchards and by well-tilled fields.

G. Kaufmann, a former member, recalled that Rapp had taught that "visibly-between 1832 and 1837," that the Lord would reappear on earth to establish his empire, "the everenduring Millennium." This doctrine and its kindred secret tenets were not publicly preached by Rapp (Arndt 1984, 193).

Zoar and Amana

Other long-lasting ventures among strict Bible-believing German immigrants included Zoar, founded in 1816 by Joseph Bimeler (1778–1853) in Ohio and named for the ancient town on the shores of the Dead Sea where Lot took refuge in his flight from Sodom, and Ebenezer, renamed Amana when they relocated to Iowa, where it lasted as a community well into the twentieth century (Noyes 1870, 135; Randall 1899, 2; Williams 1866, 19). Like the followers of Father Rapp, they were Pietists, among the strongest antagonists to the state church of Lutheranism. Pietism originated from the writings and teachings of Johann Arndt (1555–1621) and Frederick Christoph Oëtinger, a disciple of the mystic philosopher Jacob Boëhme and contemporary of Swedenborg, who translated some of the latter's writings into German. They fostered a species of dissent known as Separatism, which rejected baptism, confirmation, and other ordinances, declining military service and the taking of legal oaths, and refusing to remove their hats to superiors—they had no superiors before the Lord.

Barbara Grubermann was the original leader of Zoar, but she died before the emigration to America. A "trance medium," she occasionally passed beyond the realms of consciousness and upon her return would report what she had seen and heard. These utterances were not written down (Hinds 1878, 35). Emigrating from Würtemberg and led by Joseph

Bimeler, the eight hundred Zoarites settled on five thousand acres in Tuscarawas County, Ohio, in 1817. They shared the same class and ideas as the Rappites, but Bimeler differed in denouncing both state and church as constituting the "great Babylon" that was to be destroyed. They abjured allegiance to church and to civil authorities, refused to pay taxes, to do military service, or to obey magistrates (Williams 1866, 19).

Ebenezer was among the last and, insofar as the mediumistic practices that bound them as a group of believers, perhaps the most interesting of the Pietistic communities. The Ebenezer community arose in New York's burned-over district at about the same time as the strange phenomena of the Davenports, A. J. Davis, and the Fox sisters were occurring in that region. Some eight hundred German immigrants led by Christian Metz (1794–1866) founded Ebenezer in 1846, eight miles from Buffalo, New York. They called themselves the "Inspired people," and their practices came closest to those of spiritualism, with which they were exactly contemporary. However, their claim that their practices were much older reinforces the view that the German states, especially during the romantic era, had a subtle but profound influence on New World mysticism and religion. They perhaps drew on the Shaker ways in their communal style of organization and, most significantly, in their belief in the Bible as it was interpreted through their mediums, similar to the practices Shakers called "Mother Ann's work." Indeed, the Shakers visited the Inspirationists on at least one occasion, which reinforced for both a belief in the power and guidance of the Holy Ghost. Christian Metz and Barbara Heinemann (1795–1883), one of the sisters, claimed to have been mediums for more than thirty years. Through both, a particular spirit, whom they regarded as the spirit of Jesus, spoke and wrote "automatic" script (Andrews 1953, 175; Shambaugh 1932, 24 and passim). They held that the Holy Ghost "leads us in spiritual matters, and in those temporal concerns which affect our spiritual life." It was this source of inspiration that had directed them to emigrate to America and then to quit Ebenezer for Iowa (Nordhoff 1961, 44, 47).

The history of the "Inspired people" is traced even further back, to the German mystics and Pietists; the society was founded in 1714 by Eberhard Ludwig Grüber (1665–1728) and Johann Friedrich Rock (1678–1749), students of the Pietism of Philipp Jakob Spener (1635–1705). They believed in the inspiration of the Bible, but also in the present day when divine guidance came through individuals especially endowed by the Lord with the "miraculous gift of Inspiration"; these were called *Werkzeuge* (instruments) (Shambaugh 1932, 23-24). Like *Sainte-Parole* at Avignon, the Ebenezers placed their trust in guidance from an afflatus, the voice of the Lord expressed through their *Werkzeuge*. In 1842, and after many tribulations, a testimony came through this medium from the Lord to the small body of believers: "Your goal and your way shall lead towards the west to the land which still is open to you and your faith. I am with you and shall lead you over the sea. Hold Me, call upon Me through your prayer when the storm or temptation arises. . . ." Through entrancement in speech and via automatic script, these inspired utterances from the Lord were responsible for the mass emigration from Germany; it approved marriages, and new members were received only by consent of this controlling spirit (Shambaugh 1932, 53; Noyes 1870, 136). Albert Brisbane (1809–1890), the American promoter of Fourier, writing in the *Harbinger* in 1845 claimed that the Ebenezers had already completed an amazing amount of work, which for him testified powerfully in favor of cooperation, if not of their religious outlook. In just two years since their migration, they had cleared and cultivated large fields; they had built forty houses and finished the framework for an equal number. When he visited, they were erecting a large woolen manufactory, and huge barns were already filled with their crops (Noyes 1870, 190).

A combination of urban growth in Buffalo, now only five miles away, and the restive Seneca Indians, from whom they had bought the property but who remained hostile, prompted another move. On August 31, 1854, a second message was received from the Lord: "You shall direct your eyes toward a distant goal in the West to find and obtain there a start and entrance or a settlement" (Shambaugh 1932, 66). Westward migration was a common feature within the broader American culture, often providing a safety valve for social discontent, and in groups like the Ebenezers and the Mormons, it enjoyed a divine mandate.

Having in faith crossed an ocean, the Inspirationists again traveled further west and crossed a continent. On advice from the Lord, like the

Berlin Illuminati who obeyed *Sainte-Parole*, Ebenezer was resettled on thirty thousand acres in Iowa, changing their name to Amana, which signifies "believe faithfully." They became the largest, richest, and most enduring religious community in the United States. One new member brought in $100 thousand, and others donated similarly stupendous sums to the society. In Iowa, at their height in 1908, they had 1800 members and property valued at $1.85 million. What the secular-minded Brisbane had failed to appreciate was that, for those who called themselves the "Society of True Inspiration," the impetus for this constructive activity, the secret of their success, was a self-sacrificing ideal based upon their particular religious vision. This was why neither the Owenite nor the Fourierist communities lasted very long, while Ephrata spanned a century or more, and the Shakers survive even to our day. The main point is that, in these latter communities, varied as they were, there existed the common practice of "mediumship," antedating the form that from the mid-nineteenth century would be popularized in spiritualism.

The Forgotten Shakers

Possibly the most important subterranean religious reform to come out of the Great Awakening was the Shaker religion. Their significance to this study lies in the fact that perhaps the earliest formulation of a new melded paradigm of cure and communication can be traced to some of their key beliefs and practices. The Shakers were significant in extending the communitarian practice of the German Pietists, which they called "Gospel Order," an exigency made necessary by life on the American frontier that drew on the example of the Labadists and others. They were also, apart from minor sects like the Ebenezers, the principal locus for the practice of spirit communication, which they called "Mother Ann's work." Mediumship permeated the small Shaker communities over a decade from 1837 and was redolent of the "magnetizing" wave going on around them, just as the revival fervor had brought them converts. Hence, this outcast band of working-class millenarians was destined to exercise an inordinate influence, given its relatively few adherents, upon two of the most significant developments in popular culture at mid-century: communitarianism and spirit intercourse.

We have seen how, especially in the provinces, the repression after the 1685 revocation of the Edict of Nantes by Louis XIV, had led to the flight of the French Camisards. Their arrival in London in 1706 fed into the Boëhmian legacy and that of the seventeenth-century English sectaries and gave rise to the English prophets (Harrison 1979, 25). The Shakers were formed in 1747 by former Quakers James and Jane Wardley in Manchester. They continued the Camisard tradition of the *trembleurs*, including the shaking and trembling incited by religious fervor, which earned them the name of "Shaking Quakers," later known simply as the Shakers. In 1758, Ann Lee joined, eventually becoming leader of the sect. Known as Mother Ann, she came to be seen as Christ reborn "in the female line."

Ann Lee was born in Toad Lane, Manchester, on February 29, 1736, one of nine children. It was in the Midlands too that Swedenborgianism began to appeal to mechanics through the evangelical sermons of the Rev. John Clowes. Her father was a blacksmith. Ann worked in a cotton factory, as a cutter of hatter's fur, then as a cook in a Manchester infirmary. Ann had been one of George Whitefield's "hearers," holding him to have "great powers & gifts of God" (Andrews 1953, 7). She began attending secret meetings of some "prophets" in Manchester, which had been reported as far back as 1712, soon after the Camisard prophets had returned to France; and to these early occurrences can be traced some of her later ideas. She became associated with the followers of these original French *trembleurs*. About thirty persons comprised the sect led by James Wardley, a tailor who had removed from Bolton, and his wife Jane Wardley, who was "evidently the spirit of John the Baptist, or Elias, operating in the female line, to prepare the way for the second appearing of Christ, in the order of the female." By vision and revelation, they believed that "the second appearing of Christ was at hand, and that the Church was rising in her full and transcendent glory, which would effect the final downfall of antichrist" (Axon 1876, 4).

In 1762, Ann Lee married Abraham Standerin, also a blacksmith. Four children were born to them, but they all died in infancy. Ann came to believe that the sexual urge was the source of all sin. Having lost several children, she interpreted their deaths as divine judgments on her "concupiscence," and thus Shakers remained unyieldingly celibate

(Andrews 1953, 8; Clifton 1995, 45). The Shaker band were persecuted in England for teaching the established Church's sinfulness, and Lee was imprisoned in 1773 after disrupting a service with some of her followers. In her cell, Jesus Christ appeared to her in open vision, revealing "the most astonishing views of divine manifestations of truth, in which she had a perfect and clear view of the mystery and iniquity, the root and foundation of all human depravity, and of the very act of transgression committed by Adam and Eve in the garden of Eden" (Axon 1876, 6–8). The spirit of Christ suffused her being, and henceforth she regarded herself as his special instrument, commissioned to preach the gospel of the stainless life (Andrews 1953, 11). Lee gave up married life, teaching that the sexual urge was the principal evil that led to the Fall.

Ann Lee was a well-proportioned woman of medium height, with a fair complexion, bright blue eyes and chestnut-brown hair. Her mild countenance was said to wear "an aspect habitually grave." She could neither read nor write, but she exuded strength of faith, a quiet conviction that was communicated to most persons. Her followers believed that she was none other than the Woman Clothed with the Sun in Revelations. One visitor remembered Mother Ann in her older age:

> She sat down in a chair, and I sat down by her side. Her eyes were shut, and it appeared that her sense was withdrawn from the things of time. She sung very melodiously, and appeared very beautiful. . . . The graceful motion of her hands, the beautiful appearance of her countenance, and the heavenly melody of her voice, made her seem like a glorious inhabitant of the heavenly world, singing praises to God. (Harrison 1979, 28; Andrews 1953, 23, 25).

They became known as the "Peculiar Peoples." Persecuted in England for teaching the Church of England's sinfulness and for practicing sabbath-breaking, dancing, shouting, shaking, "speaking with new tongues," and all the other wild evidences of religious fervor, in 1774, she emigrated with eight others to America. First they lived in New York City, where for a period they took in washing to survive; then removed to "Niskeyuna" or "Watervliet," seven miles north of Albany at New Lebanon (Axon 1876, 5).

This emigration led to the collapse of the Shakers in Manchester; the Wardleys went to the almshouse, where they died as paupers. Lee's husband Abraham was not a convert, and he soon "married" another woman. At Niskeyuna, the Shakers steadily increased in numbers. Around 1780, they benefited from a local religious revival, when the Baptist "New Light" revival that turned Jemima Wilkinson to more serious concerns was underway in New York and New England, but they were also greatly persecuted on account of their testimony against war and oath-taking. Suspected of being British loyalists, they were released from durance vile on one occasion only on direct orders from the governor, George Clinton (Harrison 1979, 164; Axon 1876, 11–12).

The first and central Shaker community, Watervliet at New Lebanon, New York spawned eighteen other settlements over the next half-century (Harrison 1979, 164). "Gospel Order" was a communal system developed by the exigencies of frontier life, and there was considerable attention to cleanliness and tidiness, dirt being regarded as a symbol of spiritual iniquity. One visitor thus described the Shaker headquarters:

> The streets are quiet; for here you have no grog-shop, no beer-house, no lock-up, no pond; of the dozen edifices rising about you—work-rooms, barns, tabernacles, stables, kitchens, schools, and dormitories—not one is either foul or noisy; and every building, whatever may be its use, has something of the air of a chapel; the paint is all fresh; the planks are all bright; the windows are all clean. A white sheen is on every thing; a happy quiet reigns around. (Hinds 1878, 82)

In 1780, they also felt the call to proclaim the millennial gospel to the world. The revival then in progress was of short duration, and many were left unsatisfied. Some of these visited Mother Ann and were immediately convinced that she and her followers were "in the very work for which they themselves had been so earnestly praying" (Hinds 1878, 85). The next year Mother Ann and some elders embarked on a missionary tour at Harvard, Massachusetts, where they gained converts among the "Shadrach Irelands," whose recently deceased founder had failed to rise on the third day as he had promised. The Shakers in these early days often suffered abuse, "being sometimes whipped out of the towns" for their ambivalence about the revolution. Mother Ann professed that she was inspired, that she carried on a continual intercourse with the invisible world, and that she conversed familiarly with angels. She predicted in the boldest terms that the world would be destroyed around the year 1783 (Axon 1876, 13–14). This apocalypse did not come to pass, but by 1784, there were some one thousand Shaker believers in New England and New York State alone. Awakened by revivalism but still dissatisfied, the "spilt" religious fervor of the Kentucky Revival between around 1799 and 1806 became another fertile ground for Shaker conversion. It considerably enlarged the Shaker church, and thus the story of the Shakers is also the story of westward expansion. They followed the general westward migratory pattern of American society, spreading to the Ohio Valley and then across the Adirondacks to the bluegrass country of Kentucky.

Shakers refused to bear arms; they welcomed Negroes as converts; and they believed that they were living in a new dispensation whose principal elements were community of interest, celibacy, nonresistance, the full equality of women, and direct guidance from the Holy Ghost. They practiced an extremely perfectionist code for individual behavior and held to mystic powers of healing. Mother Ann herself practiced a form of spiritually inspired healing. In August 1783, Mary Southwick, of the Hancock, Massachusetts family, was healed of a cancer in her mouth that had been growing for two years; Ann Lee put a finger into Southwick's mouth upon the cancer, at which instant the pain left her and she was restored to health (Nordhoff 1961, 119, 127).[5] Lee advised Southwick to "do all your work as though you had a thousand years to live, and as though you were going to die to-morrow." This small band of Manchester millenarians were looking for the Second Advent, and the impression was that the Messiah would appear in the female form. The Shaker books speak of "a second appearing [that] was to be manifested in woman, which completed the desire of all nations, by the revelation of the Mother Spirit in Christ, an emanation from the eternal Mother." Some years after her

---

5. On the laying on of hands, see Andrews 1953, 194.

death, Elder Frederick W. Evans would pronounce her to be the female aspect of Christ (Harrison 1979, 166).

As with the Mormons and Metz's Inspired People, over time literal adherence to the Bible was supplanted by direct revelation (Cross 1965, 32). At the North Union Ohio "family," they would read the Bible "when they have a gift for it," but depended much upon their own revelations from the spirit-land. At South Union, Kentucky, from 1807, following the revival, some who joined were slaveholders; and as Shakers always consistently opposed slavery, these new members set their slaves free, and forty of these former slaves were induced also to become Shakers; there was even a "colored" Elder. Soon Shakerism comprised fifty-eight families, including the Philadelphia Family of twenty "colored" persons (Nordhoff 1961, 205–207).

Mother Ann died quietly at Watervliet on September 8, 1784, aged 48 years. Over the next decades, James Whittaker (1751–1787), Joseph Meacham (1742–1796), and then Mother Lucy Wright (1760–1821) took charge (Walters 1978, 45; Harrison 1979, 166). Joseph Meacham was an American convert who organized the society on the basis of community of labor and property. He also introduced the greater part of the spiritualist portion of the Shaker creed and doctrine, putting great store in speaking in tongues. The leadership eventually passed to Elder Frederick W. Evans, an English immigrant converted from Owenism.

By the mid-nineteenth century, Shaker villages were established from Maine to Kentucky, with around seven thousand believers. At its height around 1870, the census recorded eighteen Shaker organizations, comprising 8,850 persons and holding an estimated wealth of $86,900 (Andrews 1953, 224; Axon 1876, 16–18). Shortly before her death, Mother Ann had said that "the next opening of the Gospel will be in the southwest; it will be at a great distance, and there will be a great work of God." Remembering her words twenty years later, when the revival in Kentucky and Ohio was in progress, the Shakers sent three messengers, John Meacham (b. 1769), Benjamin Youngs (b. 1773?) and Isschar Bates (1758–1837), to open the testimony of salvation and the Second Coming. Setting out on foot on January 1, 1805, they trekked over 1000 miles; in Ohio, they came to the house of Malcham Worley in Lebanon, who received the messengers almost as angels of God. Worley was converted; but when he left his property to the Shakers, his relatives contested the will, setting up the plea of insanity (M'Nemar 1807, 73–108; Hinds 1878, 96, 109).

The former Owenite Frederick W. Evans was among those whom the Shakers attracted, having been awakened by revivalism, or in his case by socialism, but still remaining dissatisfied. Evans had first joined the Owenites at the Kendal Community, near Canton, Ohio. When their experiment collapsed, he became disillusioned with secular reform. In June 1826, Evans and other Owenites took in several families from the failed Cossackie Community, and together the regrouped membership of 150 survived by producing woolen goods and hops. While searching for a new location in upper New York State, Evans came upon the Shakers at New Lebanon (Noyes 1870, 13, 78; Walters 1978, 45–46). With fifty other members of the failing Owenite colony, Evans then joined the Shakers. He became a powerful elder, who declared Mother Ann as the Second Advent and announced that the Millennium had begun in 1792 (Cross 1965; 32; Harrison 1979, 166).

The Shaker religion is generally associated with a plain and unadorned, but beautiful style of furniture: all ornamentation was considered sinful (Clifton 1995, 46). The Shakers followed a daily routine that included work and union meetings. All expected to leave the world behind; it was their boast that their habits and manners were the same as had existed sixty years before. The plan of their buildings, the style of their furniture, the pattern of their coats and pants, even the cut of their hair were all regulated according to communications sent from heaven by Mother Ann through their "instruments" (Noyes 1870, 602–603).

The four pillars of the Shaker faith are virgin purity, Christian communism, confession of sin, and separation from the world. They believed that Deity is both male and female; that the second appearing of Christ, not Jesus, whom they regarded as only a man, took place in Mother Ann. There is no resurrection of the body but a progressive resurrection of the spirit. This new birth requires the united influence of spiritual parents, in the order of male and female; and as the eternal Christ in Jesus is the male, so the eternal Christ in Mother Ann is the female, constituting the father and mother of all the children of God. They fervently believed that the millennial reign and the final judgment had begun: hence, their formal name is the Millennial Church. In each family, two elder brethren and two elder sisters had charge of the spiritual affairs, along with two deacons and two deaconesses, who cared for temporal matters. The ministry at Mt. Lebanon was called the "Head of Influence." Sovereign over all the Shaker communities, it was composed of three advisers and one head elder, who might appoint his own successor. Three times a week they held "union meetings," when brethren and sisters, ten to twenty in number, could come together and, forming two ranks, would sit opposite each other and spend an hour or so in conversation, or in reading or singing, as they chose (Hinds 1878, 89, 93, 110).

By emphasizing Lee's revelations, the Shakers, like the Ebenezers, had moved beyond scriptural authority (Clifton 1995, 46). This trend was reflected also in the practices of the Jemimakins and the most well known, the Mormons. As we have seen, "The Publick Universal Friend," while not claiming to be Christ, insisted that she had become a different and divine person after suffering an illness as a young adult. Wilkinson also drew adherents from disenchanted revivalists. Later this trend continued with the prophetic career of Joseph Smith and the Mormons and the brief existence of the Millerites during the 1840s.

The Shaker Gospel Order, or communal system, was developed by the rough, independent frontier life. Their most striking precept was that the source of all evil is ultimately sex, and their community ideal was a new form of family (Harrison 1979, 169). Shaker worship was like that of other inner-light sects, the French prophets, and also the Schismatics of the Kentucky Revival. One secret of the Shaker appeal was how they alternated privation and enthusiasm, a pattern of self-denial and emotional release through ritual dancing, trances, and the like, albeit a highly ritualized enthusiasm, as in the "Whirling Gift." "Spiritual labors" were undertaken to mortify the flesh and debase the body. This led to a ritual form of dancing, and other complex rituals in the period of spiritualism, between 1837 and 1847 (Walters 1978, 47; Harrison 1979, 171). Most important at the psychological level as a means of deriving continuing aid from their departed charismatic leader was "Mother Ann's Work."

Mother Ann's Work. Shaker practices gradually developed beyond singing in unison and engaging in synchronized dances. Mother Ann's work, as this new practice was called, bore fruit mostly among adolescent girls; their trances were welcomed and controlled by the elders. After Philemon Stewart became the first prominent instrument or medium, who spoke with the words of Jesus and Mother Ann, this practice was taken up among young girls. After a dervish-like round of dancing by one of the girls, communications would be received from Mother Ann and others in the spiritual world through these instruments. In these bizarre sessions, angels and famous personages spoke. At times, the girls would be possessed by Indians, when they danced, whooped, and waved imaginary tomahawks. The fundamental point is that, by emphasizing Lee's revelations, they had moved beyond scriptural authority (Clifton 1995, 46-47; Andrews 1953, chapter 8).

As has been previously stated, Mother Ann Lee came to be regarded as the female incarnation of Christ, and many later enthusiasms can be traced to these Shaker practices (Cross 1965, 33). Communications from Mother Ann and others in the spiritual world through instruments produced visions, trances, and ecstatic states (Harrison 1979, 172). This demonstrates a pattern of communications from their late millennial teacher that was generalized to include a wider pantheon of communicators. Among the Shaker practices can be found the germs of communism, premillennialism, spiritualism, and perfectionism.

When Shaker adolescents fell into trances, like the earlier *somnambules*, they would sometimes prophesy. Among the most startling prophecies given in this state was that, from 1848, there would be a great outpouring of spirit-truth and the discovery of material wealth. These prophecies, which some believed were referring to the rise of the spiritualist movement and to the California Gold Rush, were unfortunately made public only after 1848 (Nelson 1969, 52). Elder Evans, writing in the *Atlantic Monthly* in May 1869, averred:

> In 1837 to 1844, there was an influx from the spirit world . . .
> extending throughout all the 18 societies, making media by the
> dozen, whose various exercises, not to be suppressed even in their

public meetings, rendered it imperatively necessary to close them all to the world during a period of seven years, in consequence of the then unprepared state of the world. . . . [T]he spirits then declared, again and again, that, when they had done their work among the inhabitants of Zion [Shakers], they would do a work in the world of such magnitude that not a place nor a hamlet upon earth should remain unvisited by them. (Noyes 1870, 596)

Then came the manifestations of Andrew Jackson Davis and of the Fox sisters in Rochester, New York, in 1848. But, Evans observed, "the rapidity of its course through the nations of the earth . . . has far exceeded the predictions."

Elspeth Buchan's followers had refused to transfer their allegiance to the Reverend Hugh White, and their American venture was fruitless. Ann Lee's Shaker migrants grew respectably, aided by the revival fever of several generations, and Jemima Wilkinson's homegrown apocalyptics continued to await the millennium for many years after her passing. What they and the German Pietists contributed to the changing purview of mind, consciousness and salvation was deeply ingrained into an apocalyptic outlook, as was a deep unease at the direction that orthodox religion was taking. Nevertheless, their efforts resulted in increasing American individualism and in lessening the influence of established religions; moreover, as Fuller has observed they prepared the way for a new psychology and a new theology, what he calls a "psychologically based pneumatology" (Fuller 1982, 46, 67).

Within the new American milieu can be discerned a pattern similar to that in the previous century, where we observed the transition from Mesmer's emphasis on curative efficacy to the psychological explorations of Puységur and the occult interests of Willermoz and his circle. In America too, mesmerism now became less a system of medical healing than "a schema demonstrating how the individual mind can establish rapport with ever more sublime levels of reality"; it promised adherents the ability to transcend the mundane and to experience ecstatic states of consciousness and paranormal mental powers (Fuller 1982, 46).

For each of these disappointed millenarians, Ephratans and Zoarites, Shakers and Buchanites, bound to a charismatic prophet or prophetess who preached a premillennial gospel, the prognosis for their faith was never good. But what they did achieve inadvertently was first to push forward an augmenting faith in supplementary revelation, together with a strong individualist ethos of religious practice; this would have untold consequences for the fortunes of future religions like the Mormons and the spiritualists. Even the staid Shaker faithful benefited from the second modality in the transformation of the paradigms of mind and consciousness: the study of the unplumbed levels of the human consciousness, principally through the residues of the new science of magnetism. For the Shakers, this was translated into the period of Mother Ann's Work, a practice they sincerely believed would keep them in contact with their blessed founder, from whom they continued to receive guidance from beyond the veil of death. This conjunction, arising from their sincere search for spiritual guidance was, along with the practices of the Ebenezers, among the earliest manifestations of a new paradigm of mediumship and the séance, destined to expand dramatically from the middle of the nineteenth century. It comprised the paradigm shift that brought forth the spiritualist movement and rejuvenated the Swedenborgian Church, while it eclipsed Magnetism.

6

TRANSFORMATION IN AMERICA:
THE EARTH AS HEAVEN

> The universe may contain a few agencies—say half a million—
> about which no man knows anything. I cannot but suspect that a
> small proportion of these agencies—say five thousand—may be
> severally competent to the production of all the phenomena, or
> may be quite up to the task among them.
>
> Sophia Elizabeth deMorgan
> Preface, *From Matter to Spirit* (1863)

In the early nineteenth century, while the apocalyptic cults were making less impact than they had in the closing decades of the previous century and even the Shakers put their idea of an imminent millennium in abeyance, a more secular trend was appearing in Mesmerism. Yet even this new phenomenon would soon be molded to religious and metaphysical ends, revealing again the fundamental importance of religion to American culture. This chapter presents another perspective on the transformation of American religious culture, focusing in the first instance on the Owenite movement and the surge of Fourierist and other secular communities in the following 1840s decade. A highlight of this was the transition then being effected among significant numbers of Americans, a transformation in popular religious culture from mystical somnambulism to spiritualism, as a parallel shift was occurring within the wider culture from "authorized" religion to the sovereignty of individual belief.

The distinctive melding of outlooks enshrined in the two alternate paradigms was in part the result of contact between Swedenborgian and mesmeric conceptions; this would in turn lead more or less directly to the establishment of spiritualism, which, by the early 1850s, was erected on the bedrock of imported European traditions and their native American variants. The surge in popular religion would ultimately result in the organization of the Society for Psychical Research (S. P. R.) in the 1880s among a transcultural intelligentsia, for the avowed scientific examination of paranormal events. This melding of paradigms was a significant cultural phenomenon, a recognizable synthesis conjoining the ontological and the alternate-consciousness paradigms into a new outlook, the new role of mediumship and the séance. The ontological or alternate-reality legacy of the occult revival would feed into the optimistic hope of a passable bridge between the "two worlds," while the alternate-consciousness paradigm, arising from the discovery of magnetic sleep by Puységur, "introduced a radically new view of the human psyche and opened up a fresh vista of psychological inquiry." Magnetic sleep had revealed the startling fact that consciousness is divided and that "there exists in human beings a second consciousness quite distinct from normal, everyday consciousness" (Crabtree 1993, 86–87).[1]

Pietistic and Post-1825 Communities

It was at this point in the second quarter of the nineteenth century that ideas long prominent among the Pietistic communities were taken up by a secular utopian, the British industrial reformer Robert Owen. Having subordinated the individual conscience, autonomy, and property rights to the community, the Pietists and Separatists like those at Amana and Zoar often altered family and sexual relationships, drawing sharp boundaries between their community and the outside world (Walters 1978, 54). The essential difference between the Pietists and the secular utopian societies envisioned by Owen, and later by Fourier, was that the latter would be based on "reason" rather than on the Bible or revelation. As Ronald Walters

---

1. Adam Crabtree argues that the leading paradigm in understanding diseases of the mind was firstly the *intrusion paradigm*, where it was believed that disease is caused by external agents, including spirits. In the sixteenth century, this was replaced by the *organic paradigm* through the work of Levinus Lemnius (1511–1550) and Johann Weyer (1505–1568). According to this understanding mental dysfunction was due to physical causes. With the advent of animal magnetism and Mesmer and Puységur, a second consciousness was discovered.

put it, Owenism was "the beginning of a secular critique of capitalistic individualism" (1978, 64).

Robert Owen was to exercise a more far-reaching influence on transatlantic culture than the religious communitarians. Born in Wales, he popularized village modes of "cooperation." After a modest beginning, he made his mark as an entrepreneur. In 1789, the Bank Top Mill factory became the first cotton mill in Manchester to be powered by a rotary steam engine and governor, recently invented by Matthew Boulton (1728–1809) and James Watt (1736–1819). There, Owen, still in his teens, introduced efficiencies. Paying 5s per pound for fine cotton, he produced thread for muslin weavers that sold at £ 9 18s (Owen 1791, x, 35). The youthful entrepreneur used these profits to buy the New Lanark factory in Scotland with partners, including Jeremy Bentham, for £60,000 from David Dale (1739–1806); he also used the occasion to gain his consent to marry his daughter Carolyn (Owen 1971, xi, xxxi). From 1817, his management of New Lanark began to attract wide attention. In 1813, Owen had written *A New View of Society*, an utopian tract that inspired American communitarians. As it was for Thomas Jefferson, environmentalism was a leading Owenite concept that served as intellectual justification for social engineering. Owen's experiments at New Lanark earned him a substantial fortune and a worldwide reputation, inspiring a host of industrial reformers. His New Harmony community in Indiana would also form the backdrop for the rash of Fourierist phalansteries that sprang up two decades later in the early 1840s.

At New Lanark, Robert Owen earned a reputation as a pioneer industrialist and reformer. In the cotton trade, his keen eye had "early noticed the great attention given to the dead machinery, and the neglect and disregard of the living machinery" (Owen 1971, 34). The factory reforms Owen implemented gave practical effect to the common utopian ideas of eighteenth-century rationalism. By 1817, New Lanark had been transformed into a factory village that was a light to the world. All religions were tolerated, and there were even clergymen preaching in Gaelic. Owen brought in remarkably enlightened modes of operation; in his *Essay Third*, he expatiated on the relaxation he provided for workers, like gardens to cultivate and public walks "for innocent pleasure," and he rather went to extremes on the significance of dancing as a healthy diversion, which he prescribed for his workers three times per week (Owen 1971, xxvi, xxix–xxx).

Owen believed it imperative to establish a pleasant working environment and to pay reasonable wages. During Napoleon's blockade, he continued to pay his workers, despite the drastic reduction in the exports of cloth. He also helped decrease child labor and opposed the corporeal punishment of children. Such efforts prompted Frederic Engels (1820–1895) to note approvingly that "every social movement, every real advance in England on behalf of the workers links itself on to the name of Robert Owen" (cited in Johnson 1970, 15). But unlike Engels, Owen had no faith in the workers as a revolutionary proletariat or in class struggle (Johnson 1970, 5, 15–16). He emphasized the importance of environment, and he appealed to the reason to produce social change. Owen's first principle was that character was formed for, and not by, humans, the main focus being on external conditions (de Giustino 1975, 140). Social engineering, not revolution, was the key to both the increased productivity and workplace harmony that would ultimately transform society. This was the reason he was eager to establish a living experiment away from the British Isles and the entrenched elites there who resisted change. New Harmony provided the opportunity.

Owen as Social Reformer

By the 1820s, Owen was looking for a means to try out his ideas, but not in England, with its high price of land and stratified society. Meanwhile, the Rappite community came up for sale. As was already discussed, emigrating in 1803, the followers of George Rapp had settled first in Beaver County, Pennsylvania, then moved to the far frontier of Indiana, where their hard work, deep religious faith, and social cohesion produced Harmony, a garden in the wilderness. Now they were planning to leave Indiana and settle back in Pennsylvania. Their leader Father George Rapp commissioned Richard Flower, an English communitarian, to find a buyer for the Harmony commune. Having heard of Owen's successes at New Lanark, Flower sought him out in England and sold him the entire town, some twenty thousand acres of arable land and nearly two hundred buildings for the bargain price of $150 thousand. It cost Owen nearly half his fortune (Bestor 1950, 101–102; Noyes 1870, 33–34).

Robert Owen left for America in October 1824, and following a somewhat cursory inspection, New Harmony was opened in May 1825. Among his new influential friends was New York Governor DeWitt Clinton (1769–1828), and along the way he visited the Shaker settlement at Niskeyuna. Advertisements had been taken out in journals and newspapers, and this led to a rapid overcrowding. Over eight hundred persons responded, whereas accommodation existed for only seven hundred. Owen remained sanguine, but it was a portent of things to come. The "boatload of knowledge" Owen brought down the Wabash River to New Harmony carried among the foremost educators and scientists of the time. These included Sir John Bowring (1792–1872), linguist, writer, and literary executor of Jeremy Bentham (Bestor 1950, 104, 106; Elliott 1969, 215)[2]; the French educator Madame Marie Duclos Fretageot (1783–1833), very much *au courant* with Fourier's works; Phiquepal D'Arusmont, a disciple of Johann Heinrich Pestalozzi (1746–1827), together with ten of his scholars; and the educator William Maclure (1763–1840), president of the Philadelphia Academy of Natural Sciences; and Owen and his son Robert Dale Owen (1801–1877). They had an eventful trip (Bestor 1950, 100; Johnson 1870, 2).

Boarding the keelboat *Philanthropist* from Pittsburgh, the group went down the Ohio River and crossed to the Wabash. Already they were receiving disturbing news from an overcrowded New Harmony. R. D. Owen noted in his journal that "on November 7 . . . Dr Price . . . gave us the latest news. These were, in general, favourable, though the impression here is that a number of the members are indolent, and that this has created very great dissatisfaction among the rest." He believed these claims to be exaggerated (Elliott 1969, 229).

Immediate difficulties surfaced at New Harmony over the issues of property rights and the selection criteria for entrants. By October 1825,

---

2. Bowring had resided for some time in New South Wales. He spoke of a mild climate there with no winter, yet a summer that was not oppressively hot. He considered the natives "a very fine race, free and happy, but daily deteriorating as they come into contact with European settlers" (Elliott 1969, 215).

the community was bursting with over nine hundred members, and the strains of inadequate planning were already telling. Owen's response was to depart immediately for Europe, leaving the nine hundred to fend for themselves (Bestor 1950, 116; Walters 1978, 65). Nevertheless, there was at first great enthusiasm at New Harmony and declamations of a new socialist world. Concerts and balls were given in the old Rappite church; an apothecary and store dispensed goods, probably at Owen's expense (Noyes 1870, 36). But apart from the scarcity of logistical detail, it was soon evident that Owen had not thought through some basic issues associated with founding a new world order.

Utopias have nearly always foundered when the enthusiasm of acolytes waned and they demanded that their contributions be returned. Maclure and others who arrived on the "boatload of knowledge," and William Owen, Robert's harried eldest son, tried to maintain order despite the great reformer's frequent absences. But the initial confusion was only exacerbated as Owen's strengths as theoretician, but not as a practical organizer, became evident. According to Robert Dale, he was "dogmatic," and his manner of presenting his ideas too vehement: "he tends to fall into the same fault which he criticizes in others" (Elliott 1969, 178). After three separate constitutions and reorganizations in 1826 that established the education, agriculture, and manufacture sections, the whole venture failed in 1827. Owen's main focus was on propaganda. Through letters of introduction, he met Thomas Jefferson and James Madison (1751–1836); and despite the parlous state of his venture, Owen continued to court the American elite, addressing the United States Congress on February 25 and March 7, 1825. Presidents John Quincy Adams (1767–1848) and James Monroe (1758–1831) both sat through his three-hour lecture given in the Capitol rotunda. Owen also delivered lectures to Choctaw and Chicasaw chiefs through an interpreter. Owen expected much to come out of these lectures to America's legislators, but nothing ever eventuated (Walters 1978, 65; Bestor 1950, 108–110, 113; Johnson 1970, 8).

Robert Owen was present at New Harmony on July 4, 1826, the fiftieth anniversary of the signing of the Declaration of Independence, made more poignant by the death on that same day of two founding fathers and signatories, Thomas Jefferson and John Adams (1735–1826). Owen used the occasion of this highly symbolic day in the American psyche to deliver a "Declaration of Mental Independence," in which he attacked what he called the "Trinity" of monstrous evils: private property, absurd and irrational systems of religion, and marriage founded on individual property. In stentorian cadences, he called for the radical reformulation of the young republic's institutions. He declared that, in 1776, "the greatest of blessing, MENTAL LIBERTY" had been won for the people. He now called for "the liberty of freely extending thought upon all subjects, secular and religious, and the right to express those thoughts openly" (Johnson 1970, 70, 67). That these rights were already guaranteed under the Constitution did not inhibit his rhetoric, as from these, he felt sure, a rationalist revolution would ensue. Especially did he loathe "that fearful unmeaning term SACRED," along with the present institutions, and in particular marriage, for their leading role in perpetuating "an aristocracy of wealth, of power, and of learning." Somewhat naively, Owen believed that "as soon as man shall be trained rationally . . . he will act only rationally," and he hoped that thereby "Man may be no longer a superstitious idiot, continually dying from the futile fear of death" (Johnson 1970, 71–73).

In June 1827, Owen left New Harmony for good after its reversion to "the old style" of the town; he was selling individual property lots, and a grocery store had opened, doing a normal retail trade. When Donald Macdonald (1791–1872), the chronicler of communitarianism, visited the remnant New Harmony 15 years later in 1842, he was cautioned "not to speak of Socialism, as the subject was unpopular" (Noyes 1870, 41–42).

Owenism did spread in some twenty ventures launched in the United States, Canada, and the British Isles, giving rise to around eleven communities in New Harmony's first year (Walters 1978, 67; Noyes 1870, 13). One unintended and important result was the defection from Owenism of Frederick Evans, who eventually became head elder of the Shaker movement. Moreover, Owenite communities provided a bridge to the second wave of communitarian activity during the 1840s, based on the Fourierist model. New Harmony, though failed as an individual utopian experiment, left some indelible marks on the social history of the nation. It was a vehicle for a concentration of the foremost educators and scientists of the time; as we have seen, Mme. Fretageot, Maclure and d'Arusmont, with their Pestalozzi teaching methods, were all gathered there. Other firsts included the first women's club, Frances Wright's Female Social Society, formed in 1825. "Fanny" Wright (1795–1852), Robert Dale Owen, and other secular radicals also derived their initial inspiration there, as did Josiah Warren (1798–1874), the "individual sovereignty" advocate and later instigator of the free love experiment at Modern Times, who lived at New Harmony as a young man (Johnson 1970, 2–3).

On his fourth trip to the United States, Owen met R. W. Emerson, holding a "freethought séance" with him. In 1834, Owen tried to exert his radical influence at home, forming the ill-fated Grand National Council of Trade Unions in England. And in 1853, to the horror of his secular adherents, the eighty-two-year-old Owen was converted to spiritualism after attending séances with the American medium Mrs. Hayden in London, from whom he received what he judged to be irrefragable proof of life after death. He now considered socialism and spiritualism as a "body with a soul." Owen confessed to the spiritualist publicist Epes Sargeant that "until he received the revelations of Spiritualism, he had been quite unaware of the necessity of good *spiritual conditions* for forming the character of men . . . the most important of all in the future development of mankind (Webb 1989, 241; Barrow 1986, 26; Noyes 1870, 58). It was a coup for the spiritualists to secure the old warhorse of socialism to their cause. Thus, the most important secular radical of his day was eventually drawn upon the wave of a cultural transformation that brought ancient concepts of mind and of cosmos together in the spiritualist movement.

Swedenborg in America

During Owen's peregrinations, he even influenced some Cincinnati Swedenborgians to turn to the communal ideal. The Swedenborgian community at Yellow Springs, Ohio, is of interest both as a rare Swedenborgian excursus into the communitarian experiment and as further evidence of the early immersion of Swedenborgian ideas into popular culture, yet another example of how inherently opposed ideologies could find common ground in that cauldron of heterodoxies of all kinds, the United States. This was evident in science, where phrenology was used extensively to map character, its strengths and weaknesses; in religion, where individualism reigned unfettered on the frontier; and in new forms of social organization, where an alternative mode to the family was eagerly sought.

Swedenborgianism and mesmerism had both been introduced into the United States in 1784, during the era of confederation. The Marquis de Lafayette, a prominent member of the Paris Harmonial Society, returned to a hero's welcome to the American Republic he had helped to liberate from the British, and he was keen also to spread the word about animal magnetism. His lectures to his old comrades in arms met with little success. In that same year, James Glen, a Scottish merchant and early convert, on his way to inspect business interests in South America stopped off at Philadelphia, where he lectured at Bell's Bookstore, then in Boston at the Green Dragon Tavern. He delivered lectures on Swedenborg's theology and left copies of some of the seer's writings. This led to the formation of small study groups that developed into the New Church in America, with Philadelphia and Boston still continuing as the centers of American Swedenborgianism.

Over the next decade, Swedenborg's works were transmitted slowly westward beyond their seedbed at Boston and Philadelphia. Miss Hetty Barclay of Philadelphia, a boarder in the house where Glen had stayed, founded with Francis Bailey (1744–1817) the first formal society in the United States, a Swedenborg study group, using the books Glen had left behind (Hindmarsh 1861, 29). In 1787, Bailey printed the *Summary View of the Heavenly Doctrines,* the first New Church work published in the United States, which was given out gratis; frequently extracts of Swedenborg's writings would be rolled up in bolts of cloth from Bailey's drapery, destined for frontier settlements. The Congregational minister the Reverend Ezra Stiles, later President of Yale College, was among those who received a copy of the *Summary View* that year (Odhner 1904 1:131; Brooke 1994, 98). By the 1810s, Swedenborgian societies had been formed as far west as Cincinnati, effectively the limits of the then-settled territories.

Reading and devotional groups had been established early around Philadelphia, connected to early exemplars like the Swedish mission on the

Delaware River and later to Rev. Jacob Duché's study group in the 1770s, before his hasty egress to England after becoming *persona non grata* with the revolutionary elite. From these, a small society was formed in Baltimore, whose most important convert was the powerful Virginia planter and scion of Nomony Hall, Colonel Robert Carter (1728–1804). In Baltimore, Carter joined the Reverend James Wilmer (1750–1814), a former Episcopal minister, who had preached the first New Church sermon in the New World in 1792. However, in these days of fluid changes between Protestant denominations, Wilmer became disillusioned with the slow progress of the society, numbering only twenty-two persons, and gave up his connection with the New Church, presumably returning to the Episcopalian fold (Block 1984, 87).

From his grandfather, the legendary "King" Carter (1663–1732), Robert Carter had inherited an estate of sixty thousand acres, and six hundred slaves. When he joined the Baltimore Swedenborgian Society in 1778, taking his clue from Swedenborg's teachings against slavery, he began freeing his slaves, 442 of them in 1791; and he also divested himself of some of his estates. Most importantly, Carter generously funded the reprinting of the English liturgy for the New Church at his own expense of $600. In 1793, the Baltimore society presented a copy of *True Christian Religion* to President George Washington, who had previously received from his loyal fellow revolutionary, the Marquis de Lafayette, news about the new science of animal magnetism. Nothing came out of either overture, although Washington responded with gentlemanly courtesy to the gift (Block 1984, 84; Odhner 1904, 1:172).

Things went badly for the New Church Society, and the main cause of dissension was animal magnetism, at this time also falling into disfavor in Stockholm with the eclipse of Silverhjelm's spiritists. Carter was opposed to animal magnetism, and this caused a split in the Baltimore society; nine members left with Carter to form a splinter society. Carter's denunciatory letter of July 7, 1794, to one of the schematics contains the first mention of animal magnetism in the New Church annals in America. He believed that "magnetisers are not receptive of the heavenly doctrines; if they in exchange are aided so as to foretell future events, and do effect a transient removal of distresses, that their cures are not permanent"; in short, he was convinced that "animal electricity and magnetism is of the devil." Like most other Swedenborgians, Carter saw the dangers of animal magnetism in the submission of the mesmeric subject's will to the operator or to the spiritual beings. "He apprehended the wicked magnetisers [sic] would apply the science unprofitably, as patients were entirely divested during the crisis of liberty or rationality, having resigned them both to the operator" (Block 1984, 88–89).

Animal magnetism, therefore, was one of the rocks on which the Baltimore society foundered, presaging a recurring pattern evident within the New Church over the next half-century. The intrusion of mesmeric and related beliefs had been exacerbated by the contentious issue of episcopal organization of the ministry, as advocated by the Hindmarsh faction in England. In 1797, Carter formed his own society, which lasted only a short time, and he became disillusioned in old age. Thus, as a result of the spiritistic interests pursued by some in the congregation, the first New Church schism occurred in Baltimore. It was at this time that a more tangible connection was made between English and American experience through the arrival of the Reverend Ralph Mather to Baltimore.

In 1785, the Reverend Ralph Mather was an original member of the Theosophical Society in London, precursor to the first English New Church. He probably first heard of Swedenborg through the Reverend John Clowes, who was then preaching to Bolton mystics. Even earlier, a Swedenborg reading group existed in nearby Whitefield, where Lancashire artisans drew on the mystical tradition in the works of Boëhme and his translator William Law. In 1787, Mather and Joseph Salmon, both former Methodists, proselytized in the familiar Wesleyan techniques of field preaching, but now to win souls for Swedenborg. Over the next few months they traveled from East London to Salisbury, Bristol, Norwich, Leeds, and Manchester (Garrett 1984, 78–79). Soon Mather felt a calling to preach in the New World. In 1792, he embarked for Philadelphia, where he served briefly as minister of a New Church chapel in nearby Germantown, but it dissolved when members returned to their former churches. After this, Mather was called to the troubled Baltimore society. In 1798, he reorganized the congregation, serving in a joint ministry with the Reverend John Hargrove (1750–1839) in the new Baltimore society formed by the Carter remnant. There the first New Church ordination in America was held, and also the first temple in the New World was dedicated in January 1800. But after many disagreements and friction with his fellow minister, Mather resigned and returned to England. The Reverend Hargrove, now solely responsible for the Baltimore congregation, was invited to Thomas Jefferson's inauguration in 1801, to whom he presented a copy of Swedenborg's *True Christian Religion*. On two subsequent occasions, Hargrove was invited to preach in the rotunda of the Capitol for the president and Congress (Garrett 1984, 80; Block 1984, 91–92).

Another path for spreading the writings to the far outposts of the republic came through the efforts of "Johnny Appleseed," perhaps the most famous of the Swedenborgian pioneers. John (Appleseed) Chapman (1775–1843) was a primitive New Church evangelist, a hardy pioneer who, from 1801 until his death traversed new settlements in the southern Ohio Valley, distributing apple seedlings and New Church literature along the way. As a result Swedenborg's texts appeared in very unlikely places (Odhner 1904, 1:200, 229, 250; Brooke 1994, 99). Born in 1775 in Boston, Johnny Appleseed, hailed as "the picturesque sower of a two-fold seed," worked as an itinerant nurseryman. His territory ranged from the Ohio River to the Great Lakes and from the Alleghenies to Indiana, then the limits of the United States' territory. Obtaining apple seeds from cider presses in Pennsylvania, he would plant them in a rough nursery, then transfer the seedlings to open fields during his wanderings. At each cabin visited, he would leave one or two chapters of Swedenborg's writings, then collect them again in reverse order on his way back. He was a compassionate if eccentric figure on the frontier, often depicted as garbed in an old coffee sack and going barefoot in all weather, with a tin pot for head gear. The Native Americans regarded him as a mighty medicine man. He was a vegetarian and pacifist who never carried a gun and a true humanitarian who rescued broken-down horses when they were abandoned by the pioneers. Chapman died in Indiana, aged 72. His greatest legacy was the pleasure of numberless tired pioneers who, coming over the rise, would unexpectedly find succulent apples, free for the taking, planted in anonymous orchards throughout the wilderness; but a little-known legacy was the dissemination of Swedenborg's works (Block 1984, 115).

Owen and Swedenborg

While the Swedenborgians achieved some degree of respectability, other imports to the New World had a more radical edge. Unlike Swedenborg's pronouncement that the Second Coming had occurred in 1757, sects like the Buchanites and the Shakers taught an imminent millennium, to be heralded by a great conflagration as prophesied in Revelations and in Daniel. Yet there were a few brief and unsatisfactory experiments in communal living even within the New Church. The first was inspired by a visit from the peripatetic Robert Owen. An event that highlights the cultural smallness of the American West, it was a further, and even unlikelier, conjunction with a religious group during Robert Owen's sojourn in the United States than his brief contact with the Rappites and the Shakers.

John Noyes wrote that "the beginning of the Owenite movement in this country was signalized by a conjunction with Swedenborgianism" (Noyes 1870, 59–61). In 1824, on his way to inspect New Harmony, Owen established contact with Swedenborgians during a visit to Cincinnati. There he lectured and became acquainted with New Church members, in whom he found congenial spirits. Daniel Roe, a determined anticleric, led a congregation that had been in existence since 1811. They soon became fascinated with Owen and his communism and, joining together with others in the city, they purchased a property at Yellow Springs, seventy-five miles north of Cincinnati, the present site of Antioch University, where they organized a community.

Around one hundred families consisting of professionals, teachers, mechanics, merchants, and farmers embarked on the noble experiment. It was to be a community based on Swedenborg's writings, where schools would be established, teaching all things deemed useful, except apparently religion (Block 1984, 118–119). As with Brook Farm at the beginning of its brief existence, a bucolic enthusiasm pervaded the scene:

> [A]ll entered into the new system with a will. Service was the order
> of the day. Men who seldom or never before labored with their
> hands, devoted themselves to agriculture and the mechanic arts,
> with a zeal which was at least commendable, though not always

according to knowledge. Ministers of the gospel guided the plough; called the swine to their corn, instead of sinners to repentance; and let patience have her perfect work over an unruly yoke of oxen. Merchants exchanged the yard-stick for the rake or pitch-fork. All appeared to labor cheerfully for the common weal. (Hinds 1878, 146)

Alas, the venture failed after only three months. The main problems were the familiar ones of class, the varying levels of individual commitment and industry, and the perennial disputes over money. Within a year, all participants had returned to their homes and professions. After the failure at Yellow Springs, Daniel Roe became a socialist. For a time, he lived at New Harmony, and when it failed he returned home (Noyes 1870, 63; Block 1984, 120). Hence, just as he had brushed briefly past the Shakers and the Rappites without learning the secret of their communal success, so in another strange encounter, Robert Owen served as catalyst for a brief and unhappy Owenite-style experiment among some New Church members on the frontier. Two decades later, a second wave of communalism would bring into existence, equally briefly, a further two communities organized along Swedenborgian lines, at Leraysville, Pennsylvania, and Canton, Illinois.

Owen had launched his grand living experiment in the United States among a "comparatively unperverted people," with their liberal institutions and inexpensive western lands (Noyes 1870, 60–61). But his lack of foresight as to the questions of land, rents and the everyday needs of some nine hundred persons descending on his utopia, bringing varying levels of education and energy, had foredoomed his experiment. Despite this, some interesting and enduring legacies arose from the unfortunate New Harmony community. One was the brilliant career of his son Robert Dale, then in his early twenties but already a committed reformer. A teetotaler and vegetarian, he was to have a rich and varied career in his adopted country, first in association with Fanny Wright, then as a lawyer and politician. R. D. Owen would serve two terms in the U. S. Congress, where he proposed the bill creating the Smithsonian Institution. He was also a champion of women's rights; and after Indiana's statehood, he was responsible for the passage of a landmark divorce law in that state. Later still, like his father, he became a convinced spiritualist and wrote *Footfalls on the Boundary of Another World* and *Debatable Land*, which both quickly became classics of the genre (Owen 1831, 11).[3]

In this early period, Robert Dale became associated with the vivacious and highly intelligent radical Frances Wright. They met in 1824 when both were visiting New Harmony. Together they wrote *Moral Physiology*, an early call for contraception, and Owen also worked with Wright as an enthusiastic co-editor of the *New Harmony Gazette*, which they moved to New York City and renamed the *Free Inquirer*. This radical, secular magazine became in the late 1820s the voice of the Working Men's Party, until the core membership fell out with Wright and Owen, rejecting her platform proposal that children should be put under state guardianship during their school years (Schlesinger 1945, 81; Lane 1972, 36). But the most radical of Fanny Wright's activities was the settlement at Nashoba in Tennessee.

Frances Wright was a pioneer secular radical and early feminist. Born in Scotland, where she imbibed the radical tradition of David Hume and John Millar (1735–1801) and always radical and anticlerical in her views, in her developing years, Wright read widely in the library of her uncle, a professor at Glasgow University. Through her reading, she discovered the United States, and like Margaret Fuller (1810–1850), immediately became enamored with Republicanism. At first, it was the republican ideal of equality that she championed, and soon she determined to do something about the suffering of the poor and the dispossessed. Wright first arrived in the United States in 1818 and published her impressions anonymously in Britain, which nonetheless got her noticed. But when she returned with Lafayette in 1824 and saw firsthand the horror of the slave system as she witnessed a slave ship being unloaded in a Virginia harbor, Wright decided then and there that she would devote herself to the amelioration of the condition of slaves. From New Harmony, she traveled south to Tennessee and bought several black slaves, men and women,

---

3. R. D. Owen, *Footfalls on the Boundary of Another World* (London: Trübner, 1860); and *The Debatable Land Between This World and the Next* (New York: G. W. Carleton & Co., 1872).

whom she set on the course to their freedom at Nashoba. Characteristically, her plan was to bring blacks up to civilized standards through education, and then to grant them manumission. Her lectures, essays, and the "Fanny Wright societies" had a minor influence on early Democratic Party politics via the Working Man's Party.

Wright, the uncompromising secular radical, promoted her increasingly complex range of concerns, now writing under her own name (Eckhardt 1984, 153; Noyes 1870, 22). When first contemplating the Nashoba venture, she had obtained introductions to the American political elite from her mentor Lafayette, and with considerable nerve, she sought their advice. The elderly Thomas Jefferson responded encouragingly, if equivocally, in August 1825; he reasoned that, if such ideas had succeeded "with certain of our white brethren, under the care of a Rapp and an Owen . . . why may it not succeed with the man of color?" (Eckhardt 1984, 109). General Andrew Jackson mischievously suggested that there was plenty of cheap land in his home state of Tennessee (Lane 1972, 21; Johnson 1970, 9). In the autumn of 1825, Wright purchased two thousand acres on the banks of the Wolf River in Shelby County, thirteen miles north of Memphis. She named it Nashoba, which means "wolf" in the local Chikasee Indian language. Her sister Camilla, together with a Quaker named Whitby, who served as foreman, and others, moved to this desolate marshland of western Tennessee.

By preparing slaves for freedom, Wright hoped to set an example for a system that would lead to the abolition of slavery in the southern states. The fifteen blacks she purchased were to share half of what they produced on the farm. But apart from a certain indifference to the hard work of clearing and planting when fear of the lash was removed and despite appeals made to their reason, this bold practical experiment foundered before long. General Jackson had failed to mention that the country was swampy, and soon Frances and the others became deathly ill with dengue fever and other diseases (Noyes 1870, 66, 68–69). Leaving for Europe in December 1826 to recover her health, she gave the lands over to a board of trustees, including Lafayette and R. D. Owen, "for the benefit of the negro race" (Noyes 1870, 69). She did keep her promise to free the blacks, despite the forlorn state into which the community had now sunk, arranging this with the government of the sole black nation, recently freed, the Republic of Haiti. Wright then took her charges herself to Haiti, where they might live out useful lives away from the incubus of the slave system (Noyes 1870, 72; Lane 1972, 28).

In June 1829, Frances Wright again visited New Harmony. Her most important contributions to reform occurred after Nashoba (Eckhardt 1984, 174–175). She broadened her outlook to write and lecture on other reform topics, especially women's rights, and to call for a change in attitudes toward sexuality and marriage. She bore a child out of wedlock to Phiquepal D'Arusmont, and she outraged the clerics in December 1828 during a famous lecture tour when her outspoken eloquence was heard in Baltimore, Philadelphia, and New York, where with R. D. Owen she edited the *Free Inquirer*.

The Marquis de Lafayette was responsible for bringing Frances Wright to the attention of the American intelligentsia, through his numerous contacts. In 1824, when the grateful nation wished again to commemorate his services during the War of the Revolution, Wright and her sister had accompanied him to America. Here also was an indirect but significant link to Swedenborg, through Carl Wädstrom of the Exegetic and Philosophic Society in Stockholm. On the basis of the seer's writings about the qualities of the ancient races, especially the Africans, Wädstrom had been responsible for forming the first antislavery society, with royal patronage. Lafayette too was profoundly opposed to slavery, having joined the *Societé Française des Amis des Noirs* and made his views known to his erstwhile American colleagues. Mesmer himself had written to Washington in June 1784, in characteristically pompous and self-serving terms: "It appeared to us," he intoned, "that the man who united most of his fellow men should be interested in the fate of every revolution which had for its object the good of humanity" (Darnton 1970, 88). Jefferson believed that Mesmer was dangerous. Ironically, on his first visit in 1784, Lafayette had given a mesmerist lecture to Franklin's American Philosophical Society (Crabtree 1993, 214–215).

Lafayette was an avant-garde aristocrat who embraced the radical streams of his time, including opposition to slavery, and he was involved with Thomas Paine in producing the Declaration of the Rights of Man, also being among the first to champion animal magnetism, both in his native France and during his visits to America (Eckhardt 1984, 55; Lopez 1967, 200). However, it was not until the visits of itinerant lecturers like those who impressed Phineas Pankhurst Quimby (1802–1866) during the 1830s that significant progress was made in the advancement of magnetism.

Arrival of Animal Magnetism in the United States

In 1829, Joseph Du Commun, an instructor at West Point, provided the real beginnings of magnetism in the United States as the first major promoter of Mesmer's system. Du Commun's writings were read by Samuel Underhill of Ohio, the champion of phrenomagnetism in America. Together with the English language edition of Joseph Philippe François Deleuze's (1753–1835) *Instructions Pratiques*, they sparked interest, and some hostility, within American society. David Meredith Reese (1801–1861) in 1838 castigated those whom he called the "Humbugs of New York" as nothing more than "itinerant mountebanks." By the time Charles Poyen (d. 1844) toured New England in 1836, mesmerism had caught the popular imagination. When he returned to France the next year, Poyen published *Progress of Animal Magnetism in New England*, and before his death in 1844, Poyen had amassed a large following, along with a number of imitators (Crabtree 1993, 217–218).

While it is difficult to assess the appeal of Mesmerism within popular culture, at least one line of influence can be inferred from the Christian Science movement. In 1836–1837, Charles Poyen had demonstrated mesmerism in many small towns along the New England coast. The following year in rural Maine, Phineas P. Quimby witnessed a mesmeric demonstration. Various experiments were tried on a young sensitive named Lucius Burkmar, who would fall into a mesmeric sleep in which condition, like Victor Race, he would diagnose the conditions of patients and make prescriptions. When Quimby stepped up for treatment, the magnetized Burkmar told him that he would treat him by reuniting "separated parts" of Quimby's kidneys. Quimby was astonished by the success of this treatment. As a result, Quimby developed as a healer himself, with a Zen-like approach to illness that involved no medication or even contact, but was dependent solely upon the mind of the patient (Silberger 1978, 99; Fuller 1986, 46). He concluded that illness is caused by faulty ideas and beliefs about health and that poor attitudes are the root causes of both physical and emotional disorders. This episode provides a link between the magnetic movement and later New Thought and Christian Science.

Phineas P. Quimby's healing practice in rural Maine might have escaped historical notice but that one of his patients, a Mrs. Paterson, a young woman suffering from internal problems, was to develop this mode of therapy and expand it into a new religion. It was Quimby who introduced that patient, later known as Mary Baker Eddy (1821–1910), the founder of Christian Science, to this form of healing (Silberger 1978, 99). Although Eddy took the extreme position of denying the reality of illness, the advent of her religious and moral system further elucidated the range of influence of the developing paradigms. As I have argued, these combined the insights of the magnetists into the mental causation of disease with those of Swedenborg regarding the spiritual basis of reality and the accessibility of higher realms of being. That this produced in the case of Christian Science a strange hybrid is testament to the variety of possible formulations that magnetism, transmogrified now into a "scientifically based pneumatology," ushered into the American culture, then back into Europe, in the course of the nineteenth century. As Podmore (1964, viii) put it in characteristically terse terms, "Animal magnetism became the fertile matrix from which sprung all the shadowy brood of latter-day mysticisms—Spiritualism, theosophy, the New thought, culminating in the Christian Science of Mrs. M. B. Eddy."

Quimby was among the first Americans involved in inducing anesthesia by hypnosis, a promising application demonstrated earlier by Charles Poyen. Soon to be overtaken by the new chemical anesthetics, hypnosis was applied to a young woman who had requested it for the removal of a polyp. Dr. A.T. Wheelock, the attending physician, was surprised that the patient "evinced not the slightest symptom of pain . . . but was in all respects precisely like a dead body"; he felt sure that "I might as well have amputated her arm" without provoking the slightest reaction (Silberger 1978, 101).

Therefore, from the late 1830s, mesmerism was receiving notice from some physicians, but another generation would pass before the practice of hypnotism, as it was now called, became respectable among the medical fraternity, when, in 1872, the eminent neurologist J. M. Charcot published his results with "hysterical female" patients at the Salpêtrière hospital in Paris (Owen 1971, 112). Among the numerous influential visitors to visit America in the 1840s was Dr. Robert Hanham Collyer (1823–1912), an English physician and pupil of the physician and phrenologist Dr. John Elliotson (1791–1868), editor of the *Zoist* magazine. In 1843, Collyer published *Psychography*, which taught that every human trait has its own physiological center in the brain, and he posited that protrusions or recesses of the skull were accurate indicators of a person's strengths and weaknesses (Crabtree 1993, 225; Fuller 1982, 28). Thus, Collyer introduced the combined practice of phrenomagnetism, soon taken up by Underhill and others.

Phrenology and phrenomagnetism were becoming respectable. The *American Phrenological Journal*, founded in 1837 by Orson and Lorenzo Fowler, was published until 1911. Persons of all classes and educational attainment used phrenological analysis to help with business and personal decisions, and some phrenologists even initiated campaigns for the reform of prisons and the criminal law to try out their theories of improvement and to treat the supposed "mental disposition" toward crime (de Giustino 1975, 145). Collyer conducted some experiments for a Boston committee with salutary results. Unlike its French counterpart of 1837, the second investigation there of mesmerism in that decade, this committee was of and for the people. They found that "certain appearances have been presented which cannot be explained upon the supposition of collusion, or by reference to any physiological principle known to them" (Fuller 1982, 29). Collyer kept a diary later published as *Lights and Shadows of American Life*, a kind of Toquevillian psychological tour of the early American Republic. He estimated that, by 1843, there were between twenty and thirty touring mesmerist lecturers in New England and more than two hundred magnetizers practicing in Boston alone (Fuller 1986, 26, 29–30).

Like phrenology, mesmerism was coming of age in America through the advocacy of a handful of medical men. Charles Caldwell (1772–1853), a noted Philadelphia physician, came out in favor in 1842 with *Facts in Mesmerism and Thoughts on its Causes and Uses*. He was among the first to advocate the medical application of mesmerism. A champion of progressive social causes like abolition and free public education, Caldwell called on women to abandon their corsets for the sake of their health (Crabtree 1993, 220; Fuller 1982, 62; de Giustino 1975, 73). He was a prolific writer and pamphleteer who worried that while phrenology and mesmerism, now often conjoined as "phrenomesmerism," had made real progress, they would suffer from the "vagabond pretenders who are over-running the country, reading heads for hay" (de Giustino 1975, 89). Following Poyen's tours, there had descended on the eastern seaboard a plethora of touring mesmeric and phrenological manipulators, who lectured and gave public demonstrations, the tenor of which was generally of the county fair and the carnival. Among these was Professor J. Stanley Grimes (1807–1903), who, while touring western New York in 1843, magnetized several persons in the hamlet of Poughkeepsie.

Andrew Jackson Davis was a gangly lad of twenty with no discernable talents or abilities, a hayseed and functional illiterate. Yet in the magnetic state, this unschooled youth was apparently transformed into a new and profoundly erudite personality. It was in the surprising new levels of consciousness alleged to manifest through Davis, more than through any other contemporary phenomena, that the melding of the alternate paradigms boding cure and communication had reached their apotheosis, synthesizing into a new formulation of the medium and the séance. Grimes's dramatic demonstrations were intended to "prove" character traits and to demonstrate some healing potency, but he did not succeed with Davis. However, Grimes did magnetize a local tailor named Levingston, who then experimented on the young shoemaker's assistant. To everyone's surprise, Davis under "control" scaled the heights of philosophic speculation, as the alleged guiding entity poured forth a stream of philosophy, of religious and even of cosmic pronouncements. Eventually, these were collected in numerous heavy tomes, the first and most famous of which, *Nature's Divine Revelations*, became the virtual bible of spiritualism.

Mesmerism was the nation's first popular psychology, and Robert Fuller's brilliant study *Mesmerism and the American Cure of Souls* confirms current perceptions within the popular culture of a synthesis, comprising both therapeutic and metaphysical aspects. Fuller demonstrates how people who decided their troubles were insufficiently addressed by either current medical science or the regnant religious doctrines "were destined to find their first expression through a vehicle such as mesmerism, whose intellectual contours were flexible enough to accommodate to the mental and emotional exigencies arising within popular culture" (Fuller 1982, xi). He argues that the background had been laid by the revival tradition which for years, beginning with the Great Awakening, had served as "the pre-eminent curator of the national psyche" (Fuller, 73).

After the ground was broken with the tours of Poyen and his successors and following the early interest of medical men like Drs. Collyer and Caldwell, mesmerism became a hot topic in popular culture. During the heady 1840s, the most widely circulated work was by the English magnetizer the Reverend Chauncy Townshend (1798–1868), whose *Facts in Mesmerism* (1844) called for their rational and dispassionate investigation while eschewing "Mesmer's clumsy theories about physical fluids" (Fuller 1982, 40). Townshend's writings signal an increasingly bold effort to translate mesmerism into a psychological science. Following Puységur, Townshend insisted that the proper object of investigation was not animal magnetism, but rather the unique state of consciousness commonly referred to as the mesmeric state. As Fuller characterizes it, mesmerism amounted to a psychological technique for moving awareness along a continuum; it began with ordinary sense perception and led toward a point where entirely new ranges of experience emerged into consciousness. Yet continuities existed between the normal waking state and the magnetic state (Fuller 1982, 40–42). An early example of the intersection of psychological and spiritual conceptions, Townshend's model implied that magnetized subjects gained an interior rapport with levels of reality far more sublime than those available to the average person. Thus it was natural that the concept of a psychological "continuum" soon gave way to that of a "hierarchy." The mesmeric state of consciousness became an analogue, heralded as the "deepest" mental state when referring to an inward transition of awareness, and/or as the "highest" state when speaking of the resultant exaltation of mental faculties. Via mesmerism,

Transformation in America: The Earth as Heaven

Townshend and other Church of England and Nonconformist clergymen discovered or extended their ministry of healing (Barrow 1986, 80).

The range of phenomena observed with magnetic somnambulists had intrigued operators since Puységur and Barberin. It was frequently reported that magnetized subjects became clairvoyant or were capable of seeing objects at any distance; some exhibited prevoyance, the capability of foreseeing future events, and intuitive knowledge or thought and character reading. Some even boasted that "[i]n truth, there is no definite limit to the range of their intuitive knowledge [whether] in medicine, mental philosophy, theology, chemistry, geology, etc." (Fuller 1982, 44). In some cases, this resulted in a stage of total insensibility to external sensation, even to the voice of the operator. In this state, surgical operations like that attended by Quimby had been performed on subjects sufficiently mesmerized to enter this deep level of consciousness, the hypnotic substratum.

We have seen that Alexandre Bertrand and others in France in the 1820s had revealed the surprising level of inner attention possible to the human mind, and with magnetists like Brillon and Louis Alphonse Cahagnet even further flights became possible. The margins between the alternate paradigms were shrinking; at times, as Mesmer had discovered early, a mystical sense of intimate rapport with the cosmos became manifest. In some individuals, this sense might attain the intensity later described by the psychologist R. M. Bucke (1837–1902) as "cosmic consciousness," a state wherein subjects feel that they are in possession of knowledge that transcends that of physical, space-time reality. Those who entered this state were able to use it, like Victor Race and Lucius Burkmar, and later exceptional mediums like Davis and Daniel Dunglas Home (1833–1886), to diagnose the nature and causes of physical illness, often perceiving the interior organs of humans as through a pane of glass.

Andrew Jackson Davis, when diagnosing disease described brilliant flame-like auras surrounding nerves and organs and luminescent protrusions, especially at the crown, that emanated from the bodies of patients. When he induced what he called the "superior state" in himself, Davis claimed to see the "emanations, the head especially being very luminous, and the whole body transparent as a sheet of glass"; with the greatest ease in this state, he could perceive the internal organs "which all gave out distinct flames of light." Especially did he note "the great sympathetic nerve, whose roots extend throughout the lower viscera, and whose topmost branches are lost in the superior strata of the sensorium, which appeared like a column of life, interwoven and super-blended with a soft and silvery fire" (Cook 1907, 595ff; Davis 1857, 215). These visions bear a striking resemblance to many reported in both Eastern mystical traditions, like, for instance, the central channel or *shushuma* of yogic Buddhism, and in the West. Sensitives were also alleged to exert such control over these magnetic healing energies that their cures could be effected from a considerable physical distance. Thus "distance healing," a feature of New Thought at the end of the century using the power of thought focused on a photograph or via other means was observed in some sensitives; its most famous modern exponent was Edgar Cayce, the "sleeping prophet." Within American popular culture, mesmerism was becoming now less a system of medical healing than "a schema demonstrating how the individual mind can establish rapport with ever more sublime levels of reality" (Fuller 1982, 45–46).

The Reverend LaRoy Sunderland, lecturer, editor of *Zion's Watchman* and a member of Theodore Weld's (1803–1895) famous coterie of religious abolitionists, also became interested in magnetism. From 1842, he published the *Magnet*, and he discovered with James Braid in England, and independently, that all phenomena of the trance could be explained as being simply the results of the subject's own mental reaction to suggestions supplied by the voice or gestures of the operator, as foreshadowed by Faria and Alexandre Bertrand a generation before. In *Pathetism* (1843), Sunderland rejected the existence of a fluid in favor of a sympathy or, as he preferred, a "pathetism" existing between magnetizer and subject, a term he used to denote mesmerism more accurately as the science of mental sympathy. By 1845, Sunderland claimed to have personally magnetized more than fifteen hundred patients (Crabtree 1993, 224; Fuller 1982, 39).

Around the same time, John Bovee Dods (1795–1872), a Universalist minister with an abiding interest in healing, was promoting "electrical psychology." For a time, he borrowed the somnambule Burkmar, the same instrument who had so impressed Quimby, for diagnostic experiments.

Dods articulated a physiological theory based on his enthusiasm for electricity as a life principle. All normal and pathological operations of the organism were caused by electricity, and the apparent weightlessness of this substance explained how the soul could exist yet be thought immaterial. He believed that the soul itself was composed of electricity and that the movement of the blood was caused by its intrinsic electrical pulsation, the heart serving only as a regulator of the flow. Electrical influences could come from within or without, and in his view "human magnetism" was one example of electrical influence coming from outside (Silberger 1978, 101). Dods published his 1843 lectures in which electrical psychology was distinguished from mesmerism. Having posited a "nervous fluid" that he linked to the aura, in 1847 when many were puzzled by the new spiritism, Dods attributed the spiritistic manifestations of Davis and others to the operation of "vital electricity" (Crabtree 1993, 222).[4]

Another variation was advanced by Dr. James S. Grimes, professor of medical jurisprudence at Castleton Medical College. His historical importance lies in the fact that it was he who introduced mesmerism to A. J. Davis and others. Grimes taught what he termed "etherology"; and while he rejected spiritism and clairvoyance, he believed in a subtle fluid, "Etherium," which he said produced the trance (Crabtree 1993, 227).

Yet another variation to the new theorizing was that of Dr. J. R. Buchanan (1814–1899). In 1843, Buchanan constructed a "neurological map" showing a new distribution of phrenological organs and suggested a substance he called "Nervaura," its nature being some way between electricity and will force and serving as the mediating link between the two. Buchanan, an advocate of phrenomagnetism, was then living at New Harmony; in 1842, he astonished the world with his experiments in mesmerism, reported by R. D. Owen in a famous letter in the *Evening Post* (Crabtree 1993, 224; Noyes 1870, 84). Robert Fuller (1982, 73) has noted that:

For all its peculiarities, mesmerism bore a strong resemblance to the religious revivals which, for years, had served as the pre-

---

4. See John Bovee Dods, *The Philosophy of Mesmerism and Electrical Psychology* (London: James Burns, 1876).

eminent curator of the national psyche. American Protestantism, with its obsession for saving souls through distinct conversion experiences, created a metaphysical climate which assured mesmerism a receptive audience.

American Revivalism and the Democracy of the Soul

The revival tradition was again on the ascendant after the lull of the War of 1812 and the subsequent economic downturn, especially in the burned-over district of western New York State. Beginning in 1825 at Western, Charles Grandison Finney stormed the frontier areas of New York with his revivals. A young Elizabeth Cady Stanton (1815–1902) remembered Finney's powerful presence at an 1830 revival in Troy, and for a time she came under his sway:

> I can see him now, his great eyes rolling around the congregation and his arms flying about in the air like those of a windmill.... He described Hell and the Devil and the long procession of sinners being swept down the rapids about to make the awful plunge into the burning depths of liquid fire below and the rejoicing hosts in the Inferno coming up to meet them with the shouts of the Devil echoing through the vaulted arches.

Suddenly he halted, and pointing a long finger he exclaimed, "There, do you not see them?" Cady Stanton "was brought up to such a pitch that I actually jumped up and gazed in the direction to which he pointed, while the picture glowed before my eyes and remained with me for months afterwards" (quoted in Goldsmith 1998, 43). The "ultraism" of these years ignited concern for individual salvation, but it generated much else beside in the area of reform. Religious revivalism encouraged an optimistic and activist spirit, by teaching that good deeds were the sure mark of godliness and that the millennium was near (Walters 1978, 3).

From the 1830s until the hiatus of the Civil War, a multitude of reforms of all kinds became manifest, abolition and temperance being the most widespread. As the South retreated into the shell of an intransigent slave-owning culture, the center for religious reform was no longer Kentucky, but the North, and now especially New England and the burned-over district, where other reforms were augmented in numbers. After William Lloyd Garrison's (1805–1879) bold launching of the *Liberator* in Boston in 1831, the antislavery movement made rapid progress, employing to good effect the well-worn system of branches and distribution networks used by the tract societies and temperance reformers. Public propagandists lectured throughout the nation for the American Antislavery Society, inaugurated and largely funded from 1833 by wealthy New York evangelists the Tappan brothers (Lewis, 1788–1873; Arthur, 1786–1865). Within five years, there existed a complex network of lecturers, with a total membership of 250 thousand, and over 1,300 auxiliaries. The efforts of Garrison and other "immediatists" like the Grimké sisters (Angelina Emily, 1805–1879; Sarah Moore, 1792–1873), who made an unprecedented lecture tour in 1837, helped other reforms such as women's rights. What made the advocacy of the Grimkés especially compelling was not only the new spectacle of women preachers in a public space outside of Quaker meetings, but that they were products of the Southern system, having been raised within a notable family on a slave-owning plantation in South Carolina (Walters 1978, 83, 87–88).

Two Forks of Reform

Whitney Cross in his pioneering study of the "burned-over" district of New York State emphasized the direction taken by reform in that region after the period of ultraism. Cross identified what he characterized as two bands of enthusiasts emerging from the late 1830s. They arose, in his view, from the ultraism induced by the powerful revivals of Finney and his many imitators from the 1820s. The burned-over district—especially the Erie Canal—was a psychic highway, the storm center of religious and social forces that emerged as the driving propellants of social movements, and thus became important for the whole country in that generation.[5] Cross argued that after the great schisms of 1837, two broad and opposed tendencies ran parallel throughout the 1840s, which he attributes to the

---

5. See Cross 1965, the introduction.

growing gap between the reform movements and their accustomed religious beliefs. Those who constituted what he called "the right of the fork in the highway out of ultraism"

> . . . could not conscientiously follow the now non- or antireligious emphasis of the abolition leaders. Disillusioned with the movements of the thirties . . . they inclined to retreat into a more strict fundamentalism, where literal adherence to Scripture and exclusive concern for spiritual regeneration of individual souls forbade any great zeal for the current style of reform. (Cross 1965, 277)

In Cross's terms, there had developed in those years a "left and right" of enthusiasm; and during the 1840s, this residue of unfulfilled ultraism brought a recognizable dichotomy: the group traveling to the right "sought an escapist's short cut to the millennium . . . [while] the crowd going left . . . [sought] a Utopia built by mortal hand and brain, of earthly materials" (Cross 1965, 322).

The secular religiosity that moves away from established religions to the sovereignty of individual belief was now accelerated, the right fork moving to a projected apocalypse, while on the left fork, the most important were the followers of Fourier. The limits were represented by the Millerites on the right, awaiting the trumpets of doom, and the Fourierists on the left, building communitarian "phalanxes" as a new form of social organization. They included those "who traveled varying distances toward liberal religion, Bible criticism, and a social gospel" (Cross 1965, 278). They became agitators both for abolition and for sinless, nonsectarian community churches, their numbers including antislavery leaders like Gerrit Smith (1797–1874) and George Ripley (1802–1880) (Cross 1965, 280). They wanted to create the "Earth as Heaven," and, for a brief period in the 1840s, the main instrument for such creation seemed to be Fourier's system. The postmillennialist New Church and its stepchild spiritualism straddled the region between, promising a new heaven but also concerned with the present life and conduct.

Transformation in America: The Earth as Heaven

The Millerites

Those who followed the Baptist minister William Miller awaited the imminent end of the world, as the prelude to the eternal glories of the saved. The Millerites originated in Vermont, which was also the scene of the former millenarian uprising of the New Israelites in 1800. Especially through the Millerite journal *Signs of the Times* and numerous camp meetings held during 1842–1843, the word spread of the arrival of the apocalypse, not only on the eastern seaboard but as far away as England, which had between two and three thousand converts (Brooke 1994, 132).[6] The complex symbolism of Revelations was now understood in a particular way. The woman who fled into the wilderness in Rev. 12:6 meant for Miller the people of God in all ages of the church, whether Jew or Gentile, symbolized as woman because she is the spouse of Christ. The great red dragon and beast that persecuted the church was the Roman government. Thus, the red dragon denoted pagan Rome, and the woman sitting on the scarlet-colored beast the Church of Rome or papal Rome; these powers, civil and papal, together made the anti-Christian abomination, which would drive the Church of Christ into the wilderness, where she would be fed 1,260 days, meaning years (Miller 1842, 204–206).

Although over a long period the church had been corrupted under the protection of the civil power, beginning with Constantine, God took care that "they should feed her there 1260 days [years]." This period Miller calculated as extending from 538 to 1798, during which time a free toleration of religious rights was forbidden in any of the kingdoms that formerly comprised the Roman empire (Miller 1842, 207). His exegetical calculations showed that the end would come in March 1844, but the passing of that date, the "stubborn continuation of time," brought a proposed new date of October 22, 1844. Some two hundred ministers and two thousand lay preachers campaigned in these preparations for the millennium, and somewhere between fifty and a hundred thousand persons withdrew from their churches and awaited the Second Coming (Cross 1965, 304; Harrison 1979, 194).

---

6. There were thirty-one camp meetings in the summer of 1843, and a total of 124 in the two years 1842–1843 (Harrison 1979, 202, 193).

In 1843 Rochester became the Millerite center in western New York. It must have been a busy place, for an association convention was also held there in August. In November, William Miller arrived at Rochester to make final preparations for the "end." But as "many prepared their white robes for an ascension to a brighter and happier life," alas, the revised date of October 22, 1844, also failed. Some disappointed former believers sought to reclaim their lives and property. In the expectation of the apocalypse, Ezekiel Hale Jr. had given away his industrial mills to a son who remained an unbeliever, which after this second failure of the advent he tried to recover, but without success (Cross 1965, 298; Chase 1888, 9; Harrison 1979, 195–197). Concerning the Millerites, Whitney Cross (308) asks, "Could any group in history have prepared for themselves a more vicious trap? a more sudden, more abysmal disenchantment? Not merely did the single doctrine of the present Advent come into question, but faith in the whole Bible, the literal reading of which had created their distinctive belief."

The New Church did not share the apocalyptic fervor. It was with some glee that *The New Church Advocate*, a London Swedenborgian periodical, reported the vagaries of Millerism. After fixing several dates for "the second personal coming of Christ in the clouds" (252), all of which had passed without a fulfillment of the prophecy, William Miller was now talking about a new date of March 1845. It concludes that "if this fixing the time be deemed satisfactory, it is evidence that the people are delighted with delusion." A later number noted that the Millerite Tabernacle in Boston had been "transformed into a THEATRE" (380).

Fourier and a "theoretical brotherhood"

The "left fork" out of ultraism had an equally brief and tendentious history, but as with the Millerite excitement, for a section of the population, it was for a time as a bright luminary in the sky, promising a new and different future. The originator of this passing but intense enthusiasm was the unlikely Charles Fourier (1772–1837), the quixotic leader of a "theoretical brotherhood." A strange loner whose most constant companions were his cats, he worked as a poor cloth merchant and died in obscurity in 1837 (Schlesinger 1945, 365; Manuel and Manuel 1979, 641). As a theoretical writer, Fourier was given his start by Pierre Ballanche (1776–1847), a leading post-Revolution mystic from Lyon, through the *Bulletin de Lyons*, in which he first announced his discovery of the principle of universal harmony.

Fourier's most important concepts were association and harmony. He postulated the universal principle of "attraction" that rules both the social and the moral world (Gladish 1983, 23). Fourier was convinced that, through his "laws of passionate Gravity," he had discovered the fundamental natural law of society. This was the gravitational pull of passion, a force that must be put to work instead of being repressed as in ordinary society, so as to organize men and women into a universal fraternity. For all the talk of harmony, Fourier was a difficult man, who quarreled with those responsible for initiating the only experiment of his system made during his life, in France in 1832.[7] John Noyes, with considerable experience in such matters, observed with acerbic detachment, "Fourier's dream that two or three thousand discordant centrifugal individuals in one great home, would fall, by natural gravitation, into a balance of passions, and realize a harmony unattainable on the small scale of familism [sic], has not been confirmed by experience" (1870, 293).

Two events in particular were integral to the brief popularity of Fourierism in America. The English language edition in 1840 of Fourier's congested opus *The Social Destiny of Man* was prepared by Albert Brisbane, a young journalist and devotee who had spent time in France studying the master's work. Horace Greeley (1811–1872) joined and briefly produced a journal with Brisbane called *The Future*. From 1843, Brisbane published *The Phalanx*, later subsumed into *The Harbinger* and edited by the Brook Farmer George Ripley. The other notable event contributing to the current craze was the opening of Horace Greeley's *New York Tribune* to Fourierist teachings. It was an immediate sensation, resulting in a gaggle of Fourier communities being formed between 1841 and 1858.

---

7. M. Baudet Dulary (1792–1878), a politician, bought an estate for 500 thousand francs ($100 thousand) to put the theory into practice. Fourier said he had waited twenty years to get a hearing which, from the importance of his discovery, he expected to obtain immediately (Walters 1978, 67).

The Covert Enlightenment

Overall, some forty phalanxes were inaugurated in the United States during the 1840s, many of them in 1843, the same year that the Millerites were gathering their ascension robes in preparation for the final conflagration. There were six phalanxes in western New York alone. When Robert Owen returned to the United States in September 1844, the Fourierists greeted him as the "Father of American Socialism." He was received with distinction by Brisbane at the *Phalanx* office in New York City. Owen stopped briefly at the Ohio phalanx, and in May 1845 he visited Brook Farm and later the Hopedale community, led by the Reverend Adin Ballou (1803–1890). Owen would make a further eight visits to America (Gladish 1983, 19; Cross 1965, 331).

Fourier's system was based on attraction and organized around the phalanstery, a three-story building to house the community, designed to make the most of this axiomatic force of attraction in humans. Ideally, it would contain 1500–1600 people pursuing those ventures that pleased and interested them most. Some five thousand acres would provide the food necessary to offer a self-contained life for the community, where the workers would be united in "groups" of seven people and "series" of at least five groups. They would compete in the friendliest way to see who could produce the most succulent pear or the most beautiful rose. Thus would competition be transformed into cooperation, using the self-interest of attraction in individuals for the common good. In a sense, it was a gloss on Adam Smith's recipe for optimizing commerce, with a similar appeal to self-interest, the currency being the passions. Fourier's view of the good life has been described as "copulation and cookery." Although a strong advocate of communism, his ideal differed from the Shakers, the Mormons, or the Oneida community, because there were no religious principles to lend credence and authority to these novel practices, including "complex marriage," and at the same time to preclude overtones of hedonism and sensual indulgence (Gladish 1983, 25–27).

For a brief instant in history, the attractions of Fourier's system were manifold. As Noyes noted, while many were "captivated with the glowing pictures of a new life" and others "inspired by the hopes of personal distinction," many devotees were "profoundly impressed by Fourier's sublime annunciation of the general destinies of globes and humanities."

The main idea was that "progressive development through careers characterized all movement and all forms" (1870, 661). Following Claude Henri, comte de St. Simon (1760–1825), Owen, Auguste Comte (1798–1857), and a host of other reformers, and like them presupposing the principles of order and progress in human societies, Fourier sought the natural principles of social organization, which he deduced from universal laws. Believing that "the law of the series" was a universal method in distributing harmonies, Fourierists felt that "human society and human activity, to be in harmony with the universe of relations, can not be an exception to the great law of the series" (Noyes 1870, 450).

When Owen had traveled down the Wabash in the *Philanthropist*, his son Robert Dale had spent his days hunting and absorbing woods lore and nights reading Fourier. This interest probably came via the French intellectuals Mme. Frategeot and Phiquepal D'Arusmont. On December 10, 1825, he noted: "Mme F. read aloud to us part of Fourier's work in the evening." He judged Fourier's congested work "a strange and most original production, containing many excellent ideas, but mixed up with much which is, I think, not practical" (Elliott 1969, 177).

The Fourierist enthusiasm was short-lived but intense and audacious in its demands. Brisbane, writing in 1842 in the *New York Tribune*, suggested that either the rich could contribute $400 to 500 thousand and/or the state legislature could donate, neither of which was likely. He made the lyrical suggestion that an association might be established with four hundred children aged between five and fifteen years, to work at "various lighter branches of agriculture, and the mechanical arts, with little tools and implements . . . which are the delight of children." This, in his view, could prove the possibility of "attractive industry" (Noyes 1870, 203–204).

The peak years of Fourierist interest were 1843–1844, when a virtual flood of phalanxes poured forth, of economic and social associations in variegated forms, loosely based on the views of the eccentric visionary. Typical of these associations was the Northampton Association of Education and Industry in Massachusetts, transformed from a commercial silk factory to a community by David Ruggles (1810–1849), the black reformer, and seven other persons in April 1842. Sojourner Truth (c. 1797–1883) also lived there. Situated close to where Jonathan

Edwards had inaugurated the Great Awakening a century before, it covered five hundred acres, with a four-story silk factory and six houses comprising a community family of around 130 members. Many years later, Frederick Douglass (1817?–1895) commented on his visit to the Northampton Association: "The people and the place struck me as the most democratic I had ever met. It was a place to extinguish all aristocratic pretensions. There was no high, no low, no masters, no servants, no white, no black.... Here, at least, my color nor my condition counted against me" (cited in Fogarty 1990, 14). They were "Nothingarians," and they dissolved in November 1846.

The Skaneateles Community, on the other hand, had very definite anarchist and separatist views and also absorbed other currents. In 1843, as the Millerites were making preparations in advance of the apocalypse, and the antislavery movement burst forth with one hundred national conventions, the flood of Fourierism was catching the imagination of talented reformers. In 1843 John A. Collins, a former antislavery agent bought a farm of 350 acres for $15 thousand. Some 150 persons joined. Like the Zoarites, they believed that governments, being based on physical force, have no rightful existence. They held conventional views on marriage and lived on a vegetable and fruit diet, mostly boiled wheat, rice, and Graham mush of unbolted flour; and they allowed no intoxicating beverages. Their published organ was *The Communitist*, and they were opposed to Fourier's opinions. Among their principles was a disbelief in any special revelation of God to humankind and in the clergy; rejecting the authority of the Bible, they held that belief in miracles was not philosophical and that salvation from sin was "a remnant of heathenism." Noyes observes that when Skaneateles was dissolved in 1846, Collins returned "to the decencies and respectabilities of orthodox Whiggery" (1870, 164–165).

A spray of small, struggling communities appeared throughout the frontier, "backwoods utopias" with romantic names like the Alphadelphia Phalanx in Michigan, which claimed over 1300 members by 1844; the Trumbull community; and the Sylvania Association. The Prairie Home Community in Logan County, Ohio, was typical; it was formed in 1843 and lasted one year. Set on five hundred acres, well timbered and with rich fields, it comprised 130 members, many of whom were former Quakers. Their meals consisted of a Grahamite supper of cornbread, apple pie, and milk. There was much discussion and practice of phrenology, magnetism, and hydropathy. During his visit, Donald Macdonald slept in a two-story frame house where he noted, ominously for the success of the community, that "the young women were most industrious . . . but the young men were mostly lounging about doing nothing" (Walters 1978, 70).

The North American Phalanx in Redbank, New Jersey, formed in that important year 1843, was the longest-surviving of these ventures, counting one hundred members including Brisbane and Greeley. Not only was it close to New York, thus providing a showcase for Fourierism, but it remained financially solvent by supplying fresh vegetables to its market (Gladish 1983, 31). On July 4, 1845, Transcendentalist editor William Henry Channing (1810–1884), who had also encouraged the Brook Farmers, and Horace Greeley, publisher of the popular *New York Tribune*, visited the North American Phalanx. In the cool shade of a walnut grove where a semicircle of seats had been arranged, they gave addresses lasting one-and-a-half hours, then adjourned to the main house for an excellent dinner. A table was spread the whole length of the hall, and "good cold water" was emphatically the only beverage for these temperance advocates. Afterwards, they were summoned to the hay field where "a merrier group never raked and pitched," and the young people formed in a dance and fashioned flower garlands in their hair. In the late afternoon, the New York visitors left. While this very romantic vision was intended for public consumption at a time when the Fourierist wave was already losing impetus, the experiment was a success of sorts. Remembered as "a genial and stable community," it was sold in 1856 (Noyes 1870, 469). As Walters asserts, "Fourierists [and Owenites] did not have a powerfully unifying creed or charismatic leader to hold them together," unlike the German Pietists, the Shakers, and other religious communists (1978, 71).

Other Types of Communities

There were numerous social experiments at this time, arising from the communitarian ideal and a widespread desire to form an alternative family structure. In 1853, Dr. Thomas L. Nichols (1815–1901) at the community Modern Times on Long Island, New York, published *Esoteric Anthropology* and issued a printed catalogue of names, a kind of early dating bureau, for the reciprocal use of affinity-hunters all over the country; he inaugurated a system of "free love" or individual sovereignty in sexual intercourse, then later went in the opposite reaction, converting to Catholicism. From 1851, Nichols and his wife Mary Gove Nichols (1810–1884), along with others like Stephen Pearl Andrews (1812–1886), became associated with Josiah Warren in promoting individual sovereignty, the opposite to New Harmony communism. They taught that "in a progressive state there is no demand for conformity. . . . [W]e build on *Individuality*" (Noyes 1870, 96).

Mary Gove Nichols was a most adventurous and individualist reformer; she illustrates the shape that reform was taking for many who chose the "right" fork. In 1838, she ran a Graham boarding house in Boston and lectured to women on physiology and related subjects. In a very varied experience over the following decades, which coincided with the communitarian experiments, she wrote fiction, was divorced, had an affair, was drawn to communitarianism, advocated free love, then after her conversion to Catholicism, practiced chastity. She became a water-cure evangelist and with her husband moved to Yellow Springs, Ohio, in 1856 to form a community. They renamed the Yellow Springs Water Cure the Mnemonia Institute (after the Egyptian god of waters). They left in 1857, when they were converted to Catholicism after a visit from a spirit (named Gonzales) during a spiritualist séance meeting. Mary Gove Nichols now claimed the power to heal. She moved to England where she died in 1884 (Walters 1978, 154; Fogarty 1990, 124–125).

At Modern Times, Warren had devised the "time store," a labor exchange based on the idea of "equitable commerce," an idea previously tried by Owen in England, with little success, and later by the Christian Socialists, which charged wholesale value plus time taken to serve customers. It was to be a utopia where all set their own labor values. They held the individual to be sovereign and independent, and thus all laws tending to "restrict the liberty he or she should enjoy, are founded in error, and should not be regarded." John Noyes, with considerable insight into these matters, commented that the secret to the success of religious communities was "*afflatus* and leadership, and of an afflatus strong enough to make Communism the home-center" (1870, 96, 99). This was the secret of the Shaker success, and it was based on a metaphysical edifice allowing that afflatus to be communicated to the faithful in meaningful ways. In fine, that meant the melding of the alternate paradigms: namely, a worldview admitting spirit presences and spirit contact, drawing on Swedenborg, along with a means of transmitting those teachings and inspiration that had been made available through the phenomena associated with magnetism.

Brook Farm and Communitarians

Transcendentalism, the best known movement of the decade, was influenced by German mystical philosophy and also by Greek and Eastern thought. In New England, it denoted vaguely all that transcended the senses. The Platonic form of its metaphysics, the conception of one vast soul of the universe that embraces all life and with which the individual soul is identical, or the idea that nature is merely the sense-garment of this one Over-Soul, or God, echo the Advaita Vedanta philosophy of India, then being brought by the merchant vessels traversing the world from Nantucket and elsewhere in New England. There was an explosion of individualism, as "numberless movements addressed themselves to the task of reforming or transforming the American polity. . . . [It was] an age filled with the rival declamations of "impassioned true believers." Vegetarians and natural food cultists, pacifists, abolitionists, socialists, total abstainers, advocates of free love agreed about little except that America suffered from some malaise and must change her ways" (McWilliams 1974, 236–237). This reformist mood was especially strong on the eastern seaboard, where progressive movements flourished: "the promotion of socialism, Fourierism, communitarianism, free love, . . . homeopathy, phrenology and Swedenborgianism all had their devoted adherents" (Adams 1960, 353; see also Gauld 1995, 179–180).

In American folk memory, Brook Farm was the most famous of the communitarian experiments of the 1840s. It was founded by two Unitarian ministers, William Ellery Channing (1817–1901) and George

The Covert Enlightenment

Ripley, who set out in November 1841 with fifteen pilgrims to begin their agrarian experiment at Brook Farm, set on 208 acres in Roxbury, Massachusetts, eight miles from Boston (Walters 1978, 51). Through Channing, there was at first a strong Transcendentalist influence in the venture. The idea was to live according to the values of "plain living and high thinking" as advanced by R. W. Emerson and others, and their enthusiasm was based on the communal ideal as a means of bringing out the best in individuals. George Ripley wrote to Emerson that the aim at Brook Farm was "to insure a more natural union between intellectual and manual labor than now exists; to combine the thinker and the worker, as far as possible, in the same individual" (cited in Raymond 1994, 32). None of the leaders of the Transcendental movement—Emerson, Margaret Fuller, Bronson Alcott (1799–1888), and Theodore Parker (1810–1860)—could be induced to join the Brook Farmers. Emerson decided not to join so as to maintain his critical role, while Margaret Fuller also kept her distance, visiting the farm on occasion, as she put it, to watch "the coral insects at work" (Gladish 1983, 11).

Brook Farm was from the first a middle class enterprise, comprising prominent Bostonians like Ripley, Elizabeth Peabody (1804–1894), and Charles A. Dana (1819–1897). Nathaniel Hawthorne (1804–1864) joined briefly and in the *Blithesdale Romance* left a stinging parody, what Noyes called a "poetico-sneering romance" in passages like the famous encounter with the manure pile. It was here that the "long haired men and short haired women" of eccentric mythologies had their brightest day. At Brook Farm, "they read *Consuelo*, munching apples before log fires and chatting, while studying Fourier's theory of the Human Passions" (DeVoto 1957, 31). They allowed unfashionably bearded and long-haired men, fads, odd attire, and there was much playfulness. Their greatest achievements were a progressive school and the publication of their organ, the *Harbinger*, which outlasted the experiment by two years. Elizabeth Peabody, writing in their newsletter the *Dial* for October 1841 declared, "There are men and women, who have claimed to say to one another, Why not have our daily life organized on Christ's own idea? . . . For each man to think and live on this method is perhaps the Second Coming of Christ" (Noyes 1870, 111). In such pronouncements can be recognized an early call for the manifestation of the moral maxim to love our neighbor more than ourselves and a postmillennial vision encapsulated in the idea of an already arrived Second Coming, both derived from Swedenborg's writings.

In January 1842, shortly after the community was set up, Peabody wrote lyrically that they had assembled as a group of men and women aiming at being wholly true to their natures, determined to live "a true life." To this Emersonian ideal was added the bucolic sentiment that this new life, while "it aims beyond the highest star, . . . is redolent of the healthy earth, the perfume of clover lingers about it. The lowing of cattle is the natural bass to the melody of human voices" (cited in Noyes 1870, 114). They worked in the fields and orchards, herded the cattle, did housework together; they danced and sang, discussed every topic under the sun, evolved a progressive school, and tried earnestly to live in the highest department of their souls. As one historian termed it, Brook Farm was "a community where a limited number of people might live on more or less cooperative lines and enjoy a better life than in the world of competition outside" (Adams 1960, 360). After three years of hazy idealism, following the current wave, they altered along the lines of Fourierism.

In 1845, the Brook Farm community, now comprising about one hundred members, was reorganized into a Fourier phalanx "according to the order of love," with three categories: mechanical, domestic, and farming groups, with subgroups such as the milking group, the haying group, etc. But it was "a charming interlude too innocent to last," and following a major fire in the phalanstery, Brook Farm was sold in 1849 for $20,000 (Walters 1978, 52).

The significance of the Brook Farm experiment, like that of Leraysville, was not their modest achievements in favor of communitarian organization, but as vehicles for the radical currents of the day. This influence came first through their publications, especially the *Harbinger*, which carried between thirty and forty articles on Swedenborg and Swedenborgian subjects, and by dint of the high social status of the Brook Farmers and their supporters, and the articulated opinions of its preponderant intellectuals and literary members. As Noyes judged it, they had become an agency in the great Swedenborgian revival of modern times. In 1868, he could reflect that "Brook Farm, in its didactic function, brought forth upon the public mind, not only a new socialism but a new religion . . . Swedenborgianism" (1870, 546). In the final, unhappy years of their venture, they had meant to propagate Fourier but succeeded only in propagating Swedenborg. Although the association soon passed away, "the surge of Swedenborgianism which they started, swept on among their constituents," according to Noyes; and he added, "under the form of Spiritualism, is sweeping on to this day" (1870, 537–538).

Swedenborgian Phalanxes

As we have seen, the earliest connection of the communitarian ideal and Swedenborgianism came with the arrival of Robert Owen, founder of the New Lanark experiment in Scotland. Some traced a definite resemblance between the ideas of Fourier and Swedenborg, especially their respective doctrines of universal analogy, correspondences, and conjugial love, although, unlike Fourier's view of natural attraction, Swedenborg was by no means a sexual libertine. The New Church interest in Fourierist experiments lasted less than a year. Only two phalanxes were formed by New Church members, and one commentator notes that "the New Church experience with Fourierism had been brief and bitter" (Gladish 1983, 35). The brief epoch of Swedenborgian phalangists was predicated among one section of the New Church convinced that, for the era of the New Jerusalem to appear on earth in its fullness, they must embrace new social forms adapted to a changed perception of human social relations, yet still based on Swedenborg's doctrine of uses and on his descriptions of heavenly society. It was this vision that the Leraysville Phalanx was attempting to address (Gladish 1983, 50). In Canton, Illinois, New Church members organized briefly into a community or phalanx, according to Fourier principles, on the farm of John F. Randolph. On his death, they split from groups and series and returned to their former homes and occupations.

Neither Fourier nor Swedenborg's ideas are easily summarized. The similarities perceived by their respective adherents were principally with regard to the sonorities of their respective concepts of universal analogy and correspondences. In Fourier, the idea of universal analogy was based on the supposed harmonies, derived from natural attraction, that are the fundament of both natural and social organization. In Swedenborg, the doctrines of degrees and correspondences reveal a harmony between the outer manifestations and their inner nature. This is based on a monistic view of influx and proceeds in a stepwise fashion from sphere to sphere, but is also deemed to be founded on harmony and dependent on explicative analogy, although one whose deepest meanings are derived from a proper interpretation of the Word and ultimately from inward illumination. Such an opinion was put forward by Parke Godwin (1816–1904), writing in the 1844 *Popular View*, where he argued for the equivalence of the doctrines of universal analogy and correspondences. That view was also proffered by William H. Channing, who in the last three numbers of his short-lived journal the *Present*, extolled Swedenborg (Noyes 1870, 541, 544). The main point of interest in the Brook Farm experiment was the change from a Swedenborgian, or at least a Transcendentalist, intent to a Fourierist system, reflecting the dominant currents of the epoch.

In short, the Fourierists felt that Swedenborg had revealed the religion that Fourier anticipated, while the Swedenborgians insisted that Fourier discovered the divine arrangement of society foreshadowed by Swedenborg. To writers like Charles Julius Hempel (1811–1879), they constituted the union of science and religion. He urged

> that Man's regeneration is impossible without a true organization of Society and the Church, based upon the law of Divine Order, which is the Series of Groups, and that this Serial law has therefore to be discovered and applied by Man before the inauguration of Peace, the Sabbath, the Conjunction of the Good and the True, can take place upon earth. (Hempel 1848, 24)

Brook Farmer and novelist Charles A. Dana averred that "whatever may be thought of the doctrines of Swedenborg or of his visions," all were agreed that "no man had ever such sincerity, such absolute freedom from intellectual selfishness" as Swedenborg. "The spirit which breathes from his works is pure and heavenly," and, he continued, "his was a grand genius, nobly disciplined. In him, a devotion to truth almost awful, was tempered by an equal love of humanity and a supreme reverence for God" (Noyes 1870, 547). The entire historical sequence, as Noyes understood it, was that Unitarianism produced Transcendentalism, which produced Brook Farm; Brook Farm married and propagated Fourierism; that Fourierism had Swedenborgianism for its religion, and that

Swedenborgianism led the way to modern spiritualism (1870, 550).

Partly in consequence of this new appreciation of Swedenborg among the Fourierists, in 1845 a movement arose in England to republish Swedenborg's scientific works, the leading protagonist being Dr. J. J. G. Wilkinson (1812–1899). Emerson's lecture "Swedenborg, the Mystic," given in England through 1847, and later collected in *Representative Men* (1849), while considering Swedenborg's visions humbug, claims for him the lofty position as a scientific discoverer, the Aristotle of the North and the last of the great Church Fathers.

Within the wider society, in the decades before the Civil War, not only "immediatism," the antislavery sentiment that demanded immediate emancipation, led by William Lloyd Garrison (1805–1879), but also temperance, women's rights, and other reforms continued to sweep the burned-over district and New England, bringing in their wake the outlooks inspired but not always fulfilled by the revivals, along with popularized versions of Swedenborgian theology concerning the accessibility of the other world. This latter trend of the 1840s finds its clearest exponent in A. J. Davis, who claimed no less than Swedenborg himself as spiritual tutor. It also marks the transition from a purely therapeutic focus to attempts to utilize the machinery of magnetism, as it were, to induce the alteration of consciousness for higher ends. This trend has been observed already in the earlier European scene when Puységur, Willermoz, and others began employing Mesmer's system for metaphysical ends. In the 1840s, Warren Chase (1813–1891) exemplified this trend toward a "psychologically based pneumatology." When the Ceresco community was founded in 1844, they were engaged in mesmerism; but upon hearing of A. J. Davis and reports of the phenomenal results he obtained, Chase and his fellow communitarians began experimenting in spiritistic mediumship.

Mesmerism, Phrenology, and Radical Politics

Warren Chase, at various times politician, communitarian, and lecturer on spiritualism, was a consistent radical and archetype of those who followed the core heterodoxies of mid-century America: communitarianism, mesmerism, and then spiritualism. Ceresco (after the corn goddess Ceres) was among the most successful communities in the Fourierist wave of the 1840s, lasting six years and, unusually for such ventures, closing with good feelings all around and a profitable balance sheet shared by all joint-stockholders (Nelson 1969, 20). Chase was a deeply anticlerical freethinker; having traversed the mesmeric and Fourierist paths, he became a secular preacher of the new spiritualist doctrine, as well as supporting female equality and opposing slavery. Of humble origins, Chase was a self-made man who became a politician reformer, an adherent of a strict diet, and a total abstainer from alcohol. He had been "for some years in favor of perfect equality between the races and sexes," and though he was not a medium, he retained an unshakeable lifelong faith in the new movement (Chase 1888, 19).

Warren Chase penned two autobiographies, *The Life-line of the Lone One*, and *Forty Years on the Spiritual Rostrum*. Though alternating in tone between the plaintive and the triumphant, these works provide a fascinating picture of the activities of those on the social and religious fringe of the era. They also render a sense of the precedence of concerns in the early 1840s (Moore 1977, 91). Chase recalled that, in that eventful year 1843, he read some published experiments in mesmerism, like those conducted by Dr. Buchanan in the revamped New Harmony, that led his mind "into that tangled maze of curious experiments," adding significantly that they "did not then open the spiritual world to my perception"; he attributes this to the more pressing and more promising socialism of Fourier and his current leadership of Ceresco or the Wisconsin Phalanx (Chase 1888, 11). He was among those who came to view magnetism as a stepping stone to the more desirable contact with other states of being that spiritualism promised.

The useful but not always reliable or unbiased chronicler of American socialisms, John Noyes, judged the Wisconsin Phalanx "one of the most conspicuous experiments of the Fourier epoch," together with the Trumbull and the North American phalanxes. To a considerable extent, this was due to Warren Chase, founder, principal manager, and spokesman of the venture, who sent regular letters in the form of progress reports to the *Southport Telegraph* (Noyes 1870, 411). Fourier's writings are nothing if not tedious to a modern reader, containing much jargon, and a fascination with numbers and petty detail; but it is an indication of the effort many persons were prepared to expend to make sense of Fourier's byzantine system. Warren Chase recalled having been "taken on the social tidal wave of Fourierism and led into it by some very able and enthusiastic writers in the *New York Tribune*, then edited by Horace Greeley" (Chase 1888, 9). Greeley gave Albert Brisbane, the enthusiastic student of Fourier, carte blanche for a regular column in his newspaper.

In the spring of 1844, the nineteen resident members bought ten sections (one section equaling 640 acres) near Green Lake, in Marquetta County, Wisconsin. At their first meeting on May 27, 1844, after a prayer had been offered, Warren Chase in the chair, they were divided according to Fourierist principles into two series: agricultural and mechanical. The agricultural series commenced plowing and planting the very next day, while the mechanical series began the excavation of a cellar and made preparations for the erection of a frame building 22 feet by 20 feet, as the central wing for a building projected at 22 feet by 120 feet, to be built according to Fourier's specifications as to the optimum dimensions for a phalanstery. Unfortunately, and despite Fourier's arcane calculations, this turned out to be a great mistake: this long, double-fronted building at a cost of $3000 was found to be poorly ventilated, which proved uncomfortable and extremely inconvenient for families who lived and did their cooking on the premises (Noyes 1870, 413, 435).

The phalanx began with no debt; and by September 1843, the members had planted twenty acres of potatoes, buckwheat, and turnips and were then sowing one hundred acres of winter wheat. Their membership had now increased to eighty members. All labored in the fields in keeping with "the class of usefulness," except that "female labor," like kitchen duties, received a reduction in outdoor work. By mid-1845, with a membership growing to 180 members and their formal incorporation into a township operating as a joint-stock company, Ceresco was flourishing. Former members of other phalanxes like Sylvania, the Swedenborgian venture Leraysville, and the secular utopia Skaneateles joined Ceresco after the dissolution of their respective ventures. They strove for equity in most respects, with a complex but workable system of labor notes organized on the basis of a labor account and stock shares, such as that attempted by Josiah Warren and later in England by the Christian Socialists, but with more success (Noyes 1870, 437, 440, 445).[8]

All Ceresco members professed temperance, but they were tolerant in other matters. There was no interference with the structure of the family, and each individual was free to follow his or her own faith. Apart from the required work on the phalanx property, many pursued interests such as alternative forms of living, including magnetic experiments. In July 1847, writing to the *New York Tribune*, Chase reported that they regularly received some thirty or forty publications like the *Water-Cure Journal*, and these were thoroughly perused; he was proud that an excellent school had recently been organized for the children and that the cultivation of music by young men and women was encouraged. There was an increasing emphasis on vegetarian food and on hydrotherapy and magnetism, for which they held subscriptions to relevant journals. They prided themselves in having no physician, lawyer, or preacher, yet enjoying good health, and every Sabbath they organized a Sunday School, a Bible class, and divine service led by different denominations in their hall (Noyes 1870, 421, 430).

Chase soon embarked on a political career. With the arrival of statehood and the opening of a protracted debate over the introduction of slavery into the new territories, the Free Soil Party was making its mark (Chase 1888, 19). Chase was a delegate to the Wisconsin state constitutional convention in 1847 and was elected state senator in 1848. The next year he ran for governor under the banner of the Free Soil Party; however, only a small vote was registered in the state for him, as the looming battle over slavery in the former territories, the heat of bad compromises like the Kansas-Nebraska Act and the Fugitive Slave Act were in the future, and Abraham Lincoln was still a frontier politician. Chase later moved to California where, in the early 1880s, he served three years in the state senate (Chase 1888, 74; Noyes 1870, 442).

---

8. At the end of the fiscal year, members drew on their individual labor account their proportion of three-quarters of the increase and products, and their stock shares, their proportion of one-quarter that was divided to stock. For instance, in December 1848, profits totaled $8,077.02; with a total valuation of $33,527.77, a dividend was given to each stockholder work 6.25 per hour of labor.

His *amour propre* came with the arrival of spiritualism, especially the publication in 1847 of A. J. Davis's first tome, *Nature's Divine Revelations*. Chase had "an order long-waiting for one dozen copies, that were sent, as soon as bound, to Milwaukee" where he collected them. Chase was always proud to have been on that first mailing list, in eager anticipation of a new revelation (1888, 14, 65). In their time in the Wisconsin State Senate, together with his colleague "Brother Sholes," he would read and discuss Davis at length during legislative sessions. And as at Strasbourg during the occult revival, their interest in Mesmer's methods that began in a therapeutic mold were now being applied more frequently, after the example of Davis, to the pursuit of truths from the spirit realms than to the cure of disease. He found the work of Davis and others to be confirmation "of the few shadowy Glimpses of the spirit world which came to us through the imperfect subjects we found in our [magnetic] experiments." Through local mediums, he received "proof of survival" of the spirits of his two deceased sons. He asserted that he "had never doubted from that day to this the spiritual origin of the intelligence received through persons mesmerized by mortals or by spirits" (Cross 1965, 33; Chase 1888, 14–15; 39).

The Fourier bubble burst early; by the mid-1840s, most ventures had met an abrupt and, in many cases, a contentious dissolution, with investors and stockholders demanding the return of their contributions. Chase notes that "soon after our enterprise was started, one after another of the twenty or more Fourier associations in the States failed, till at last all were gone, the Brook Farm in Massachusetts, and the North American Phalanx in Red Bank, N. J., going last. All but ours were financial failures" (Chase 1888, 12). He related, somewhat sadly, in a letter to the *Democrat* dated October 22, 1855, a visit to the North American Phalanx, which he called "the last lingering remnant of the many Phalanxes." The North American soon after succumbed, to await "a renewal in the other world, as society here was not ready for that state of social life." Chase judged part of the reason for the demise of association that, "as none of them tolerated tobacco or liquor, gambling or laziness, they were sadly out of sorts with popular society and soon dried up" (Chase 1888, 179).

Nevertheless, by the autumn of 1849, it was evident that the dissolution of Ceresco itself was inevitable. Differences of feeling had arisen over what buildings should be erected, whether as combined dwellings or as separate family houses. Moreover, the school was deemed inadequate by some members. Yet the breakup was due to no flagging energy, but rather to the opposite. Their hard work had yielded an abundance of crops, and the improvements had made the property extremely valuable. By then the enthusiasm for Fourier and his strange ideas had waned almost universally, but at Ceresco many maintained a strong faith in the ultimate practicability of association. Noyes believed that Ceresco failed principally because its leading minds became satisfied that, under existing circumstances, no further important progress could be made in association, while Macdonald concluded that Ceresco dissolved because their property became valuable and was sold to make a profit. In 1850, the land was cut up into small lots and sold, and the stock was cancelled in that way (Noyes 1870, 446–447).

For the rest of his long life, Warren Chase turned to lecturing and became a prolific writer of articles on spiritualism and related subjects. He traveled almost constantly throughout the Midwest and most of the large eastern cities from 1860 until his retirement in 1887, averaging some one hundred annual lectures and trekking thousands of miles each year. As a freethinker, he had a strong dislike for all forms of sacerdotal authority. He had felt unable to adopt Swedenborg because of what he perceived as the "churchiness" of his system. On the Bible and revivals, he remarked testily, "I was not affected by this religious tidal wave, never having been a Christian, and never having believed the Bible to be the 'Word of God,' or more sacred than other old books written in the ages of scientific ignorance" (Chase 1888, 9). He was typical of a class of believers that spiritualism drew in the 1850s. Largely self-taught and resolutely anticlerical, he became a champion of the spiritualist message on public platforms throughout the land, often traveling the whole circuit from New England to the Great Lakes region and further west.

Warren Chase's active work on the platform circuit took him all over the country. In 1862, for instance, he delivered 136 lectures, mostly on spiritualism, but some also on the war. In his second career as essayist for the spiritualist press, especially the most successful of these journals, the magazine *Light* in Boston, Chase exhibited a strong if artless literary style and equally definite convictions on a number of reform related topics, in particular on spiritualism. He was of that breed of autodidacts and self-improvers that throve in England and America at the mid-century, often being admirers of Thomas Paine and freethinkers on most issues. In religion, they applied the same careful common-sense approach to investigating the nether worlds as to their ledgers and balance sheets, and thus would become the mainstays of the spiritualist movement, decent and honest persons of the humbler sort with a high regard for the methods of science and an unsatisfied religious sensibility. Having read often enough of the crisis of religion, and seeking to prove its truths to themselves, for these individual seekers first magnetism, then spiritualism, held an irresistible appeal.

In general, Chase repeated the nostrums with that particular blend of scientific interest, antisacerdotal feeling and self-learning that was a common feature among the working classes in the West involved early on with movements like spiritualism and secularism. He resembled men like his contemporary, the Australian politician Graham Berry (1822–1904) who as a young man, while shaving would commit to memory whole stanzas of works like Pope's *Essay on Man* (Deakin 1957, chapter 1). Warren Chase had a deep aversion to Christianity, and he was especially hard on Catholicism. He wrote, or recorded in his journal, a parody of the Pater Noster that begins, "Our Father, who art in the Vatican; Infallible be thy name. . . ." He condemned the illogicality of biblical injunctions, of a God who forbade killing, yet soon after "ordered his chosen people to commit the most cruel and unjustifiable murders" (1888, 215, 226). Chase also had an exaggerated respect for science and for its capacity to explain the universe. He traces a peculiar and somewhat reductive sacred history: "the grand work" of which spiritualism was the culmination had become possible only when the fogs of Christian superstition were lifting; it began with "the telescope . . . soon followed by the microscope, the crucible, and the retort, the scalpel and the cabinet of fossils collected from the crust of the earth. . . ." Geology had turned humankind's attention to theology, ultimately leading to "Spiritualism, with its intercourse and correspondence with the denizens of the other life, which is to be our next revealement" (Chase 1888, 232). This is familiar ground, the idea that science will serve to confirm the facts of a continued life beyond the grave.

An article dated March 20, 1848, which Chase later claimed to have been an anticipation of the theory of evolution, was published a decade before Darwin's book and ten days before the Fox sisters' manifestations in the hamlet of Auburn in western New York, generally marked as the inauguration of spiritualism. He wrote of "the new philosophy which shadows forth a brighter day, indicating our connection in this physical sphere with a succeeding spirit life" (1888, 215, 226). In another article, he relished the prospect that "the outward form will die, and man pass another transition, to commence a new and higher and more Glorious sphere of development." Thus would "every lover of goodness and truth . . . hail with joy the new philosophy, as the positive sign of a good time coming"; these truths had been shadowed forth distinctly in Isaiah and Daniel, and by Jesus, Swedenborg, and Fourier (Chase 1888, 24–26).

At times, Chase's personal reminiscences are bizarre, even startling, as in his declaration that President Abraham Lincoln (1809–1865) was a spiritualist. It was well known that Mary Todd Lincoln (1818–1882) used mediums to contact her dead son Willie, but the President's involvement has been less publicized (Crabtree 1993, 234).[9] Chase recalled being in Washington, D.C., on Sunday, January 1, 1865, where after lecturing to good audiences, he met many old friends, among them several mediums who were then giving private sittings to the president. He remembered especially Nettie Colburn (1841–1892), later Mrs. Cora Maynard (later Richmond), and a Mrs. Colchester. He took care to mention this "because many prejudiced people deny that Lincoln was a Spiritualist, and I know he was, as also were Senators B. F. Wade, Henry Wilson, Senator Howard of Indiana, and many others of our prominent public men of that time" (Chase 1888, 96). Another astounding assertion was that Lincoln's 1862 Emancipation Proclamation had been issued from his guardians!

Chase was also active on social questions such as temperance. In August 1873, he spoke at the great camp meeting at Silver Lake, Massachusetts, where 15,000 people attended (Chase 1888, 148). There he met Victoria Woodhull (1838–1927), the notorious free-love advocate, whom he

---

9. On Lincoln and spiritualism, see also Goldsmith 1998, 78.

regarded as "the greatest social agitator this country has produced" (103). Modern spiritualism in his view also had a social function; it would "elevate and purify the race till angels and men, unfettered by present untoward conditions, would clasp hands in practical efforts to rid the world of poverty and crime" (210).

Chase's phalanx was flourishing around the same time that the Ebenezers were preparing to heed the injunction of the Lord and move farther west to Iowa, where they were renamed Amana and became the wealthiest communal venture in American history. Though coming from vastly different cultural milieux, both of these ventures shared in the American dream, where the possibility of new beginnings drew numerous adventurers of all kinds to travel west, even before the gold rushes of the late 1840s and the glut of new frontier land brought on by the annexation of Texas and the Mexican War. Theirs was a cultural outpost of European heterodoxy, but their ideas and concepts carried the seeds of earlier radicalisms, now merging imperceptibly across the nation even as the telegraph and the penny post were shrinking the West culturally. Thus could Chase eagerly await the arrival of the Davis book, with its heavy reliance on Swedenborg, while he experimented with practices deriving from the Mesmerian epoch of the covert Enlightenment.

The most egregious example of this heady *mélange* of cultural forms in America is Mormonism. J. F. C. Harrison (1979, 183) argues that the *Book of Mormon* can be understood as a projection of the beliefs and attitudes of postrevival, sectarian religion. John Brooke (1994, 210) has demonstrated that the Mormons were in their native Vermont heirs to a tradition of scrying, of European hermeticism, and of searching for buried treasure, most famously in the discovery by Joseph Smith of the Golden Tablets near Palmyra, New York. The Mormons were also part of a general trend toward individualism in religion, along with Israelitism. In pronouncing the literal gathering of Israel and the restoration of the Ten Tribes, Smith drew on local as well as on biblical lore and overseas prophets like "the nephew of the Almighty," Richard Brothers. Moreover, in asserting that Zion would be built upon the American continent and Christ would reign on the earth, whereupon "the earth will be renewed, and receive its paradisiacal glory," Smith was in the millennial, Bible-based tradition, heir to the chiliasm of Joseph Mede and William Whiston. Finally, native doctrines such as the special place of the Native Americans in America's history, caused as great a hostility among the broader American society as their polygamy and tight communal solidarity. Joseph Smith produced for the laboring peoples an additional scripture that was to be taken literally (Harrison 1979, 180, 184).

Near Palmyra, in the hamlet of Poughkeepsie at around the same time, Andrew Jackson Davis in mesmeric trance appeared to supplant or at least to supplement Swedenborg with his own teachings. The differences between them, as some pointed out, was that Swedenborg had not received his revelation in any trance and had frequently warned against the dangers of such a state if the subject was not "in the faith of Love,"[10] that is, sufficiently morally regenerated to be protected from evil influences. Yet many within the New Church were hungry for new or supplementary Revelations, like Professor George Bush, the eminent Orientalist who joined the New Church in 1845 and the ministry in 1848. Bush at first supported some of Davis's claims, especially that his works were dictated through him by a spirit who claimed to be Swedenborg himself. The Reverend Samuel Worcester was a later dissenter within the New Church. In the early 1840s, Worcester led members in New York and Boston into the New Era movement. Other *soi-disant* or latter day Swedenborgs arose in the New Church, like the Reverend Henry Weller, and the most famous and interesting of all, the Reverend Thomas Lake Harris (1823–1906). These examples of the theological ructions within the New Church and the interest in social reform increasingly witnessed within the broader American society suggest the immediacy of the atmosphere of reform from which spiritualism was forged at the end of that decade.

---

10. See, for instance, Swedenborg's *Other Planets* §123.

7

SWEDENBORG REDIVIVUS

The cherished ones for whom we mourn
As lost in death's embrace,
Are living still in realms of bliss,
In God's eternal space.
Then let your voices sweetly blend,
This grand old anthem sing,
'O grave, where is thy victory?
O death, where is thy sting?'
                    Alfred Lord Tennyson, *In Memoriam*

Professor George Bush

In early 1847, Professor George Bush, eminent Orientalist, biblical expositor, professor of Hebrew at New York University, and a leading American Swedenborgian theologian, published *Mesmer and Swedenborg*, a treatise drawing on the alleged similarities and continuities between the systems and practices of these eighteenth-century savants. In a rather convoluted essay of some 250 pages, Bush argued that the animal magnetism Mesmer claimed to have discovered confirmed Swedenborg's teachings. The leading idea was that

> [i]f Mesmerism is true, Swedenborg is true, and if Swedenborg is true, the spiritual world is laid open, and a new and sublime era has dawned upon the earth. . . . The divine hand itself has, in the teachings of this illuminated seer, lifted the veil interposed for ages between the world of matter and the world of mind. (Bush 1847, 161)

For Bush, the arrival of mesmerism was divinely timed. He asked whether "it be more than merely plausible . . . that the ultimate design, in Providence, of the development of Mesmerism at the present era, is in fact nothing less than to pave the way for the universal admission of Swedenborg's claims" (1847, 168).

Born in Norwich, Vermont, in 1796, George Bush attended Dartmouth College and read theology at Princeton. After being ordained as a Presbyterian minister, he served as a home missionary in Indiana and was appointed professor of Hebrew and Oriental Literature at New York University in 1831. His learned publications include a *Life of Mohammed* and *Notes on Genesis and Exodus*. From 1842, he published *The Hierophant* magazine. He made a public profession of his Swedenborgian faith in 1845, upon realizing the similarities in their theological views, and received ordination in 1848; he was later appointed pastor of the New Church in New York (Gladish 1983, 53; Obituary 1860, 402–409).

Many among Bush's co-religionists in the New Church found this narrative neither theologically sound nor flattering to their eponymous founder. Especially galling to them were the long appendices, where Bush gave sanction firstly to the miracles of the "Seeress of Prevost" and more significantly, to the contemporary mesmeric "revelations" being poured out through the "Poughkeepsie seer," Andrew Jackson Davis. In a state of trance, Davis was then producing a lengthy series of "mesmeric lectures." Bush attended some of these lectures, which Davis published later in the year as a massive, rambling work in three volumes, modestly entitled *The Principles of Nature, Her Divine Revelations, and A Voice to Mankind.*

Bush did enjoy some support within the New Church in the United States and in England, with whom the American Swedenborgians retained close ties. But as we shall see, he quickly changed his mind on the status of Davis as supplementary Revelator when, in late 1847, he read the finished product of these mesmeric séances. The enduring mystery is why he lent his name and authority to them in the first place. Most New Church men and women were eager to distance Swedenborg from any claim that he had been a "mesmeric medium" or that his writings required any contemporary confirmation.[1] New Church publications labored the crucial distinction

---

1. See Swedenborg's *Heaven and Hell* §249 on warnings regarding contact with spirits by the unregenerate.

between Swedenborg and Davis: Swedenborg's divinely ordained revelation required that the Swedish seer should, perforce and by divine command, experience "intromissions" into the afterworld; by contrast, the mesmeric clairvoyance practiced by Davis and others, that had originated in a technique for tapping into the human consciousness to effect healing cures, was often accompanied, as in Mesmer's day, by strange phenomena that some claimed to result from, or to manifest through, contact with another world. There were opinions on both sides of the question within the New Church.

This debate within the Swedenborgian Church was short-lived. It was only one of a series of dissensions among the New Church membership during the heady 1840s, having little direct or lasting influence upon the wider American community. However, the proto-spiritualism of Davis and Bush's transient claims on his behalf do signal broader debates over religion in this era, both within the New Church and in the wider American society, especially regarding the possibility and forms of religious gnosis.

Swedenborg as a Barometer for Radical Movements

During the 1840s, more than in any other decade in the nineteenth century, the New Church was associated with progressive movements, either directly or as a major influence on these other movements. Thus, along with Universalist ministers, mesmerists, and others, Swedenborgians figured prominently in the general mood of reform. In England and Australia, they spearheaded anti-mourning societies. The Brook Farm communitarians drank at the fount of both Swedenborg and Fourier, the former preponderant in the early part of the decade, the latter after 1845; and we have seen that at least two Swedenborgian phalanxes were formed during this period, both having a brief existence, at Leraysville, Pennsylvania, and Canton, Illinois. But it was spiritualism that incurred the deepest debt and on which the seer's legacy exercised the broadest influence, especially in direct borrowings from Swedenborg's witness to the other world; this aroused the greatest frictions among New Church people from 1845 onward, in the few years before the spiritualist movement became institutionalized.

The Covert Enlightenment

After 1848, despite spiritualism itself becoming the focus for official condemnation within the New Church, some members became attracted to the new movement. The main issue was not so much a loss of membership as the undermining of the unique status of Swedenborg's revelation. The New Era movement within the New Church and the involvement of Bush and some Universalists in the coming out of A. J. Davis turned many New Church stalwarts against these reconstructed mesmerists within their communion, now attracted to the fledgling spiritualist movement. While many Swedenborgians, especially in England, cooperated with the new movement, others, jealous of the primacy of Swedenborg, warned against deceiving or personating spirits who claimed to be Swedenborg or to speak with his authority. By 1860, a formal denunciation of spiritualism was passed in the Massachusetts Council, due partly to the excesses of former Universalist and Swedenborgian divine Thomas Lake Harris and partly to their previous experiences of Davis and his purported revelations. It is instructive to give some consideration now to the minor schisms within the New Church during this decade and the consequent growing disfavor with which the Swedenborgians viewed firstly the magnetic phenomena and then the career and claims of A. J. Davis and the burgeoning spiritualist movement.

An examination of the transition from mesmeric to spiritistic phenomena can render only a partial idea of the multitude of reform movements extant in the United States at this time. It is worthwhile nonetheless to review the reactions of leading Swedenborgians to what they considered threats to an absolute theological standard. In abstract terms, they demonstrate again how the paradigms of alternate-reality and alternate-consciousness were shifting and accommodating each other, leading to ever-new interpretations. In the popular imagination, spiritualism as a movement supplanted both mesmerism and Swedenborgianism. Within the broader society, this new mixture of psychological, scientific, and religious modes of thought, altered by lived experience, was to yield new formulations that would soon spill back into England and beyond. As a result, from the 1850s onward, a new spiral of cultural influence was produced across the Atlantic that culminated in the formation of English spiritualism and in the new respectability of hypnosis, and that led indirectly to the formation of the S. P. R.

Magnetism in the 1830s

Around the same time as medical men and divines in England and America were cautiously advancing theories on electricity and magnetism, Swedenborgians were grappling with a different aspect of the new craze: its perceived dangers to their faith and especially to the unique status of Swedenborg's revelations. The most important confirmation for the synthesis of the paradigms initiated through the pervasive influence of Mesmer and Swedenborg was in the fusion of scientific and religious concepts. Mesmerism, both in its doctrines—its belief system—and its therapeutic practices—its ritual—"framed symbolic processes through which individuals might learn to participate in some ultimate reality" (Fuller 1982, xii). For many this did not constitute an abandonment of religion; on the contrary, it signaled a divorce from apparently outmoded ecclesiastical and scriptural forms, along with a yearning for direct spiritual experience already quickened by revivalism, that was now being satisfied for an increasing minority by Swedenborg's teachings and later by spiritualism.

It is instructive to follow the rise of mesmerism and the reaction within the New Church from the 1830s. As an avant-garde theology, Swedenborgianism exerted a far wider influence than seems warranted by the numbers of its adherents. We have seen the ructions generated by animal magnetism within the Exegetic and Philanthropic society in Stockholm, and the hostility of Col. Robert Carter's group in Baltimore in the 1790s (Block 1984, 131). These disastrous effects were repeated on a larger scale in the 1840s, as magnetism was again held responsible for schisms within the New Church, first in the "New Era" movement, then more seriously, over the activities of A. J. Davis and the Reverend Thomas Lake Harris.

In New Church publications from the 1830s, the new magnetic phenomena, which were then reaching the United States largely via French and English experience, were vigorously debated. There were definite contrasting opinions arising within the fold regarding the nature and desirability of these new phenomena, as applied to New Church values and beliefs. A number of articles appeared on the topic. For instance *The New Jerusalem Magazine* for August 1833 recounts a case reported in the current *Lancet*, where a woman, though of limited education had "under the cataleptic influence" succeeded *inter alia* in extracting several roots of numbers and, with much lucidity, had given expositions of several philosophical systems, while she also "discovered and described the phases of her own disease." In the same issue appeared "Singular Effects of Disease," an article that renders a positive account of the recent 1831 French commission experiments. It relates that, in these experiments, "colors, or the position of the hands of a watch beneath the watch glass, were ascertained by the touch of the fingers" of magnetic subjects, and that "psychometric" demonstrations were conducted, whereby articles placed on the pit of a subject's stomach evinced knowledge ostensibly "captured" in the vibrations emanating from the object, these being of "remote places and circumstances, or of the internal condition . . . of their own bodies [and] those of other persons." The author, giving a New Church twist to the undoubted facts of mesmerism and relating them to the Swedenborgian concept of influx, argues that these and similar phenomena should be expected at this time, "because revelations have been made of that world which lies within the natural and gives it form and energy and governs its changes" ("Singular Effects" 1833, 451–455).

Magnetism was now being seen by some believers as complementary to New Church teachings, but others were more wary. A contrary opinion is expressed on the French experiments in *The New Jerusalem Magazine* for February 1834. "Somnambulism and Animal Magnetism" also comments on the celebrated 1831 French report on animal magnetism, and this is followed by editorial comments on their significance to New Church practice. The author worried that "the whole process of magnetizing seemed to be a 'leap in the dark' without a distinct end or aim" and that it bore too near a resemblance to magic and sorcery ("Somnambulism" 1834, 226).

Swedenborg's revelations had taught "that there is an intimate and indissoluble connexion between the spirit of every man, and societies of spirits in the spiritual world," on which he is dependent for his whole power of thinking, of willing and of acting (see *Heaven and Hell* §247). As his character changes, so the individual comes into association with spirits of a corresponding character. It is explained that the regeneration of the human being, a fundamental article of Swedenborg's teachings, is accomplished by the influence and operation of a succession of different societies of spirits, each adapted to a person's various and successive states.

Thus "every change of state is a choice of new spiritual associates, and necessarily subjects us to a new spiritual influence" ("Somnambulism" 1834, 227). The perceived danger was that, in yielding to the influence of the magnetizer and especially in falling into a trance or a sleep that precludes the unfettered exercise of the will, regeneration could not occur. A person cannot be "saved by compulsion," since the Lord "receives and blesses all who can be made to come unto Him, voluntarily and as of themselves." New Church men and women should remain vigilant against any loss of freedom and rationality. In summation, the article states that it seemed "hardly possible that any person could submit to the operation of animal magnetism, without a very great change of internal state, involving, and indeed produced by the proximity and influence of spirits, whose character and quality he has no legitimate means of ascertaining" ("Somnambulism" 1834, 228–230).

For this dominant section of the New Church membership, as for Col. Carter a generation before, magnetic phenomena were regarded as dangerous because they were believed to interfere with regeneration and free will. This was exactly the reverse of the conclusions reached by the magnetic spiritists in their 1787 Exegetic and Philanthropic Society letter.

Over the next decade, the internal battle over mesmeric phenomena would gain further momentum, as a result of their increasing general popularity on public platforms. One example of this trend was in the May 1842 *New Church Advocate*, based in London, which sounded a more alarmist note in "Observations on Animal Magnetism and the Doctrines of Swedenborg." It puts forward a more doctrinaire interpretation of Swedenborg's views on spirit contact and mesmerism: "Now in natural sleep, the power of the will is suspended . . . as it were surrendered to the Lord himself. No angel would take possession of it, and no devil is permitted to do it." But in mesmeric sleep, the concern especially was that "the will of the patient is completely subject to that of the mesmeriser" ("Observations . . ." 1842–1843, 35–36).

The whole matter is assessed later by a Swedenborgian writer, identified only as E. A. B. who sought to strike a middle ground. "Man a Microcosm," published in *The New Jerusalem Magazine* for April 1845, is mostly an unfavorable critique of phrenology, which the author links with other "so-called sciences" like mesmerism and neurology. While there was so much in these practices that is "repulsive" and given through "questionable mediums," E. A. B. insisted that "we need not therefore reject the facts, which each of these sciences may be capable of revealing concerning the constitution and organization of man, to say nothing of the practical benefits with which they claim to be able to assist mankind." With a nice elision, he urged caution, stating that these practices should remain under the "active and constant influence of the light of the Heavenly Doctrines, making them always a test of what else we receive" (E. A. B. 1845, 295).

Nevertheless, for a sizable number within both the English and American New Church communions, these dangers seemed exaggerated. The Reverend C. E. Fernald's article on "Supernaturalism" in the *New Church Repository and Monthly Review* for May 1848, stood firm:

> We would not deny that Animal Magnetism has its dangers. . . . But it has also its high uses in the relief of suffering humanity, and in the confirmation which it lends, as a fact, to the disclosures of Swedenborg. (266)

Fernald, a former Universalist and sometime spiritualist, had great difficulties within his communion. He was among those who gathered around A. J. Davis and *The Univercoelum* from December 1847, along with Universalist ministers S. B. Brittan (d. 1883), William Fishbough (1814–1881), and T. L. Harris. *Heat and Light*, published in 1851 in Boston included a review of the Davis philosophy written by Fernald; and Fernald later became more strident with an 1858 article on "spiritualism," where he asserted that "even those who are not necromancers or magicians may profit from spirit intercourse" (Fernald 1858, 420–422). An unsigned letter in the same issue reflected the majority opinion, repudiating the practice and its introduction within the pale of the New Church. Fernald was suspended from the ministry in 1860 for his increasingly positive comments on spiritualist phenomena, and for his devotion to the teachings of T. L. Harris.

The 1840s: A Crucial Decade of Change
The 1840s decade was the era of the Humanitarians, when social movements for reform of all kinds were burgeoning and the aura of the

"newness" was everywhere (Higginson 1968(a), 77–78); it was a brief halcyon period, a time when the opening of the West and the notion of Manifest Destiny guided a naive optimism about the possibilities of human experience. In New England, a literary renaissance was occurring, before the dissensions of the 1850s would turn minds to darker pursuits, leading to the carnage of the Civil War. It was a time when young Harvard students could spend a summer vacation translating Novalis and when Thoreau could turn his back on industrialism and contemplate in solitude at Walden Pond (Higginson 1968(b), 102). By 1840, a social transformation had been achieved from the seedbed of the young Republic. As Robert Wiebe succinctly characterizes these massive changes: "from impulses to find better farms and higher profit, Americans developed unique popular schemes of land distribution and internal commerce. From continuing attempts to widen access to republican politics, they fashioned a democratic politics;" and most significant for the purposes of this study, "from a Protestant quest in the West, they devised an [sic] universally available salvation" (1984, 164).

From the 1820s, the Erie Canal, "Clinton's folly," had transformed the northeastern United States, linking New York City to Lake Ontario and beyond. The burned-over district was an outgrowth of economic and social factors, including the spread of revivalism and ultraism in the new West from the turn of the century onwards, and especially in the towns and cities that sprang up along the canal route. While the Erie Canal dramatically reduced freight costs with a rapid rise in shipping on the Great Lakes, a flux in attitudes was also occurring, due mainly to factors like western migrations, the increasing waves of immigration, and the effects of eastern industrialism. As canal and rail systems opened vast domestic markets, farmers and manufacturers looked to merchant capitalists for capital and outlets, who, in turn, tried to force down labor costs. It was an age when workingmen were fighting for higher wages and shorter hours and also when anti-slavery and efforts at reform in education, temperance, and the rights of women, along with a host of other reforms were gaining ground.[2]

---

2. Freight rates were reduced from $1,000 per ton to around $15 to $25; Nelson 1969, 59; Adams 1960, 339.

The Covert Enlightenment

The immigration surge was at its height during 1845–1850, when the Irish fleeing the famine and Germans and other refugees of the 1848 revolutions swarmed to the New World. Many were Catholics, and deep prejudices arose against them. The 1840s also saw a tide of nativism in the "Know Nothings" movement. In this highly literate society, by June 1850 some 2,800 newspapers and periodicals were published, with a circulation of over five million (Nelson 1969, 62, 65). The spiritualist press was part of this wave. Spiritualism became a spreading fervor and rapidly developed a viable press. In 1851, it was reported in the *Spiritualist World* that there were over one hundred mediums in New York City and between fifty and sixty private circles in Philadelphia. By 1851, fifty circles were estimated in Brooklyn and twice that number in nearby Williamsburg, along with several spiritualist papers and magazines. In 1850, Apollos Munn (d. 1852) and R. P. Ambler inaugurated the *Spirit Messenger*, the first paper wholly devoted to publicizing open intercourse between the two worlds (Nelson 1969, 8; Chase 1888, 41). Periodical titles reflect the eclipse of magnetism and the rise of spiritism; Laroy Sunderland's Boston paper the *Spiritual Philosopher*, replacing the *Magnet*, was founded in 1850 and changed its name again the next year to *Spirit World*. From Auburn in 1851 came *The Spiritual and Moral Instructor*, edited by T.S. Hiatt; and in the same year, *Heat and Light*, originating in Boston, featured a review of A. J. Davis's philosophy by C. E. Fernald. *Shekinah* lasted only eighteen months, but *The Spiritual Telegraph*, founded in 1853 and edited by S. B. Brittan and Charles Partridge, endured for eight years. The most popular and successful ventures were the *Univercoelum* and the Boston magazine *Light*, published for well over a half century by Luther Colby (1814–1894) (Podmore 1963, 1:204).

During this brief springtime for Americans, when they could and did experiment with the variations in the social forms that the American dream might take, Ralph Waldo Emerson could write to Thomas Carlyle (1795–1881): "We are all a little wild here with numberless projects of social reform; not a reading man but has a draft of a new community in his waistcoat pocket" (quoted in Higginson 1968(a), 77; Gladish 1983, 3). Elsewhere in that era, Chartists were striving for a new wave of parliamentary reform as the 1848 revolutions burst over most of Europe. Even though these ventures were mostly failed, at that time they gave the impression of newness. This was especially so in the United States, where the Humanitarians and Transcendentalists in New England and the middle states were attracting attention. Communitarianism was another outgrowth of the current enthusiasm for reform. As Walters (1978, 19) has written, antebellum reformers "in their best moments . . . believed in harmony and human unity. They thought the glorious and perfect time was near when men and women would behave morally because they wanted to, not because they were forced to." But instead "imperialism, industrialization and war advanced upon the modern world." An era of optimism, self-reliance, and confidence in the infinite possibilities inherent in the individual were preached by Emerson and lesser men. At the same time, altruism developed in experiments in living such as Brook Farm, with its lyric note of "youthful buoyancy and confidence (Adams 1960, 353)."

The influence of the New Church in this general mood of reform was manifold and complex. The conjunction of Fourier and Swedenborg was short-lived, while that of Swedenborg and Mesmer yielded a broader legacy. Swedenborg had taught a scientific theology; his claim was a new revelation, granted through divine favor. Mesmer doggedly promoted his own rediscovery, through the agency of nature, of a new fluid and a new curative therapy. The merging of their respective paradigms emanated from two distinct traditions: from seventeenth-century science, especially of Newton and William Maxwell, and from hermeticism, traced through Paracelsus, Boëhme, and Fludd to Swedenborg. Crabtree argues that the alternate-consciousness paradigm supplanted the "intrusion" and "organic" paradigms, revealing a layered consciousness (Crabtree 1993, 86). It was the early magnetists who brought this concept forward most forcefully. The metaphysical analogue to Mesmer was the new vista of a greater world offered by Swedenborg's writings. The rise of the spiritualist movement in the United States and its transmission to England and Europe were principally the result of the collision between the Mesmerists and the Swedenborgians, along with Universalists and other dispensational religious movements during the 1840s. Hence, the secularization of the soul, or at least the means to communicate with another level of being, had commenced in earnest.[3]

---

3. See J. Cerullo, *The Secularization of the Soul: Psychical Research in Modern Britain* (Philadelphia: Institute for the Study of Human Issues, 1982) for a good discussion of the effects of secular ideas on the S. P. R.

The Covert Enlightenment

From around 1845, Swedenborg's teachings experienced a resurgence of popularity, due partly to factors like the publication of a new edition of his works in England, to the publicity given by the Brook Farm's *Harbinger*, and the congenial attitude of prominent thinkers like Emerson and the wealthy Bostonian Henry James Sr. (1811–1882), father of Henry (1843–1916) and William James (1842–1910). Regarding the increasing popularity of Swedenborg during the 1840s, John Humphrey Noyes, the chronicler of what he called "American Socialisms," commented in 1870:

> He suited all sorts. The scientific were charmed, because he was primarily a son of science, and seemed to reduce the universe to scientific order. The mystics were charmed, because he led them boldly into all the mysteries of intuition and invisible worlds. The Unitarians liked him, because, while he declared Christ to be Jehovah himself, he displaced the orthodox views of Sonship and Tri-personality, and evidently meant only that Christ was an illusive representation of the Father. Even the infidels liked him, because he discarded about half the Bible, including all Paul's writings, as "not belonging to the Word." (Noyes 1870, 538–539)

Except for the determined German Pietists, communitarianism was in brief flower in American society only during the Owenite incursion of the 1820s and again more dramatically with the Fourierist phalansteries of the turbulent 1840s. American communitarians formed a linkage between European and native traditions, whose diversity illustrates the current mood of experimentation. We have traced the variegations of the ontological or alternate-reality paradigm through several generations from the European millennial ideal, with succeeding waves of secular, socialist, and Christian permutations. Communitarianism represents an important linkage between European and native traditions in religion and social thought, wherein are found also phrenology and Mesmerism, along with perfectionism and revivalism in a bewildering range of mixtures. From the Shakers and Jemimakins to the quasi-religious, the secular, and even the anti-religious, we arrive finally to the Swedenborgian and spiritualist experiments of the 1840s and 1850s. Brook Farm and the spray of Fourierist phalanxes that flourished briefly in the 1840s have shown how

European systems not only survived under American skies but developed in different and unsuspected directions. With the progressive secularization of the American soul from the mid-nineteenth century, many among the reform-minded who had previously been devotees of phrenology or magnetism and their variants, many of them also children of the Great Revival, coalesced into a new and distinctively American quasi-religio-philosophical movement in modern spiritualism.

Schisms within the New Church

In 1760, a Baron von Hatzel, intending to translate Swedenborg's works into German and French, asked the seer for the means of communication with spirits. Swedenborg's reply on August 11 warned against intercourse with spirits, and explained his own exceptional case (Odhner 1904, 1:72). From the time of Swedenborg's death in 1772, there had been occasional controversy over the thorny issue of spirit intercourse; and with the New Church's establishment was added another issue, relating to the ordination of the New Church ministry. Col. Robert Carter and other American Swedenborgians over these years rejected the "casting of lots" by which the foundational ministry had been decided in 1788, when it fell on James Hindmarsh. Edward Brotherton (1860, 9) wrote that at that time "the casting of lots was the only expedient which bore the aspect of an appeal to invisible powers to decide." As we shall see, for Brotherton, this implied an early New Church tradition of "spirit" help and provided a wedge for both supplementary Revelation and for the claims of the Reverend T. L. Harris in that role.

The ordination issue, along with spirit intercourse, would assume especial poignancy in the 1840s and 1850s decades when first Andrew Jackson Davis and then the charismatic Thomas Lake Harris claimed to be speaking with the authority of the great Swedish teacher. Moreover, they both claimed to be receiving divine instructions directly from Swedenborg himself, now translated to the sublime celestial spheres.

We have seen the differences over magnetism within the New Church of the 1830s; with the changing paradigms over the next decade, the issues concerning free will and the magnetic phenomena became expanded into one of spiritual authority. Some claimed that other noble spirits and celestial angels were invoked, as in Stockholm of the 1780s, while others insisted that Swedenborg himself was communicating through "sensitives." With some exceptions, the issue was not so much a challenge to Swedenborg's revelation as a questioning of its finality, with a perceived need in some quarters to update his message for the modern age. These ructions surfaced within the New Church membership from time to time; and as spiritistic practices became more widespread throughout New England and the Middle states, a growing minority within the New Church was caught up in the contagion of priesthoods and modernized revelations.

In one New York Society, such an "attack of spiritualism" occurred in 1844. Many New Church members in New York and also in other places were drawn into the "New Era" movement, a spiritistic development instituted by Silas Jones, who claimed to have gained open intercourse with heaven through the aid of an astrologer and sorcerer in Brooklyn. Its adherents met privately for worship, for the administration of the sacraments "in a new and better way," and for the reception of immediate revelations from spirits and angels. The Reverend Samuel Worcester, the same who in the 1820s had contemplated founding a Swedenborgian community similar to the Rappites, became an adherent and claimed ordination as high priest in a ceremony allegedly performed by the spirit of Swedenborg (Duss 1972, 54). He instituted a new priesthood, beginning with himself and passing it on to his son, Samuel H. Worcester (1824–1891); both of these ordinations were quickly repudiated by the Massachusetts Association. The issue was of special poignancy because of the pedigree of its malefactors. The Worcesters were an eminent family whose ancestors included the Reverend Thomas Worcester (1795–1878), who had been responsible for establishing the Swedenborgian Church in Boston (Odhner 1904, 1:264; Silberger 1978, 111).

Not much is known about Silas Jones, but he appears to have taken an interest in phrenology as well as astrology. In 1836, he published *Practical Phrenology*, which teaches among other things that "philoprog-enitiveness," or love of offspring, is a characteristic of Negroes, in whom "the organ is generally large, and that race are proverbially fond of offspring." In the "more cultivated Europeans, and the educated classes, this instinct is less predominating, and at the same time better assisted by intellect, and the higher sentiments" (Jones 1836, 46–48).

Two related issues of pressing concern within the New Church came together in this time of crisis: spirit contact and the controversy over the casting of lots in the establishment of the Swedenborgian ministry. The elder Worcester died the following year, but not before repudiating New Era and returning to the New Church fold. After his death, his son Samuel H. Worcester wrote an apologia of sorts, in a public letter published as a small volume in 1845, that was set out in the form of twenty-four points.

It was claimed that Samuel Worcester senior, for some for six or seven months prior to his death, "had his spiritual senses opened." On October 20, 1844, the elder Worcester, emulating Swedenborg's own language, had written, "The LORD HIMSELF was pleased in His divine Mercy to show Himself to me in a most glorious manner. . . . I looked, and beheld a light at a distance, which approached towards me. As it approached, all the spirits and angels who were with me receded, and at length even Swedenborg left me. Every cloud sank below the horizon. I was aware what was meant by this" (1845, 5–6). The implication was that he had ascended even further than the great revelator himself. Then referring to the other contentious issue, the casting of lots by Robert Hindmarsh in 1788, Swedenborg himself had informed Worcester "that the commissions are not complete—not full—not entirely orderly" (3). These terms, "orderly" and "disorderly," are important within the New Church theology. Apparently these deficiencies in Worcester's commission were then "supplied in a very interior manner by Swedenborg," and he was told henceforward "to regard the present time as the commencement of a new era in the Church" (24).

Then came the younger Worcester's turn. In a scene startlingly reminiscent of Bunyan's Pilgrim, having been informed that he also was to receive a commission as a priest in the new era of the Church, "two angels, females, approached, and seemed to remove something from my eyes, and I then saw more clearly. Emanuel Swedenborg advanced in front of me, holding a roll in his hand. This he seemed to unroll before me from top to bottom, and then presented it to me" (Worcester 1845, 10). It contained the junior Worcester's commission as priest.

The letter then addresses the issue of supplementary or progressive revelation. The younger Worcester rhetorically asks, "May it not be that no system of order [of the degrees of the priesthood] was revealed during Swedenborg's natural life, so that the new heavens might become more fully formed, and more able to give forth light and strength for the reception of true order?" (Worcester 1945, 17). We recall that the main purpose of the arrival of the final Judgment in 1757 had been to clear the obstructions from the overpopulated world of spirits so as to allow the unimpeded flow of influx to the Earth. In essence, the issue that concerned New Era seemed to be one of apostolic succession and theological legitimacy, that is, whether "a ministry which has derived its existence, and its authority from a layman, is not to prepare the way for a more perfect order" (19). The meaning is clear: the authority for a priesthood is derived from the spiritual source, in fact from Swedenborg himself in conformity with the Lord's will, rather than from any layman, which act was judged "disorderly." And since the New Church was established by open intercourse with the spirit realms, the junior Worcester asks, "Will it not be preserved in the same manner in which it was created?" (19)

The final points in this lengthy letter relate to the use of clairvoyance, but these matters were minimized. Many had expressed fears that these new developments would lead to a schism within the church; this fear came from those in the New Church "who do not yet belong to the Circle," meaning those

> both of heaven and earth, by whom E. Swedenborg is acknowledged as the High Priest of the Church, and by whom the present time is regarded as the commencement of a new era in the Church, in which open intercourse with the spiritual world will be given. (Worcester 1845, 24)

The energetic Reverend B. F. Barrett responded indirectly to these assertions in a cautious article entitled "Open intercourse with the spiritual world—its dangers and the cautions which they naturally suggest," published in serial form between September and November 1845; it was a reasoned response to New Era. He began by calling attention to *Arcana*

Coelestia §9438, which cautioned against discourse with angels and spirits by any individual:

> unless he be of such a quality that he can consociate with them as to faith and love; nor can he consociate unless the faith be directed to the Lord, and the love to the Lord, inasmuch as man by faith in Him, thus by truths of doctrine, and by love to Him, is conjoined, and when he is conjoined to Him, he is secure from the assaults of evil spirits from hell ...

Barrett argued sensibly that, since different degrees of the mind are opened, up to the inmost level, according to an individual's moral fitness, then "in order to hold open intercourse with the angels of heaven . . . they must be like the angels" (1845, 15). Swedenborg had taught in *Arcana Coelestia* §5863 that "unless he be in the good of faith," it is dangerous for anyone to consort with spirits. There are various ways in which the barrier that separates the natural from the spiritual world may be broken down within us: through excess, disease, prolonged meditation on the things of religion, a strong desire for spiritual intercourse, *delirium tremens*, or by hereditary predisposition. It follows then that "the class of spirits with whom we should find ourselves in open communication, if our spiritual senses were opened, would depend wholly upon our own characters." This is why it is necessary that an individual "be far advanced in the regenerate life" before it would be safe to have his spiritual senses opened (1845, 22, 24).

When Swedenborg was asked by some spirits, "Why did your Lord reveal those secrets to you who are a layman, and not to some one of the clergy?" he replied, "This was the Lord's decision; ever since I was a young adult he has been preparing me for this mission" (*True Christian Religion* §850). If, therefore, such intercourse should be attained by irregular means, merely by a strong effort of their own will and without adequate preparation by the Lord, this would "manifestly be a disorderly thing, and therefore dangerous and hurtful" (Barrett 1845, 52). This was by way of response to Worcester on the issue of ordination; Swedenborg himself was a layman and a revelator, but he had been prepared all his life for his appointed role. Barrett implies, moreover, that the clergy of that day were too narrow in outlook to have been proper vehicles for this revelation.

Barrett cautioned against overweening egotism and being overawed by alleged spiritual presences. He urged those believers likely to be imbued with an exaggerated sense of solemnity and awe to retain a critical distance and to eschew superstitious beliefs, since there is no way of knowing directly what might be the real character of these spirits. Especially would this be the case if the spirits we saw should be counterfeit "angels of light," as they very possibly would be: "And if some one of them should pretend to be Swedenborg, and would appear clad in such garments," he continues, "we should then feel like reposing unlimited confidence in whatever they might say" (Barrett 1845, 62). Barrett argued that, if one's state of mind were not sufficiently motivated by the doctrine of uses, by a love of one's neighbor more than oneself, the real danger is that "a spirit assuming to be Swedenborg would flow into, and feed and foster that love and conceit." Such an entity would be likely to tell the individual that "the Lord had chosen him to be the medium of some new and important instruction to His church, and that his spiritual senses had been opened for that purpose" (54). Clearly Barrett's comments are only a thinly veiled criticism directed at Worcester and his acolytes.

Nothing more is known of Silas Jones and little more of New Era or its later history. The Worcesters later renounced spiritualism and the Reverend Richard DeCharms (1796–1864) of Philadelphia came up to New York to reclaim the lost sheep by means of a course of sermons on the evils of "pseudo-spiritualism." Only one further article came out of this controversy, penned by Silas Jones three years later, but it did not appear to make much of an impact, as by then the more serious threats of Davis and Harris had surfaced (Odhner 1904, 1:500–501; Block 1984, 99).

Another minor schism, occurring in the Midwest in 1852, was led by the Reverend Henry Weller, pastor of the Grand Rapids Society in Michigan. Weller also claimed to be in personal communication with Swedenborg and began to call himself the "Lord's High Priest," although it is not clear whether he was associated with the New Era movement. He gathered a small group of followers among whom he introduced the "spiritual wife system." He and his followers sought direct intercourse with spirits. The Michigan Association soon repudiated this movement and dismissed him as leader. Weller moved to LaPorte, Indiana, where he founded another society and a magazine, *The Crisis*, before disappearing from historical sight (Block 1984, 127).

These minor schisms, along with later episodes involving A. J. Davis, and later still the ructions caused within the New Church by the poet and mystic T. L. Harris, reveal the lineaments of objections within the New Church to spirit contact, just as earlier it had advised against magnetic sleep, although a fairly large body of believers accepted these techniques for the advancement of Swedenborgian tenets, and they minimized the potential dangers.

Another related issue was the "Third Testament" controversy. This issue surfaced in far-flung New Church congregations, as at Adelaide in South Australia, where, in 1900, the Reverend Percy Billings caused a schism in the Hanson Street society. The central issue was the authority to be given to the theological writings of Swedenborg, but now this was a theological rather than a spirit-related controversy. Two approaches had emerged: whether Swedenborg's writings were the product of a human instrument, giving a faithful and divinely revealed interpretation of the Word as contained in the Scriptures, or whether they formed part of the Word itself, as the "Third Testament." Billings inclined to the latter view, which was rejected by the members, and by 1905 this caused a ruction and eventually a general decline in church attendance (Hilliard 1988, 80–81). While it differs somewhat from the mid-century schisms over episcopal organization and supplementary revelation and belongs, like the brief but intense controversy over Swedenborg's views on "concubinage," to a later era, this issue can be seen as a related attempt to reconsider the substance of the revelator's message, or to shift its emphasis in another direction. The "Third Testament" issue created a serious schism in the General Church at Bryn Athyn, Pennsylvania, which has endured to the present day (Block 1984, 214, 229).

Swedenborgian Revival, 1845

A great change had occurred in attitudes within the New Church between 1787, when the Exegetic and Philosophic Society had invited cooperation with the harmonial societies, and the 1840s, when the New Church leadership was attempting to rein in dissidents and to preserve the uniqueness of the message and of the experiences of its revelator. The irony was that Swedenborg's writings had long been held up as the primal authority for the existence of other levels of being, communications with which were now being discouraged. Their defensive tone is an indication too of the ferment that American spiritual sensibilities were undergoing, especially during the 1840s. Its main significance is the furor it caused in the New Church's published organs and the indications that, rather than having its genesis in 1848, spiritualism had antecedants within the New Church as well as among the Shakers and other groups, who though small in numbers, were instrumental in bringing forward the spiritualist movement over that decade. Most important was the melding, or catalytic, function of the work of Andrew Jackson Davis.

The investigators of spiritistic phenomena at the London circle of William Howitt during the 1850s were a distinguished group, in sharp contrast to the working-class men and women who became the mainstays of the later movement. Among them were old friends like Dr. J. J. Garth Wilkinson, a leading Swedenborgian; the evolutionary theorist Dr. Robert Chambers (1802–1871); Augustus DeMorgan, professor of Mathematics at University College London; Robert Dale Owen; and the royal physician Dr. John Ashburner (1793–1878), who regarded animal magnetism as "a revelation of God's bounty" and proclaimed that "it is owing to it [that] we receive communications from the world of spirits" (Nelson 1969, 90; Watts 1883, 246; Ashburner 1867, 276). Wilkinson, a distinguished homeopathic physician at Wimpole Street, was a member of the Royal College of Surgeons. An intimate of Thomas Carlyle, Charles Dickens (1812–1870), and Alfred Tennyson (1809–1892), he moved in London intellectual and literary circles that were already acquainted with the ideas of Mesmer and Swedenborg. In 1845, he translated some of Swedenborg's works and wrote a *Life of Swedenborg*. Garth Wilkinson, whose treatises Emerson greatly admired, was recognized as the one writer "who directly and avowedly connected the New Church with current literature and living writers." He arranged for Swedenborg's works to be sent to, among others, Thomas Carlyle, Dr. Thomas Arnold (1795–1842), J. S. Mill (1806–1873), and Charles Dickens (Griffith 1960, 17, 35; Owen 1989, 21, 79).

Swedenborg Redivivus

The republication of Swedenborg's scientific and other works, in which Garth Wilkinson was active, helped to generate a Swedenborgian revival in the trans-Atlantic community around 1845. The mid-1840s were the years of the Fourierist collapse and the Millerite disenchantment, but they also brought new ideas, leading to a new hypothesis and a succeeding era of religious excitement. Cross avers that at this time in New England and the burned-over district Swedenborgianism "composed a new synthesis, utilizing both the heritage of ultraism and the newer notions of mesmerism, Fourierism, and phrenology. Swedenborgianism in turn yielded place to spiritualism" (1965, 341–342).

This was in part because of the New English edition of Swedenborg's works in 1845, but the most important factor was "the growth in interest in mesmerism during the preceding decade [which] probably did most to create the Swedenborgian vogue." The sequence and the relation of the elements in this process were thus:

> Mesmerism led to Swedenborgianism, and Swedenborgianism to spiritualism, not because of the degree of intrinsic relationship between the three propositions but because of the assumptions according to which American adherents understood them. The religious liberals of the forties had grown beyond dependence on the letter of Scripture. (Cross 1965, 342)

We are back to a "scientifically based pneumatology." In the burned-over district of New York in particular, Swedenborg served as a catalytic agent, "a great if rather vague, synthesis of more liberal religious doctrines, and many of the scientific and sociological ideas of its day" (Cross 1965, 343). Noyes comments on Swedenborg's appeal, which he traces back to the Brook Farmers:

> Swedenborgianism went deeper into the hearts of the people than the socialism that introduced it, because it was a religion. The Bible and revivals had made men hungry for something more than social reconstruction. Swedenborg's offer of a new heaven as well as a new earth, met the demand magnificently. (1870, 538–539)

Hence in the lengthening of its trajectory, in the synthesis of the ontological and alternate-consciousness paradigms, Swedenborgianism and later spiritualism, were situated between the two "forks," promising a new heaven as well as a new earth.

A. J. Davis and the Harmonial Philosophy

Andrew Jackson Davis was the harbinger and principal prophet of spiritualism, destined to play a most important part in its future history, though in time he became increasingly contemptuous of the direction the movement was taking. Like many primal religious personalities, his life has assumed mythological dimensions, where truth and fiction are difficult to separate. He has been both reviled and reified; Noyes regarded him as "the great American Swedenborg," while others have perceived him to be a fraud, albeit a very successful one (Noyes 1870, 539). One commentator considered his activities "another episode in the well-worn saga of the wide-eyed American countryboy who goes to the city and wins fame and fortune by hoodwinking his far better educated and infinitely more gullible brethren." There was then a vast market "for wondrous nonsense conveyed in theosophical jargon and in the trappings of 'Science,' which Davis and his many imitators did their best to satisfy (Gladish 1983, 90).

A. J. Davis was born in 1826 into a family of poor farmers. His father Samuel Davis eked out a precarious existence also as a weaver and shoemaker. Named after the populist hero "Old Hickory," the boy had a mere five months of formal education. His father was fond of liquor, and this prompted "Jackson" to become a lifelong temperance man. Davis recalled how "poverty, with its hideous train, dwelt in our habitation. . . . Oft and again I have seen my mother busy baking the last handful of Indian meal in our possession—without meat, or potatoes, or the flour of other grains." He remembered that in his family "each felt that intensely fearful desire to eat which only the really famishing can ever fully comprehend" (Davis 1857, 25, 68).

From an early age, Jackson was apprenticed to a shoemaker named Armstrong in the hamlet of Poughkeepsie, in the heart of the burned-over district. In 1843, when Professor Stanley Grimes was giving lectures on animal magnetism in the district, a local tailor named Levingston began practicing the new sensation. Geoffrey Nelson has called attention to the role of itinerant mesmeric lecturers in preparing individuals for the claims of spiritualism within these newly settled districts, along with the teachings of Swedenborg and Christian mysticism, alchemy and American Indian traditions of guardian spirits and shamanism. Levingston experimented on the seventeen-year-old Davis, who quickly became deeply entranced; to the amazement of those assembled, he became "possessed" by a higher intelligence that began to dispense a series of wordy and elevated discourses on metaphysical, scientific and religious topics (Nelson 1969, 53; Podmore 1963, 1:158; Moore 1977, 11). Of this first experience with Levingston, Davis wrote, "What surprised me more than anything else was the gushing forth of novel and brilliant thoughts— extending apparently over the vast landscape of some unknown world of indescribable beauty [and] comprehending more than it is possible for me even now to relate." These conceptions, he was now fully persuaded "were an influx of many interior and immortal truths." He awoke to see several acquaintances, who had been sent for by Levingston, "sitting near and around me, with countenances beaming with pleasure and astonishment" (Davis 1857, 208–209).

Almost immediately, a mythology began to develop around Davis. He developed the ability to diagnose disease, as well as performing minor feats such as reading newspapers through his forehead and telling the time by placing his hand on a watch while blindfolded. Of this early period, he commented that, like the poet "I awoke and found myself famous." The events leading to his spiritual ministry began on March 6, 1844, when, after a session at Levingston's, Davis obeyed a spontaneous impulse to wander away to the country and he seemed to float above the ground: "My feet clung to nothing. There was no friction. They were like wings, and I fled with a fleetness indescribable. My exuberant joy was ecstatic" (Davis 1857, 210, 228). Soon he found himself among wild mountains, where he encountered two venerable spirits with whom he held an intimate and elevating communion, the one upon medicine and the other upon morals. Falling into a spontaneous trance, this experience evolved into an epiphany during which these spirits, Galen and Swedenborg, reflecting Davis's interests in healing and in mystical philosophy, instructed him concerning his mission to humankind. He noted that the second spirit especially "possessed perfect symmetry of cerebral structure, and was seemingly about six feet in stature. His head particularly attracted my attention, for I had never beheld such an harmonious combination of moral and intellectual developments. The cerebrum indicated a most vigorous and gigantic intellect—as also an exalted power of conception, great ease of expression—and a high degree of spirituality." This was Emanuel Swedenborg, who drew near and spoke these words:

> By thee will a new light appear; it shall be new because it will brighten and purify that already in being, and reflect intellectually upon that heretofore conceived; and it will establish that which has been, and still is supposed to be the wildest hallucination, viz., the law and "kingdom of heaven" on earth—Peace on earth and good will to men. (Davis 1857, 242)

The next day Davis discovered that he had traveled in this semi-dissociated state to the Catskill Mountains, some forty miles distant from his home (Doyle 1926, 1:40). It appears that, at this first meeting, he was advised by the spirit of Swedenborg to establish contact with Professor George Bush, to whom he wrote on June 16, 1846.

Davis then met Dr. Silis Lyon and Universalist minister the Reverend William Fishbough, who served respectively as magnetizer and scribe to help with a series of lectures on philosophy to be given in clairvoyant trance. Dr. Lyon was a medical practitioner in Bridgeport, Connecticut, who gave up his practice and moved to New York for this purpose. Davis chose three witnesses, and between one and six visitors were also admitted to each lecture; at various times, these included George Bush himself, Albert Brisbane, and on at least one occasion Edgar Allan Poe (1809–1848). Other attendees like George Ripley and Parke Godwin were also impressed, writing favorable reviews in Brook Farm's *Harbinger*. From November 1845 through the next fifteen months, 157 public "lectures" were produced at 92 Green Street, Manhattan, in New York City (Davis 1857, 333, 303). The procedure followed was that, after Lyon had induced the "magnetic state," a few words would be uttered at a time, which were then repeated by Dr. Lyon and recorded by Fishbough. Davis recalled:

When delivering these lectures, I would receive impressions from the invisible world; and then, with my natural organs of speech, I would slowly, distinctly, and audibly deliver them to the Scribe, in order that they should be accurately recorded. I would then return to the invisible world for another impression. (1868, 43)

This laborious process meant that the delivery of a single lecture could occupy from forty minutes to about four hours (Moore 1977, 11; Review 1848, 58, 60). The lectures were published in 1847 as *The Principles of Nature, Her Divine Revelations, and A Voice to Mankind*. Money for their sustenance during the dictation of these revelations was gained by Davis's prescriptions for patients while in the clairvoyant state and contributions from a Mrs. Silone Dodge, a wealthy middle-aged woman whom he later married (Doyle 1926, 1:47–48; Gladish 1983, 89).

George Bush and A. J. Davis

The Reverend George Bush frequently attended the circle while these revelations were dictated, although other accounts say that he was present at only two or three sessions and read the remainder in manuscript form. At any rate, it is clear that Bush was enthusiastic about the project: he advertised the work, which thus met with a favorable reception, and he lent his authority in vouching for the good faith of the author, or amanuensis, who answered impromptu questions put to him as tests and quoted Hebrew and other ancient languages unknown to him in the waking state. Bush could "most solemnly affirm that I have heard him correctly quote the Hebrew language in his Lectures" (Bush 1847, 215; Podmore 1963, 1:159). He added that there were numerous instances when an entranced Davis, in reply to impromptu questions, would launch into extended digressions that do not appear in the volume, "showing a complete mastery of the subject in its various ramifications and relations" (Chapman 1847, 8). One instance given was in response to a question posed by Bush regarding the import of the Hebrew word for "firmament"; this, he averred, was answered "with the utmost correctness" (Chapman 1847, 9). Writing to the poet Sarah Helen Whitman (1803–1878), Bush declared Davis "as the most astonishing prodigy the world has ever seen next to Swedenborg's oracles" (More 1977, 11). The most decisive factor in the nascent career of Davis was that Bush took him under his patronage and concluded in *Mesmer and Swedenborg*, published in late 1847, that Davis was the true medium of Swedenborg "providentially raised up to confirm his divine mission and teachings" (Noyes 1870, 540).

That there were early connections between the surging interest in magnetism and the New Church over these years is patent; indeed, this appears to have been how the former Presbyterian minister George Bush came into the Swedenborgian communion in 1845 (Odhner 1904, 1:512). His neighbor Louisa Ogden, in a letter to Anna Cora Mowatt (1819–1870), a well-known actress, related how her friend George Bush became interested in these matters: "Our household chanced to be equally interested in the discovery of magnetism, and I think it was through this gate that he entered (as we did) into the 'City of the New Jerusalem.'" Lucius Lyon (1800–1851), United States senator from Michigan, reflected on similar circumstances in a letter to Bush: "In looking back on my own state of mind five years ago, I do not see how I could ever have been brought to recognize and acknowledge the psychological truths given to the world by Swedenborg, but for the confirmation afforded by the phenomenon of Mesmerism." He added that, of the fifty or sixty persons he knew personally who had since embraced the Heavenly Doctrines, "there is not one who has not been more or less aided in the same way" (Block 1984, 131–132).

In regard to philosophy and theology, George Bush testified that *The Principles of Nature* . . . for the most part accurately reflected Swedenborg's views and that the coincidence in language between them in several cases was "all but absolutely verbal"; we will return to this point (Podmore 1963, 1:166). Bush first championed Davis and then just as definitely rejected his revelations within a year. Some consideration of the reasons for this dramatic change of mind will render an idea of tensions existing within the New Church at this epoch, exacerbating the already strained atmosphere engendered by the apostasies of Samuel Worcester and Henry Weller. For that purpose, we shall focus on the period 1847–1848.

Davis's work *The Principles of Nature* is an encyclopedic work in three volumes, a colossal enterprise that includes an evolutionary account of the origin and growth of the universe, along with a system of mystical philosophy and a description of the relations between the spirit realms and the material world, and a plan for the reorganization of society along socialist lines. Adam Crabtree, whose interest in these events is their part in the history of dynamic psychiatry, pondered the many mysteries of A. J. Davis's writings, such as how this unlettered youth, with only a minimal education, could have obtained the vast knowledge of history, geology, languages, mythology, and theology they display. There is no evidence that he had read any books other than a few religious works or that he had plagiarized from any. Whatever their source, Davis's works struck a note that was right for the time. *The Principles of Nature* went through thirty-four editions over the next thirty years (Crabtree 1993, 232; Nelson 1969, 53). Others have suspected trickery, or like Podmore, an extraordinarily retentive memory.

The Principles of Nature is too large and diffuse a work to be easily summarized or to allow any definite conclusions. Putting aside its alleged spiritual origins, the three parts of the work show how closely Davis, or his amanuensis, was steeped in the currents of his time. The first part demonstrates that the universe is one and outlines a vast system of correspondences, or analogies, and degrees, throughout the universe, where things in general are arranged in series of three (Podmore 1963, 1:164). The second part, *Her Divine Revelations*, opens with the nebular theory in the formation of the universe from what Davis calls the "Great Positive Mind" and offers an account of the origins of our solar system, somewhat like LaPlace. In this section, there appears a prophecy of the discovery of an eighth planet; Bush said he was willing to testify under oath that this prophecy had been made months before U.-J. Le Verrier's (1811–1877) calculations proved the existence of Neptune and led to its discovery (Chapman 1847, 16). In the most often-quoted part of the work, Davis then gives an account of the relations of the human being with the world of spirits and a description of the six spirit spheres and their societies. He concludes with a prophecy, delivered in Swedenborgian language, though the meanings of the principal terms are dramatically altered from Swedenborg's usage:

> It is a truth that spirits commune with one another while one is in the body and the other in the higher spheres—and this, too, when the person in the body is unconscious of the influx, and hence

cannot be convinced of the fact; and this truth will ere long present itself in the form of a living demonstration, and the world will hail with delight the ushering in of that era when the interiors of men will be opened, and the spiritual communion will be established such as is now being enjoyed by the inhabitants of Mars, Jupiter, and Saturn. (quoted in Podmore 1963, 1:163)

This and similar passages were taken as prophesying the advent of spiritualism. It is undeniable that, within three years, the phenomena burst upon a startled rural population in the burned-over district with the manifestations of the Fox sisters, then spread rapidly throughout the Republic and thence to Europe and elsewhere.

The theology and seership of Swedenborg permeate Davis's work from beginning to end. Like Swedenborg, Davis speculates on life on the other planets of this system. He avers that Saturn was the first planet on which animal life developed, hence their "organization is of the most perfect kind, both mental and physical; and their intellect being expansive and powerful, judgment controls them entirely, insomuch that weakness and disease are not existing among them" (Chapman 1847, 19). Davis's cosmology too draws heavily on Swedenborg. He describes a series of six celestial spheres of increasing harmony, beauty, and wisdom through which the soul advances after death. Swedenborg had also outlined six progressive spheres following death, three hells and three heavens. Davis corrected the seer, explaining that these were actually six heavens but that the first sphere after earth (the second sphere) was relatively chaotic and so had been misperceived as a hell by Swedenborg. The more spiritually advanced one became during life on earth, the more progressed would be the sphere one would enter at death (Braude 1989, 40). There follows a dense history of the migrations of humankind, including the peopling of America. Like Swedenborg also, Davis asserts that, in the earliest ages, human beings communicated their ideas by expressions of the countenance. Along with much else, such as the origin of evil, this book concludes with sections on the history and criticism of each book of the Old and New Testaments. These include descriptions of the character and ministry of Christ, which one commentator found "marked by great profoundness, insight, and self-evident truthfulness, and expressed in language of no less appropriateness and beauty" (Chapman 1847, 23). It was principally on this point, and on the unsalutary depiction of the great Swede himself, that Bush and the New Church would soon part company with Davis.

The third book, *A Voice to Mankind*, puts forth a rather crude socialism, ending with a scheme for the salvation of humankind by the organization of society into phalanxes of co-operators. It advocates Fourier's views, which had recently spread in the eastern United States where they had excited extraordinary enthusiasm. Among the passages that distressed Bush and his co-religionists was the assertion by Davis's "control" that Christ was to be regarded as a great moral reformer but in no special sense divine. The mistakes throughout this massive work are frequent, gross, and palpable, and many passages are pretentious nonsense; but Podmore judges that "nevetherless, at its best, there is a certain stately rhythm and grandiloquence which partly explains the favorable impression produced on Bush and others" (1963, 1:166).

Whatever its deficiencies, *The Principles of Nature. . .* was a stupendous achievement for a man not yet twenty-one years of age and barely schooled. John Chapman, the original publisher, concludes that, after stripping the book of all its claims to a supernatural origin, "there still remains a work of no ordinary scientific and theological pretension; displaying a knowledge so profound and comprehensive, and generalisations so eminently philosophical and vast, that it must inevitably . . . command the respectful attention of learned and inquiring minds" (1847, 9). On its completion, Davis renounced all claims to copyright in the work or its proceeds, simply claiming a just remuneration for the time he had employed in its delivery (Cook 1907, 595).

Although Davis protested little education and admitted having done little reading, others who had known him earlier, like the Reverend A. R. Bartlett, insisted that "he possessed an inquiring mind—loved books, especially controversial religious works" (Podmore 1963, 1:165). And Bush relates how, in a letter received long before the outpouring of his revelations, Davis had quoted a passage from Swedenborg's *Arcana Coelestia*, giving the exact reference. This was probably the letter prompted by his first meeting with Swedenborg and Galen. There is also some evidence of parallelism in passages from Davis's *Great Harmonia* (1852) and Sunderland's *Pathetism* (1847). Podmore suggests this was not plagiarism but due to an extroadinarily retentive memory, such as that often associated with the somnambulic state (Podmore 1963, 1:166). Podmore was an acute psychical researcher; and though he never accepted the theory of spirit survival, he did conduct experiments in the 1880s that convinced him of the reality of hypnotic phenomena and mental telepathy.

The main impression garnered from Davis's revelations, and possibly the secret of their success, was in the moral attitude of the author. "The whole book is transfused by a vague enthusiasm—an enthusiasm not always according to knowledge—for the regeneration of mankind" (Podmore 1963 1:169). There are, however, occasional striking passages, as in *The Penetralia*, published in 1856, where Davis intones the following prophecy in response to the question "Will utilitarianism make any discoveries in other locomotive directions?":

> Yes; look out about these days for carriages and travelling saloons on country roads—without horses, without steam, without any visible motive power moving with greater speed and far more safety than at present. Carriages will be moved by a strange and beautiful and simple admixture of aqueous and atmospheric gases—so easily condensed, so simply ignited, and so imparted by a machine somewhat resembling our engines, as to be entirely concealed and manageable between the forward wheels. . . . These carriages seem to me of uncomplicated construction. (cited in Doyle 1926, 1:47–48)

Arguments within the New Church on Spiritualism

We now return to the Reverend George Bush's 1847 defense of Davis in *Mesmer and Swedenborg*. It may help to recall that Bush was a bit of an *arriviste* in the Swedenborgian movement, having joined only two years previously. This production was clearly resented by a sizeable majority among the New Church membership. In the preface, dated November 19, 1846, Bush discusses first the various levels of "spiritual attunement" among magnetizers, dismissing the garden variety, and stakes his claim for the highest manifestations; "as the development of an interior state which puts the subject into a new relation with the spiritual world," he regarded magnetism "fraught with a sanctity with which no right mind will trifle" and A. J. Davis as a special case "altogether unique and unprecedented." But he was careful to note: "Still even this is not a case of direct revelation of the facts of the spiritual world, like those of Swedenborg . . . which can only be explained on the ground of the influx of the minds of spirits into his mind" (Bush 1847, ixx).

Some two thousand publications were dedicated to Mesmerism by 1846, which was now found in a surprising variety of milieux, from the frontier settlement to the Philadelphia mansion. The ultimate scope of Bush's work was "to evince that all the higher or mental manifestations brought out in the Mesmeric processes were well known, though not under this name, to Swedenborg" (1847, 20). Bush argued that the indubitable facts of Mesmerism were affording to the very senses of the human being a demonstration that "Swedenborg has told the truth of the other life." His main argument was that the higher mesmeric phenomena fall into the same category with Swedenborg's seership and that the truth of the former establishes that of the latter. The converse, however, that if Mesmerism is false, then Swedenborg is false, does not hold true (69).

Bush posited an invisible aura or sphere exhaling from individual persons. The first effect of the magnetic condition was to blend the respective spheres of operator and subject. This he put into a Swedenborgian context, for this sphere "is not merely the efflux of the corporeal system, but . . . [it] emanates also from the interior spirit, the seat of sentiments and intellectual sympathies" (71). Thus does he neatly imbed magnetic practices, based on concepts like community of sensation, into a Swedenborgian universe where the "exhalations" of spirits and angels have a direct effect on spiritual regeneration. To many of his co-religionists, this would have seemed a travesty and a reductionist analysis based on physical effects, rather than spiritual causes. He held that "these spheres are the grand media of conjunction between spirits, being the emanations of their interior affections" (82). Further confusing the argument, Bush asserts that these mental phenomena "are in some mysterious manner connected with the influences and agencies, electric and magnetic, which, in some of their forms, come under the cognizance of the senses" (85).

In fine, Bush saw the coming of Mesmerism as divinely timed and its development as providential, its purpose being "nothing less than to pave the way for the universal admission of Swedenborg's claims." At this point, Bush regarded Davis as a kind of John the Baptist figure, a confirming voice for the truth of Swedenborg's revelation. It is not surprising that he drew the ire of a number of persons within the New Church communion, who saw no need for confirmation of either the revelator or his revelations. Continuing in this vein, Bush asks whether it is it not reasonable to conjecture that some striking and palpable authentication should be given to Swedenborg's mission:

> And how could this be more effectually accomplished than by an unexpected and providential discovery, clearly ascertaining that the psychological structure of the human mind and its interior manifestations in the present world, are in strict accordance with what Swedenborg, from supernatural insight, assures us are the laws of spiritual existence in the world to come? (168)

To strengthen this audacious claim, in an appendix, Bush considers the "revelations of A. J. Davis." Davis was not simply a stalking horse for his broader theories but seemed to be at this time their principal exemplar. Davis claimed he had never read Swedenborg, but according to Bush his "enunciations coincide with his teachings, sometimes to a surprising degree" (172). For instance, all *Arcana Coelestia* references in the 1846 Davis letter to Bush were correct except one, "and that one was found in the original Latin of Swedenborg to also be in error" (178). It cannot be that Bush was simply naive about the possibility of plagiarism, but that he was so keen to prove that Davis was the true medium of Swedenborg that even errors transposed from Latin to English were made to serve his purpose.

Bush interrogated Davis under the mesmeric state, with eyes bandaged, and affirmed that he had heard him correctly quote Hebrew and display a knowledge of geology "which would have been astonishing in a person of his age, even if he had devoted years to the study . . . [with] access to all the libraries of Christendom" (215). Could it be that Davis was gifted with a prodigious memory and that he "crammed" for sessions beforehand?

Swedenborg Redivivus

Using Swedenborg's letter to Prelate Oetinger, where the revelator mentions that the truths of his doctrine will be conveyed not by miracles, but through the revealed Word and "some *speaking illustration* of certain persons," George Bush suggests that a magnetized Davis may be one of these illustrators (211). Though yet insisting on the fundamental differences between Swedenborgian and mesmeric visions, Bush seems thereby to undermine his own argument as to Swedenborg's primacy and uniqueness: "if common clairvoyants are gifted with the opening of spiritual sense . . . there is no need to consider Swedenborg's prerogative in any other light." However, he hastens to add that "there is an immense disparity in the two on the score of solidity, gravity, reality, and a certain indescribable air of truth" (204).

The ticklish issue of plagiarism was skirted in a number of ways. For instance, a comparison of Swedenborg's *Earths of the Universe* and the Davis letter revealed a suspicious concurrence; but as Bush saw it, this accusation may be invalid if the communicator was indeed Swedenborg (185). It was an ingenious but for many an unconvincing apologia. There is much special pleading as Bush laboriously contrasts the passages in A. J. Davis's letter with Swedenborg's writings, noting small verbal changes. For his part, Davis asserted that the quotations from Swedenborg's *Earths of the Universe* were supernaturally dictated to his mind, not plagiarized (214). To demonstrate Davis's moral integrity, Bush states that "the most urgent solicitations have been made to him to aid individuals in the accomplishment of schemes of private interest, but all in vain." As to the lectures, which were then being delivered through his agency, Bush notes approvingly that for Davis, "in their grand scope they aim directly at the regeneration of society; that a great moral crisis is impending in this world's history; and that he is selected as a humble instrument to aid, in a particular sphere, in its accomplishment" (210, note).

As we have seen already, the question of any similarities between mesmeric trances and Swedenborg's state of illumination as proposed by Bush, was already contentious after New Era. But once *The Principles of Nature* . . . was published, he and other New Churchmen were incensed not only by Davis's gross distortions of Swedenborg's principles, but at the cavalier way in which he handled Swedenborg himself. In one passage, the "control" asserts that "[Swedenborg's] writings do not unfold a germ of spiritual truth in those primitive pages . . . because it is impossible for them to contain such, inasmuch as they are only historical accounts and not spiritual revelations" (quoted in Gladish 1983, 91–92).

Within a few months, Bush's prose revealed a rapid change of tone. In September 1847, he published a pamphlet with B. F. Barrett entitled *"Davis's Revelations" revealed*. This strongly suggests great tension within the theological edifice of the New Church and a vigorous attempt on Bush's part to reinstate himself. Warning the public not to be misled by Davis's numerous errors, he now asserted that, viewed in light of Swedenborg's teachings, Davis had been made the mouthpiece of uninstructed and deceiving spirits. Bush pointed to Davis's pretended revelation as no isolated phenomenon, since other media like the Davenport brothers were now appearing. He warned darkly that "the indications are rife of a general demonstration about to be made, or now being made, of the most pernicious delirium breaking forth from the world of spirits upon that of men." Frank Podmore suggests that this rapid change of tone arose principally from a change in Davis's attitude toward Christianity (1963, 1:170). Bush was concerned that Davis "turns the Ark and the Cherubim out of the sanctuary by denying the divinity and true inspiration of the Word, and by representing Christ as merely a great Social Reformer, though the most perfect type of humanity" (quoted in Block 1984, 136). From this point, Bush back pedaled over Davis; his theology, such as there was, was mostly radical and not Swedenborgian; and to a friend, he confided, "In point of talent and scientific mind it far transcends my most sanguine expectations, but in the theological department it is absolutely destructive" (quoted in Block, 136).

The sticking point for many in the New Church was not simply a theological one. A review article of Bush's book, provocatively entitled "Bush's Mesmerism," totally rejected "the supposed analogy between the phenomena and disclosures of Mesmerism and those set forth in the works of Swedenborg." For this reviewer, their two states differed not merely in degree, as Bush had implied, but in kind; and moreover, they "differ so much, that we regard them as opposite, rather than similar." Among the fundamental differences between Swedenborg and Davis were that Swedenborg had been carefully prepared for his illumination by a thoroughly moral and religious character, by many years devoted to the acquisition of a vast fund of knowledge, and through a long and careful intellectual discipline. Moreover, between the state of Swedenborg when under illumination and his normal condition, there was "no separation, no disunion, no impassable abyss" ("Bush's Mesmerism" 1847, 171, 174–175).

George Bush, while accepting its spiritual origins, now rejected Davis's work as any kind of revelation. *The New Church Quarterly Review* for 1848 contains two pieces on Davis, the first an editorial review article, the second an unsigned review penned by Bush and Barrett, and both dedicated to reviewing Davis's book. The editor noted the great contrast in the book between "the imposing splendor of the promises, and the huge, interminable verbosity of the fulfillment" ("Professed Revelations" 1848, 36); he found in particular that its criticisms of the Scriptures are "throughout stale, puerile, and most impiously offensive (45). [The joint article by Bush and Barrett now referred to the book as "this masterpiece of infernal cunning against the immovable fabric of revelation," and they railed against the proposition that "such crudities could be digested by the gastric potencies of the stomach of any Christian community" ("Publication of Strictures" 1848, 111). From his own biblical scholarship, Bush recognized the absurdity of opinions advanced in Davis's tome, such as the proposition that the Hebrew Scriptures had been translated from a Persian manuscript during the Babylonian captivity or the frightening assertion that the mythos of the Biblical Trinity was derived "from the Hindoo [sic] legends respecting Brahmah [sic], Vishnu, and Siva [etc]" ("Publication of Strictures" 1848, 111). The latter was in fact a popular idea in later writers like M. Denon and Louis Jacolliot (1837–1890), but these opinions were too much for the Church of the New Jerusalem.

It appears that considerable pressure was placed upon Bush for his former supportive comments on Davis. The next year Barrett returned to a dissection of Davis's opus at a public lecture in Cincinnati, published as a pamphlet "Davis's Revelations Sifted." Davis had said that "the Savior was a good man, but nothing more." He insisted that Jesus was not the Son of God and classed him together with Confucius, Zoroaster, Brahma, Mohammed and (amazingly) Fourier. This familiar attack now takes an interesting twist, for since Davis was subject to impressions, Barrett averred that these expressed opinions "would be according to the character of the spirits that were around him for the time." He concludes that, due to the varied influences brought to play in those lectures, "Mr. Davis's book . . . is a perfect chaos of contradiction—a strange compound of Swedenborgianism, Universalism, Naturalism, Materialism, Infidelity and Fourierism," which in his view proved the truth of Swedenborg's theory of spiritual affinity (Barrett 1849, 4, 10, 11).

Some four years later, in 1852, over several issues of *The New Church Repository and Monthly Review*, of which he was now editor, Bush returned to Davis and "Pseudo-Spiritualism." By that time, spiritualist phenomena had surfaced among numberless "home circles" throughout the land and spread to England and elsewhere, and they now assumed for some the nature of an epidemic of media. Bush had clearly changed his mind and even become hostile to the new revelations coming through Davis or others. He asked what a New Church man should think of the reliability of communications "which so generally—we do not say universally—lead the 'circles' to deny the supreme divinity of Jesus, to reject the Bible-Word as the grand authoritative embodiment of Divine Truth, to scout the eternity, not to say, in many cases, the existence of the hells, to ignore the necessity of regeneration, and to inculcate a system of ethics which makes little or no account of the relations of genuine charity to genuine truth?" (Bush 1852, 547).

Alan Gauld (1995, 190) believes A. J. Davis paved the way for American spiritualism in four important ways:

> He accustomed a wide public to the idea that a clairvoyant somanmbule might engage not just in medical diagnosis and travelling clairvoyance, but in the transmission of social, religious and cosmological teachings; he propounded neo-Swedenborgian doctrines about the future state and the spirit spheres and about the features and inhabitants of the planets; he propagated the view that some new and stirring revelation was about to rock mankind; and he implied that this revelation would involve a bursting of the barriers that separate our world from the spiritual one.

Gauld appears to miss the significance of the altered style and singular focus in events from this time onward. It might be added that Davis also precipitated the merging of the paradigms that had been coming into confluence since the covert Enlightenment and especially over the last few years through the magnetic movement and the cautious application of medical men. Most significant was the transformation of the magnetic sessions into a religious performance, with only the slightest variation in the activities of the participants, but with a correspondingly greater change in their mental and emotional perspective. What had commenced as the scientific application of a curative regimen had moved with the magnetic movement into a "scientifically based pneumatology" and lastly in spiritualism to a fully fledged religion and philosophy of life.

Whitney Cross comments that "American Swedenborgianism provided a leadership, a theology, and a set of social concepts which required only a mechanism for communication with the dead to become spiritualism" (1965, 344–345). This mechanism, as we have seen, was provided by mesmeric practice. A natural outcome of the *rapprochement* between spiritualism and mesmerism was the metamorphosis of the "magnetic trance" into the "mediumistic trance" in which the "sensitive" or medium is especially open to spiritual influences (Gauld 1968, 18). The changes that transformed these events from magnetic to spiritistic séances were subtle but significant; they involved a reversal of the bacquet sessions, where, instead of receiving the curative effects of a healing fluid, participants now gave "power" to the central figure of the medium for the furtherance of "communion" with higher entities. They no longer involved an individual magnetizer and a magnetic subject *en rapport*, but now a group—in spiritualist parlance, a "circle"—and thus became a corporate venture focused principally on a mutual search for illumination or, at the very least, "proof" for the continued survival of deceased loved ones. Similarly, the role of the medium, from acting as passive instrument to becoming a vehicle providing a liminal connection to a greater life, was thus transformed into that of a religious figure. Important also was the ritual of the séance as a private family experience that illustrates a democratic ethos. The séance became a unique religious practice, with a new ritual atmosphere befitting what was now less a scientific or curative enterprise and more a form of orison or communication with divine spheres. The merging of the alternate paradigms had now become complete, and the medium and the séance were born into religious discourse (Crabtree 1993, 232; Gabay 2001, chap. 6).

After the first book of his three-volume opus was completed, Davis discovered that he was able to enter the magnetic state unaided, and he dispensed with the services of Dr. Lyon, as he could now achieve a deeper state that henceforth he called "the Superior condition." If we are to search for the fulcrum of the new practice of mediumship, the moment when magnetism yields to spiritualism, it was this moment. No longer would the medium be a mere passive instrument, but he or she would now become the focus of "power" for those assembled. In truth, a similar transformation occurred to that of Puységur, Willermoz, and St. Martin, at Avignon and at other quasi-Masonic societies: therapeutic interests were subsumed within a metaphysical quest, but now that quest regarded the instrument—the medium—as the liminal connection between this world and a greater reality, the spirit spheres that, according to Davis and others, surround and interpenetrate this earthly sphere. Therefore, the merging of the alternate-consciousness paradigm, a scientific practice for inducing varying levels of consciousness within the human mind, and the alternate-reality paradigm, the worldview that recognizes the existence and fosters the accessibility of greater intelligences within the universe, occurred at this moment and were soon to be appropriated by the Fox sisters and a host of other mediums over the next few years.

The practice of mediumship differed in these subtle ways from that of the magnetic subjects and also from the practices of the Shaker instruments, principally in the conceptions that informed their understanding regarding the nature and purposes of their practices. For the early magnetizers, this practice was based on the existence and manipulation of a quasi-physical fluid that had salutary effects on health, dependent on a rapport with the subject and on the will of the operator. For the Shakers, it provided continued guidance and succor from Mother Ann for the proper conduct of Shaker life, whereas, for Davis and those who followed, the practice of psychic mediumship comprised no less than a breaking of the veil between this sphere and an afterworld. Davis makes the point forcefully in his autobiography. He bemoaned the misapprehension as to what his mediumship consisted of, "as if my mind (while in the superior condition) were an insensible, unintelligent, and passive substance, or spout, through which disembodied personages express or promulgate their own specific opinions! This is an egregious error—a most unwholesome representation." He insisted that mediums were "not . . . playing the part of insensate automatons under incessant inspirations from spirits, but that we are self-existent and responsible beings" (Davis 1857, 311).

From this point on, Davis became involved in a number of reformist ventures. He endorsed virtually every contemporary reform, including antislavery, temperance, and women's rights. His radical anticlericalism was palpable and did much to influence this trend within the early spiritualist movement. Davis was equally hostile to Protestants and Catholics, commenting, "It is hard to determine which is the worst enemy of freedom and humanity, the party that would make the church our master, or those who would give to us the Bible as sovereign" (1854, 26). In this 1854 speech, he was especially hard on Christianity:

> It may be argued that civilization is not a child of Christianity— that its authority leads to bigotry and intolerance—that it is no better than the best part of any other religion—that it does not satisfy but stultifies the heart, and confounds the head—that from the Bible we get our worst ideas of God—that the scheme of salvation does not save the world from sin, slavery and discords— that its authority is good only so far as its contents stand the test of conscience and of scientific principles. (20)

Davis kept aloof from the new trends in spiritualism, especially after the hiatus of the Civil War. Like many of the leading figures in the movement during the 1850s, he was primarily interested in spiritualism as a new philosophy and religious dispensation. Davis sincerely believed that higher spheres were trying to help humans transform this one (Walters 1978, 168). Eventually he obtained an M.D. degree and practiced as a doctor and herbalist in Boston until his death in 1910. In 1886, a request from the Seybert commission, then investigating spiritualist phenomena, to exhibit his powers was declined. In a letter written to H. Furness, dated March 24, 1886, he stated, "[I]t is not apparent to me that I can subserve any of the purposes of your valued Commission." He then related how, from 1843 to 1846, his "days and evenings were frequently given to *tests* of Clairvoyance at short range, so to speak": this included the usual fare of seeing without physical eyes into closed books, perceiving objects at a distance, and reading thoughts a few miles away. But then a change came upon him as to the exercise of the clairvoyant faculty:

> [I]n 1846, when I commenced the "Revelations," and from that time to the present my perceptions are at long range, and during all this long period my state, mentally, is what I have in my books defined and elucidated as "The Superior Condition," which rarely calls for the exercise of clairvoyance.

He added, somewhat condescendingly, that, although he could truthfully say that he now possessed no powers of that kind, "there are, I think, several short range clairvoyants—sometimes "fortune tellers" perhaps, which signifies their method of earning daily bread—who could, doubtless, demonstrate for you and your Committee the *reality* of the faculty" (Davis 1886, Furness Papers).

In this second convergence of mesmeric and Swedenborgian influences, a Swedenborgian cosmology was so palpable that Arthur Conan Doyle, a later champion of spiritualism, could ask, "Is it not a feasible hypothesis that the power which controlled Davis was actually Swedenborg?" (1926, 1:54–55). The influence of Davis on the spiritualist movement was pervasive, although he kept an aloof distance from the mainstream of mediums that arose after the 1850s. His *Principles of Nature . . .* became the virtual bible of the movement, even though spiritualists rejected sacerdotalism in all its forms, including the acceptance of specific doctrines.

Moreover, Davis provided a vocabulary, coining common terms like the "Summerland" as a name for the modern paradise. In 1863, he devised a system of Lyceum schools, based on similar establishments he had visited in heaven. These spiritualist Sunday schools operated in America and throughout the British Empire and remained popular well into the twentieth century. Following his advice, spiritualists wore white at funerals and in other ways transformed internments into events that emphasized continuity rather than separation. Instead of delivering eulogies, mediums, usually entranced, would convey messages from the recently deceased. Often these would describe the journey away from earth, enjoining those left behind to consider the beautiful destination arrived at and the continuing concern and love of the deceased for those who had survived them (Braude 1989, 54).

Certainly Davis deplored the "body snatchers" of the following decades, mediums who channeled the banal reassurances from departed loved ones that later jammed the psychic airwaves, and he had little time for the physical phenomena that became popular in England and America from the 1870s. By 1878, Davis had broken off with mainstream spiritualism, which he saw flowing off into magic and superstition. It seems that he rejected attempts by some of those like S. B. Brittan, along with Lyon, Fishbough, and C. E. Fernald, all connected with the *Univercoelum and Spiritual Philosopher*, to found a new religious sect and to retain Davis as their oracle. He rebelled and broke up their plans (Fuller 1982, 99; Walters 1978, 168; Chase 1888, 27).

Thomas Lake Harris

A postscript to Davis in this early period of spiritualism's advent was the career of Reverend Thomas Lake Harris. His metaphysical pretensions were grand, and he straddled the tendentious region between Universalism, Swedenborgianism, and spiritualism, all of which he declaimed at various times. As spiritualism became institutionalized, bringing a greater curiosity for the immediate questions of "survival," this eclipsed the influence not only of Davis and Harris but of others like the Howitt group in England, whose main interests were in the philosophical basis of a regenerated faith.

Thomas Lake Harris was perhaps the last of the long line of prophets from the British Isles to come within our period of study. Harris regarded himself as a prophet and a visionary. Born in Stratford, his family immigrated to the United States when he was a boy. Harris trained first for the Baptist ministry but converted to Universalism in 1843. Adopting the teachings of Andrew Jackson Davis, for a time he became a fanatical spiritualist. Through the mediumship of a Mrs. Benedict, the Apostolic Circle at Auburn, New York, obtained communications from various apostles and biblical prophets; its spiritual leader was said to be the Apostle Paul. In 1849, James D. Scott, a Seventh Day Baptist minister from Brooklyn, joined this circle, now known as the Apostolic Movement. Scott was joined by Thomas Lake Harris, and together they established a religious community at Mountain Cove, Virginia, one of the few spiritualist ventures into communitarianism, a cooperative agricultural colony with about a hundred members. Harris served as spiritualist medium along with Scott, and both received "divine Instructions" about the direction that the colony should take (Nelson 1969, 18–19).

When the Mountain Cove community failed, Harris came to New York where he threw himself violently into the spiritualistic movement. He moved away from spiritualism when "manifestations" began to be emphasized with the Fox sisters and a host of other mediums who surfaced in the 1850s. He was repelled by this trend to external manifestations, along with the democratic style of the emerging movement. Harris believed that mediumship should be practiced only by consecrated vessels like himself and that the emphasis should be in the "spirit of Christ, which descends to be immanent in the heart." After breaking with Davis, Harris organized the Independent Church congregation in New York City and rejected spiritualism in favor of Christianity. In this early period, Harris was in religious turmoil, as his faith now encompassed Jesus, Davis, and Swedenborg (Doyle 1926, 1:120-121; Moore 1977, 17–18; Fogarty 1990, 30–31).

At the invitation of New Church members there, Harris removed to New Orleans in 1854, where he organized a pseudo-New Church society, the Church of the Good Shepherd, a spiritualistically inclined Swedenborgian congregation condemned by the New Church as "disorderly and containing spiritistic proceedings" (Odhner 1904, 1:590). During the late 1850s, Harris was turning toward Swedenborgianism. Soon, however, he developed his own variant on the New Church creed. He believed certain truths about the spiritual world had been revealed to him, as they had been revealed to Swedenborg. He claimed to be adhering to Swedenborg's original doctrines and to the philosophical basis of his faith. Christ was taught as the true God, but Harris now believed he had been led by providence "to add other and vital matters which were unknown until they were revealed through him." Like Davis, he viewed the trance state as a means to discover one's own true divinity. And like Worcester, and then Davis, he believed himself to be guided by the spirit of the great Swede. After a troubling period when he was beset by frightening daemons, he began preaching a mystical doctrine of "Two-in-One."

In 1859, Harris announced to a congregation in New York that he had now developed into the third apostolic, or missionary, degree and was called to preach in England. His preaching, set forth in language of vague grandiloquence, now promoted a mystical Christianity colored by Swedenborgian and spiritistic notions (Fogarty 1990, 42; Podmore 1963, 2:26). He made the grandiose assertion that he was now a "pivotal man" operating between the forces of heaven and hell and between body and spirit. He taught that certitude of our divine estate would come by a process he called "divine respiration," a reconnection with God through the breath, a state of consciousness that consecrated the senses (Noyes 1870, 580–581; Fuller 1982, 96). This idea draws vaguely on the doctrine of influx, although in this formulation it seems to have more closely resembled the Hindu notion of *prana*. Swedenborg had taught external and internal breathing; he had seen how this internal breath, which comes from the spiritual world, constitutes the very life of the spirit (Suzuki 1996, 51-52). Harris preached by these means the "final entrance into eternal conjugal love," a merging with one's spiritual counterpart.

In the same year, 1859, Harris returned to England, with the support of his American congregations, where he gained fame for his eloquence. William Howitt was among those who attended these lectures, which he regarded as "abundant proofs of the magnificent results [of "inner breathing"]. His extempore sermons were the only realisation of my conceptions of eloquence; at once full, unforced, outgushing, unstinted, and absorbing. They were triumphant embodiments of sublime poetry, and a stern, unsparing, yet loving and burning theology" (Doyle 1926, 122–123; Watts 1883, 281). While lecturing at Steinway Hall, London, in 1860, he met Lady Oliphant. His wild eloquence so affected her that she brought her son, Laurence Oliphant (1829–1888), who came to regard Harris as "the greatest poet of the age as yet unknown to fame." Both mother and son surrendered themselves entirely to Harris and went forth to a long period of manual labor in yet another new colony at Brocton, New York, recently commenced by Harris, the Brotherhood of the New Life. Eventually, Harris and his devotees, numbering about one hundred, moved further West. From 1875, the Brotherhood was situated at Fountain Grove, California, on seven hundred acres near Santa Rosa, where he ran a prosperous vineyard (Fogarty 1990, 30–31).

Harris is worthy of note chiefly for his attempts to synthesize conceptions drawn from spiritualism and Swedenborg. For a brief period at the end of the 1850s, during his lecture tour in England, he was the cause of yet further dissension within the New Church. In 1861, he became associated with the London New Church society in Bloomsbury. William White (1831?–1890) was agent and manager, and along with the secretary W. M. Wilkinson, brother of Garth Wilkinson, and other members he became attracted to spiritism through the activities of T. L. Harris. White began publishing some of Harris's works and made the Swedenborg Society's premises a depository of spiritualistic publications. He and Wilkinson defied the committee's request to cease this practice and even hired some toughs to attack the bailiffs whom the committee had installed. The matter was eventually resolved in the courts (Griffith 1960, 22).

Among Harris's supporters was Edward Brotherton, an English member of the New Church. William White published an apologia penned by Brotherton, *Spiritualism, Swedenborg and the New Church*. There is something familiar about the tone and the comments, as in his assertion that "Mr Harris's opponents do not deny the reality of his spiritual experiences, but think he is deceived unconsciously by spirits." He agreed that in much of what other spiritualists wrote "pantheism lies at the heart, . . . [and] the idea of development takes the place of regeneration." But he insists that this was not the case with Harris, who "recognises the divine Humanity." As Brotherton notes, the conundrum for Harris was that "if he agrees with Swedenborg, he has of course plagiarised; if he disagrees, he is [regarded as] a heretic" (Brotherton 1860, 25–26).

The contentious issue of spirit contact was again raised, wondering whether Harris's opponents would "wish to exclude all spirit-dictations and spirit-writing" (Brotherton 1860, 41), given that even the venerable Reverend John Clowes had written some of his sermons and published works under spirit influence. He asserts that Swedenborg never imagined that his gift was unique or that it was disorderly for all others but himself to exercise spiritual vision. Among the most interesting of Brotherton's arguments is that even "Disorderly Spiritualism," if rightly seen, was a far more important phenomenon than most readers of Swedenborg suppose, for it would have its uses in proving that "it is man's birthright to know both worlds" (Brotherton 1860, 41, 43). By means of external evidence, spiritualism would help to destroy the old theological beliefs, so that the "Old Church already decayed in its outward power and influence, will become a wreck from the explosion of its own spiritual forces" (46–47).

Brotherton's main contention was that spiritual intercourse should be allowed within the New Church, and that this "will bring the new Heaven." Brotherton, White, and W. M. Wilkinson, among others, were worried that, with the arrival of the new spiritualist phenomena, "a contagion of pantheism and absolute selfishness" was spreading. In America especially, the teachings of spirit-communicators were singularly uniform, and included

> a denial of any divine authority in the Word,—pretended acknowledgement of Christ as an advanced medium,— assumption of superiority to Him,—a claim for this New Era of an exaltation above all former ages,—scorn of any notions of moral evil,—universal progression and continual development, —and liberty to break off the marriage bond where not congenial (Brotherton 1860, 48).

Brotherton and his fellow schismatics reasoned that it was far better for the New Church to take the lead in this new wave of spirit contact than to leave it to the "disorderly" hordes of spiritualism. He also took a swipe at the protagonists of the established New Church: "how shall we classify the casting of lots to obtain the authority to ordain ministers?" Was this to be regarded as "disorderly, or a false pretence?" (49).

The Covert Enlightenment

Social Change in the Burned-over District

According to Whitney Cross, the instrumental role played by the revivalists in the 1830s had been to establish "the notion that special efforts under a person of particular talents would create a keener spirituality than the ordinary course of events could achieve" (quoted in Fuller 1982, 77). Shakerism, Mormonism, Adventism, communitarianism, and millenarianism all emerged among those engaged in a protracted search for new ways of securing what he calls "the automatically operant Holy Spirit to descend and symbolize the start of the New Life" (Cross 1965, 181). Cross and Fuller are agreed that mesmerism entered into American cultural life as but one more permutation of the nation's revivalist heritage. Like revivalism, Mesmerism "provided confused individuals with an intense experience thought to bring them into an interior harmony with unseen spiritual forces" (Fuller 1982, 77–79). But whereas the evangelical spirit placed absolute faith in God and his ways, the mesmerists, breaking forever with the Calvinist heritage, actually encouraged "the tendency to impose human reason onto the ways of God" (Fuller 1982, 77–79). In this continuing cultural trend toward the secularization of the soul, it now became possible to speak of the difference between the human being's higher and lower natures in nontheological language.

So it was that from among the leftward-tending former ultraists, together with numerous Universalists, Quakers, and other seekers, the study of lowly animal magnetism was made to point to higher things. The cultural product was the synthesis of the paradigms emanating from the covert Enlightenment, the advent of mediumship, and the séance. Magnetic phenomena were explicable only by "some grand and fundamental law of our being that has hitherto escaped detection," and clairvoyance was regarded as a new science, "the true philosophy" of the age, wherein the spiritual was the "region of causes" and "the worlds of matter and of mind" were conjoined (Cross 1965, 342). To many of the spiritualist faithful, and more transiently among some adherents of the New Church, the trance seemed "so near an approximation to the state of spirits divested of the body" (quoted in Cross 1965, 342) that it illustrated the basic laws of the spiritual world. Indeed, it had seemed to George Bush at an early phase as if mesmerism had "been developed in this age with the express design of confirming the message of Swedenborg" (Bush 1847, 168). But even in his most enthusiastic moments, he insisted on the important caveat that the proof of its truth and the breadth of its appeal depended ultimately upon its attestation by "the voice of Reason and the voice of revelation" (quoted in Cross 1965, 342).

Robert Fuller's insightful analysis enables mesmerism in its American variants to be located within the revivalist tradition and shows how the growing dichotomy between "religion" and "science" then yawning for many earnest people, those who, in Marcus Clarke's apt phrase "would fain believe, but for their reason ... and reason, but for their belief" was bridged (1876, 65). During the 1840s and 1850s, many former revivalists transferred their attention to religious causes they considered more progressive. In particular, spiritualism, Universalism, and Swedenborgianism all responded to a growing concern to unite the forms of both ecstatic experience and "scientific" thinking into a single religious system (Fuller 1982, 81). Thus was born the spiritualist movement.

CONCLUSION

The developing paradigms of mind and cosmos that are the principal focus of this book would lead to a radical new understanding that "discovered" the unconscious in the course of the nineteenth century. These were puissant phenomena, covering the whole of the culture of the West and extending in both "inner" and "outer" directions: to the infinite Cosmos with Boëhme and Swedenborg and to the deepest, or highest, regions of the individual consciousness with the work of Mesmer, Puységur, F.W.H. Myers (1843–1901), and Freud. The former ushered in a new theology and the latter a new psychology. Along the way, current paradigms were transformed as they filtered through the minds of mystics and mesmerists, "groaners," prophets and prophetesses, "men with beards," and other agents, until they became the basis of the new religious phenomenon of the séance and the medium.

This study has endeavored to elaborate the transformation of two sets of ideas arising from the work of the extraordinary savants of the eighteenth-century Enlightenment, F. A. Mesmer and Emanuel Swedenborg. With the advent of the mediumistic séance, the resultant synthesis of their systems of ideas into a new form in the nineteenth century would hold great appeal to a wide array of religious seekers, mostly among the working classes. This by no means implies a notion of paradigms self-existing as entities on their own, but that they are shared, frequently confused, sometimes contradictory, but always changing phenomena that, occurring among significant groups of individuals, constituted a cultural transformation. This analogical connection or cultural transformation resulted in a paradigm shift that in significant ways guided the worldview and the values of numbers of persons for well over a century. Although they remained a miniscule minority of the total populace—at its peak, spiritualism drew somewhat less than five million according to the most generous estimates—the transformation thus generated would have collateral significance in a number of fields, including theology, medicine, and psychology.

That influence would persist and increase over future generations. More than any other religious teacher, Emanuel Swedenborg opened the popular imagination of the thinking and reading public to what he called the spiritual and celestial worlds, just as Franz Anton Mesmer indirectly opened the way for the discovery of states and levels within the human mind and consciousness. Together their conceptions subtly transformed ways of thinking about the human organism, both in its mental and in its spiritual aspects. The result was nothing less than a revolution, first in popular theology, especially in respect to the conditions of a future life and the destiny of the human spirit, and second in the clinical, theoretical, and practical applications of mesmerism, later known as hypnotism. In this way, the evolving paradigms of alternate-consciousness and alternate-reality, whose contours we have traced, effected a subtle yet potent transformation in conceptions both of the inner world of mind and the infinite outer cosmos.

As the influence of Mesmer declined in Europe after the heightened excitement in Paris during the mid-1780s and as the French *revolutionnaires* turned most people to thinking of more immediate matters, both mesmerism and Swedenborgianism went increasingly underground. In the Philosophic and Exegetic Society's letter of June 1787, we have seen how their views were becoming entwined in the minds of occultists, freemasons, and *Illuminati*. They had always been a

Conclusion

significant part of the European intelligentsia; and with a ready conduit of the *Societés de L'Harmonie* and certain other hermetic, cabalistic, and similar groups in Germany, England, and France, a merging of ideas and beliefs drawn from a wide realm of traditions were now witnessed. Into this occult and dispensational grab-bag went a mixture of new and old traditions, such as the lineage of Paracelsus and Böehme, and most importantly in this lineage, the writings of Emanuel Swedenborg. Minor conclaves like the Buchanites and the followers of Richard Brothers in Britain, as well as quasi-Masonic societies like the Avignon Society in France, all drew on cabalistic and hermetic lore, but also on Catholic mysticism in the cult of the Virgin Mary, on spiritualism in its numerous variegations, and on Swedenborg's cosmological writings, along with the theories and practices of animal magnetism. This process was part of the continuing merging of ideas ostensibly dealing with different orders of reality, but now adapted to other purposes, within differing frameworks and under changing conditions.

Whereas curative therapies were the chief concern of the originators of magnetic somnambulism, the fashion for direct knowledge of other levels of being, surely an Enlightenment concern in its quest for empirical certitude, led to the appropriation of this ready conduit to the inner self (not yet widely known as the unconscious or subconscious), so as to communicate with the denizens of those alleged spheres. There was also a large seepage of selected parts of Swedenborg's writings that eventually found their way into both secularized and pantheistic versions of plebeian spiritualism and in the Christian spiritualism that flourished briefly during the 1850s. It was during this first decade of the organized movement, especially in England, that middle-class spiritualists like the Howitt circle flourished, well acquainted both with the system of Swedenborg and with mesmeric phenomena.

Thus a new occult or dispensational movement took root in Europe, while at the same time German mystical somnambulism grew as the French adherents were being terrorized or were scattering to England and elsewhere. The movement of persons and ideas was still very much from East to West shortly after the American war of independence. Within two decades, migrants and visitors like Lafayette had brought over the mesmeric system, which did not take root until the 1830s.

The Covert Enlightenment

The appeal of Swedenborg's complex system to a broad spectrum of enquirers occurred, like all human experience, within an historical and cultural context. In the milieu of the high Enlightenment, its ineluctable connection at this period was with mesmerism and the occult revival. The hostility of the Lutheran clergy in Sweden meant that the main body of adherents was gathered elsewhere for at least a generation. In England, Swedenborg's teachings attracted a small but influential body of followers, leading to the early diffusion of his works throughout the Atlantic world and even to organized missionary work. In the late 1770s, Swedenborg's teachings on human regeneration, in particular, led to the formation of small and scattered assemblies, usually study groups within existing denominations, like those of the Reverend John Clowes at Manchester and the Reverend Jacob Duché at Philadelphia. In France, a more occult understanding of Swedenborg was transmitted through the conduit of the Scottish freemasonic fraternities and other societies, which in turn bred organizations like Dom Antoine Pernety's Avignon Society (Garrett 1975, 104ff). The Avignon Society became increasingly millenarian, a trend soon exacerbated by the chaos and repression of the French Revolution. As an occultist branch of Swedenborg's influence, it would not outlast the century, but it did have a considerable effect during its last two decades, when it attracted interested persons from England, Sweden, and other European countries.

From the early 1780s, the Swedenborgian movement became slowly established in the United States. John Brooke in a recent study has linked Mormonism to the European hermetic tradition and freemasonry, arguing that Joseph Smith and his acolytes had strong links with European hermeticism. Both Swedenborg and Mesmer are located within this tradition, its latest phase emanating from the 1730s, and Chevalier Ramsay's reformed Scottish Freemasonry in France. Brooke argues that a hermetic brotherhood ensconced in freemasonry and the *Illuminati* indirectly provided Smith with some of his heterodox opinions and that, after 1730, religious hermeticism became grounded principally in Swedenborg, whose thought fused hermetic philosophy, in the sense of being based on secret or hidden lore, and religious dispensentionalism, in his claims to be the harbinger of a new Christian revelation. It is claimed also that Mesmer's discovery of a universal fluid drew upon the hermetic knowledge of previous centuries. While no strong evidence is adduced for either Swedenborg's or Mesmer's participation in secret societies, a valid inference is drawn, in that Masonic and other secret or quasi-secret associations did provide a ready conduit for the transmission of heterodox ideas of all kinds. These are perhaps the first indications of the close if shadowy relations existing between Swedenborgian and other underground movements throughout the Enlightenment, while it also strengthens the suggestion of European influence on the cultural geography of the northeastern United States and especially the burned-over district of western New York, where Mormonism and a host of other religious reforms had their origins (Brooke 1994, 94–97; Schuchard 1988, 369).

In the United States, the secular, communitarian impulse, the "right fork" of reform, although its main aims were neither other worlds nor alternative curative therapies, brought forward the basis of the paradigms inherited from the eighteenth-century covert Enlightenment in culturally significant ways. From the Shakers and the Owenite experiments to Brook Farm, considerable attention was paid in various ways to the occult inheritance from Swedenborg and Mesmer. Just as the magnetic movement helped the ultraist revivals by making seekers hungry for more immediate fare, so the Swedenborgian outlook helped them to break free of a view of the universe based upon a supposed chasm between God and humankind, to be bridged only by God's grace and to be manifest in a righteous providence that on the American frontier was not always self-evident. While adherents of Fourier and Swedenborg discerned parallels between their principal doctrines, the idea of emanations of spirit life interposing between the Deity and his creation, since the advent of the startling phenomena associated with magnetism, had acquired a more tangible provenance in the minds of many persons on the cultural fringe, both in Europe and America.

Established in 1792, Swedenborgians in America were among the first to propound a doctrine of spiritual influence, intimately related to the theology and moral imperatives of spiritual regeneration. "Consociation" with spirits and angels, in Swedenborg's understanding was a fact of the inner life (*Heaven and Hell* §247). It required of the believer the constant uplifting of thought and motive, lest infernal influences should lead him or her away from the path of righteousness. Perhaps to realize their fundamental teaching that the purpose of existence was to make an angelic heaven on earth, some Swedenborgians were drawn into various social reforms. We have seen their brief 1820s experiment at Yellow Springs, while Brook Farm was the most famous of the communities that sprang up in rural New England and in the West during the optimistic decade of the 1840s.

Soon contention broke out in the New Church when the eternal status of Swedenborg's revelation was being questioned by some members. They argued that it might now be updated in view of the vastly changed state of society since his day, and they believed that the induction of magnetism or artificial somnambulism into instruments could yield such supplementary teachings. Others even revisited the origins of the New Church and posited Swedenborg's as a "Third Testament." In these middle decades of the nineteenth century, there was much questioning of the status of the Swedenborgian ministry, since it had been instituted by the layman Robert Hindmarsh in London on the casting of lots, the role of minister which fell to his brother James Hindmarsh being deemed by some as inappropriate. Questions arose also as to the very status of Swedenborg as "final" revelator. This prompted the arising of schisms like New Era, the activities of the Reverend Henry Weller, then indirectly the claims of A. J. Davis and T. L. Harris as harbingers from the great Swede for an updated, but not necessarily a New Church, message of regeneration. At the same time, an induced mechanism of magnetic phenomena was invoked to bridge the liminal zone with a greater reality, repeating a pattern discerned more than a century before in Puységur, Barberin, and St. Martin.

Influence is, of course, difficult to assess. How much the beliefs and practices of one sect or social grouping affect those with whom they come into contact depends on how that contact is made: through writing or polemics or, in the nineteenth century, via the platform and the pulpit. I have argued that the diffusion of leading occult ideas in late eighteenth-century Europe was not only instrumental not only to the direct lineal groupings of believers like the harmonial societies or the New Church, but

Conclusion

moreover that they were revitalized and, in the systems of Swedenborg and Mesmer, transformed through their exposure to American conditions. There they took a new form, congenial to the secular and reform-drenched *mentalitées* of the generation of Americans who came of age in the 1840s. This conjunction brought forward the spiritualist movement.

In thus tracing the complex webs of significant interactions between occultism, mesmerism, and popular culture, we have set the scene for the reversal of that cultural trend whereby European systems were introduced to the New World; through this peculiar amalgam of the 1840s, the secular religion of spiritualism came back to England and the Continent, which resulted in turn in a new range of reactions and formulations. Among the most significant were the taking up by one small branch of science, mostly physicists, in the Old World of the investigation of spiritualist phenomena. This brought strong denunciations of the alleged phenomena by the majority of scientists in Europe. A few years later, the medical branch of European science took up the study and practice of what was now called hypnotism. We therefore face an interesting cyclic phenomenon in the two disparate world views of Mesmer, the medical scientist, and Swedenborg, the scientist turned theologian: they merged in the understandings first of an educated elite of occultists, then poured forth in the maelstrom of popular culture as carnival hypnotism and popular mysticism and daemonism, to be finally reconsidered by an educated and professional class for their therapeutic efficacy and their theoretical implications.

In America, with no state church, a rugged individualism flourished that made every person his or her own popular psychologist and the judge of all doctrines. Here new social reforms and new religions abounded, whereas in Catholic France, much of the Swedenborgian influence stayed within Masonic or mystical organizations. And with a strong physiological and medical tradition, the rediscovery of mesmeric phenomena in France—with Charles Richet's studies in the 1870s, which were then given university recognition in Charcot's famous demonstrations and his paper in 1882—was tied firmly to the medical model. Understood as a manifestation of pathological conditions, hypnotism was employed by these researchers as a means of curing those pathologies by the artificial induction of crises. Thus we are back at the insights of Mesmer and

Puységur. Put another way, the alternate-consciousness paradigm in France was medicalized, while the alternate-reality paradigm did not make much impact except upon a small elite. The spiritism of Allan Kardec (1804–1869) and his followers never gained the wide audience that spiritualism did in England and the United States during these same years. Nevertheless, the mediumistic paradigm had effects even in France: the bold introduction of hypnotism into medical practice by Charcot ushered in a new era for French psychology and psychiatry, while the Nancy School of Ambrose-August Liébeault (1823–1904) and Hippolyte Bernheim brought "suggestion" into broader application. The effects of this new wave of interest in the therapeutic possibilities of artificial somnambulism stimulated the work of the French psychotherapist Pierre Janet, who had studied with Charcot. That decisive event in the history of psychotherapy on the Continent, in turn, had a stimulating effect on others, especially on the work of Josef Breuer (1842–1925) and Sigmund Freud.

In the longer term, other results would follow from the mediumistic paradigm, the resultant synthesis of the alternate-consciousness and alternate-reality paradigms. In England, the French research stimulated the independent efforts of Edmund Gurney (1847–1888), F.W.H. Myers and the Sidgwicks (Eleanor M., 1845–1936; Henry, 1938–1900), in other cognate directions (Broad 1965, passim; Myers 1913, introduction). When the Society for Psychical Research was formed in London in 1882, talk of hypnotism and spiritualism engaged the curiosity of numbers of educated persons. Although many could not accept the assumptions of "community of sensation" of the former or the spiritualist theory of survival, an increasing interest in the nature of the human mind and consciousness was evident in a number of ways. If the universe were friendly, it would exhibit a teleology or divine purpose. The spirits of the departed would not be lost, nor would they have failed to learn lessons from their physical existence. A sense of order and continuity in the cosmos implied also the continuing discovery of laws, both in the physical world, and in what Myers called the "metetherial worlds" (Myers 1913, 9 and passim). Some of their labors were devoted to the establishment of laws for telepathic communication and hypnotic trance. Again, if the universe were a friendly and hospitable place, ultimately the knowledge of the soul—and its nature and destiny—would be revealed to patient enquiry. Hence, the concepts of human individuality and those concerning the destiny of human existence were closely related to the S. P. R.'s larger aims of divulging new powers inherent in the human personality understood in its totality. A radical and extended notion of the human individuality arose out of their early work with telepathy and hypnotism in the "Subliminal Self" theory of Myers and William James, but this was connected also with the possibility of establishing a bridge between this world and the next, through trance mediumship. In the efforts at least of Myers and Richard Hodgson (1855–1905), and less intensively in those of the Sidgwicks, these two aims can be seen in inherent tension, the metaphysical and the scientific, in their experiments conducted according to what they regarded as strictly scientific canons.

From its formation in the early 1880s until World War I, the S. P. R. conducted the principal inquiries concerning human experience and beliefs about altered states of consciousness and reality; it became the locus for addressing a wide variety of interrelated concerns, including hypnotism, telepathy, and mental and physical mediumship. These detailed and time-consuming inquiries were conducted by a small band of energetic researchers in the United States and in Great Britain. In these series of investigations into a wide variety of alleged phenomena, the common basis was that they pointed to powers or means of communication between mind and mind that seemed to transcend those acknowledged by science. The S. P. R.'s experimental work, published in its own *Proceedings* and *Journal*, exerted a significant influence upon many professional and academic minds of that generation, helping to shape current ideas regarding the human mind and its capacities, along with a somewhat lesser, yet still significant, influence on current social and religious debates.

While they were less interested in therapeutics, the S. P. R. group was intimately concerned with the implications, if such phenomena could be scientifically verified, to a wider realm of speculation: how were these influences being witnessed at the Salpêtrière and with Janet at LeHavre possible, and what were the implications for metaphysical inquiry of phenomena like distant viewing or traveling clairvoyance (*sommeil à distance*)? The psychical aspects of these phenomena that they regarded as their mandate to explore, and thus the psychological developments in France, turned minds to the wider questions of the nature of consciousness and the means of communication directly between mind and mind. It was only a short step from artificial somnambulism to mediumship and from telepathy between the living to the positing of telepathic communication between the living and the departed. Whether this were effected, as Gurney believed, through a fluid, or as Myers preferred, via the higher subliminal aspects of the total human personality, they point again to an implicit *rapprochement* between two seminal paradigms, extant now within the high culture of England (Cerullo 1982, 65; Moore 1977, 138, 149, and passim).

To those core members of the S. P. R., appalled by the materialism of the wider scientific community and wishing to place all of these alleged phenomena before the tribune of science, the most important subsequent development, crucial to the future history of the S. P. R., was the discovery in Boston by Harvard psychologist William James of the medium Mrs. Leonora Piper (1857–1950). With the advent of Piper, they had "on tap," as it were, a closed and continuing experiment of a living somnambulistic medium. She became the principal focus for the S. P. R.'s labors in the 1880s and beyond, and the psychological and metaphysical problems that they took as their mandate to consider could now be studied in considerable depth and over an extended period. R. L. Moore notes the ironic conclusion that their attempts to convince the scientific community "were doomed to fail because spirit communication and E.S.P. could not be proved with the means of scientific verification Spiritualists and Psychical Researchers had at their disposal" (Moore 1977, xv).

This was the path that the rise of spiritualism betokened in the latter decades of the nineteenth century. Spiritualism, along with Darwin and geology, had loosened the hold of traditional religious forms on men and women, and now the S. P. R. in England and in the United States sought confirmation for the scientific efficacy of the methods that Mesmer and his followers had inadvertently brought into existence a century before for tapping into levels or stages of consciousness, as they pondered the ultimate purpose and destiny of human beings, which Swedenborg's theology and seership declared with pronounced emphasis.

Conclusion

One pattern that has emerged clearly in this discussion of changing paradigms was what might be called the "fragmentation of the ideal." An important difference between the millennial eighteenth- and nineteenth-century radicals of all kinds was in the perceived unity of the religious ideal. While they retained a religious orientation insofar as the object of all salvific work was the work of God, nineteenth-century spiritualists and other heterodox groups were intent on providing a bridge between the sphere of deity and the mundane sphere served by the spirits intermediate between God and humanity. Alfred Russell Wallace (1823–1913), pioneer scientist and spiritualist, put the moral and teleological aspects succinctly in a May 1874 article in the *Fortnightly*. The world, and the whole material universe, Wallace averred,

> exist for the purpose of developing spiritual beings; death is simply a transition from material existence to the first grade of spirit life—and the happiness and the degree of our progress will be wholly dependent upon the use we have made of our faculties and opportunities here.

Such an assault on the cosmos required a mechanism to realize this accessibility; the magnetists provided the method and moreover prepared the popular psyche for this "psychologically based pneumatology." Ancient biblical prophecies were abetted, or replaced, in the 1790s by a new breed of millenarian prophets and prophetesses, then by magnetic subjects, and later by spiritualist mediums. The result was a fragmentation of spiritual authority, as simple faith in the Bible or in the clergy no longer sufficed for that significant section of trans-Atlantic popular culture whose religious sensibilities had been quickened by the revivals and who had moved on to more personal evidences of the glory of Nature and the redeeming hopes of the faithful. It was another aspect of the growth of individualism in religious faith, and these new paradigms provided both a new cosmology of beings intermediate between God and humanity, derived from Swedenborg, and a means for the accession of higher beings, in the first instance through the higher or deeper levels of one's own consciousness, a method derived principally from Mesmer and Puységur.

The Covert Enlightenment

The long-term influence of Swedenborg, who founded no church and who had only a handful of adherents in his lifetime, on all shades of heterodox opinion is difficult to gauge definitively. When Mesmer took Paris by storm in 1778, Swedenborg had been dead for six years. It was not long before some among their adherents began to infer conjunctions between the ideas and practices of their respective innovators. As the new science of animal magnetism came briefly into direct conjunction with Swedenborg's metaphysics, especially his ideas concerning the existence and geography of an afterlife, there resulted a new cultural configuration, whose most potent expression appears around the mid-nineteenth century in spiritualism, especially in the "new" phenomenon of mediumship. Through their discovery of induced somnambulism, Mesmer's followers almost accidentally had provided the mechanism wherewith generations of magnetizers and mediums, whose principal aim was to provide a vehicle for the exploration of other levels of being, produced in the process new raw material making it possible to apply increasingly sophisticated methods to explore the untapped potential of the human mind and consciousness. How this conjunction occurred and its implications for religion and science in the nineteenth century have been the principal concern of this study, to understand better the origins of this conjunction of theological and empirical modes braced within an architectonic of a resurgent interest in biblical prophecy and millenarianism, the events that led to and the effects precipitating from the rediscovery of induced somnambulism, as one important aftermath of the covert Enlightenment.

From the old magnetizers to the revelations of Andrew Jackson Davis, to the spiritualist movement, and finally in the S. P. R.'s attempts to formulate a scientific assessment of all claims of transcendence in the sensory modes of communication and understanding, there is a direct line and something of a mixed lineage. The transformation of ideas and values arising from the changing mental and emotional field of individuals is the stuff of cultural histories, and the premise of this study has been the slow and fitful transformation of two sets of ideas, originating in different intellectual compartments and stemming from the widely disparate interests of two roughly contemporary geniuses of the Enlightenment: the therapeutic, scientific, and ostensibly rationalist line of the physician

Conclusion

Mesmer; and the dispensational, revelatory, and rejuvenating line of the great seer Swedenborg. These were melded into a synthesis of the medium and the séance that in time would yield a new soteriology as well as a new psychological practice. While the latter led to the spiritualist movement, the former heralded a new era in dynamic psychiatry, first in hypnosis, then in the complex work of Janet, Freud, and others in the area of the subconscious causes of mental illness, in multiple personalities, and a whole range of psychological phenomena that now came under their scrutiny. Finally, this new trend was made possible to a large extent due to the pioneering work on hypnosis, mental telepathy, and latterly, mediumship undertaken from the early 1880s by the S. P .R. These were among the seeds sown by these eighteenth-century savants, germinated by several generations of apocalyptic visionaries, millenarians, magnetists, Shakers, and others; and bearing fruit finally in the modern scientific treatment of psychological illness, along with a deepening appreciation of other levels of being, such as have informed both ancient and modern religions and New Age philosophies.

References

Adams, J.T. 1960. *New England in the republic, 1776–1850*. Gloucester, MA: Peter Smith.

Andrews, Edward Deming. 1953. *The people called Shakers*. New York: Oxford University Press.

Arndt, Karl J. 1984. *Economy on the Ohio 1826–1834*. Worcester, MA: The Harmony Society Press.

Ashburner, John. 1867. *Notes and studies in the philosophy of animal magnetism and spiritualism*. London: Bailliere.

Axon, William E. A. 1876. *Biographical notice of Ann Lee, a Manchester prophetess and foundress of the American sect of the Shakers*. Liverpool: T. Brackell.

Barrett, B.F. 1845. Open intercourse with the spiritual world—its dangers and the cautions which they naturally suggest. *The New Jerusalem Magazine* CCXVII (September): 13–28; CCXVII (October): 50–64; CCXIX (November): 89–104.

———. 1849. *Davis's revelations sifted: A review of Rev. T.L. Harris's lectures on "spiritual philosophy."* Cincinnati: n. p.

Barrow, Logie . 1986. *Independent spirits, spiritualism and English plebeians 1850–1910*. London: Routledge & Kegan Paul.

Beilby Porteus Papers. 1787–1809. Lambeth Place Library, London.

Bestor, Arthur E. 1950. *Backwoods utopias*. Philadelphia: University of Pennsylvania Press.

Block, Marguerite Beck. 1984. *The New Church in the new world*. New York: Swedenborg Publishing Association. First published 1932 by Holt, Rinehart and Winston.

Braude, Ann. 1989. *Radical spirits, spiritualism and women's rights in 19th century America*. Oston: Beacon Press.

Bricaud, Joanny. 1927. *Les Illuminés D'Avignon: Étude sur Dom Pernety et son groupe*. Paris, Librairie Critique Émile Nourry.

References

Broad, C.D. 1965. *The life, work and death of Edmund Gurney*. Ph.D. diss., Cambridge University, Trinity College.

Brooke, John L. 1994. *The refiner's fire: The making of Mormon cosmology, 1644-1844*. New York: Cambridge University Press.

Brotherton, Edward. 1860. *Spiritualism, Swedenborg and the New Church*. London: William White.

Bryan, William. 1795. *A testimony of the spirit of truth, concerning Richard Brothers*. London: J. Wright.

Bucke, R. M. 1923. *Cosmic consciousness*. New York: E.P. Dutton.

Bullock, Steven C. 1996. *Revolutionary brotherhood: Freemasonry and the transformation of the American social order, 1730–1840*. Chapel Hill: University of North Carolina Press.

Buranelli, Vincent. 1976. *The wizard from Vienna*. London: Peter Owen.

Bush, George. 1847. *Mesmer and Swedenborg, or the relation of the developments of Mesmerism to the doctrines and disclosures of Swedenborg*. New York: J. Allen.

———. 1852. Pseudo-spiritualism. *The New Church Repository and Monthly Review* 5, no. 7 (July): 334–338; no. 8 (August): 373–377; no. 11 (November): 509–511; no. 12 (December): 533–548.

Bush, George, and B. F. Barrett. 1847. *"Davis's revelations" revealed*. New York: Allen.

Bush's mesmerism. 1847. *The New Church Quarterly Review* I, no.2: 165–185.

Cerullo, J. 1982. *The secularization of the soul: Pyschical research in modern Britain*. Philadelphia: Institute for the Study of Human Issues.

Chapman, John. 1847. *Brief outlines of a work entitled "the principles of nature, her divine revelations and a voice to mankind," by and through Andrew Jackson Davis . . . being the substance of a preface to that work*. London: John Chapman.

Charcot, J. M. 1889 *Lectures on diseases of the nervous system*. London: New Sydenham Society.

Chase, Warren. 1857. *The life-line of the lone one: or, autobiography of the world's child*. Boston: Bela Marsh.

References

———. 1888. *Forty years on the spiritual rostrum.* Boston: Colby & Rich.

Clifton, Charles S. 1995. The forgotten Shakers. *Gnosis* 95: 45–49.

Clowes, J. 1845, [Letter on deceiving spirits.] *New Jerusalem Magazine* XIX (November): 96–97.

———. 1873. *Outlines of Swedenborg's doctrines.* London: Longmans, Green & Co.

Collected Tracts. [1757–1785]. British Library.

Conyngham, Redmond. 1827. An account of the settlement of the Dunkers at Ephrata, in Lancaster County, Pennsylvania. *Memoirs of the Historical Society of Pennsylvania* 2: 135–153.

Cook, E. Wake. 1907. Andrew Jackson Davis and the harmonial philosophy. *Light* 14 (Dec.): 595–597.

Crabtree, Adam. 1985. *Multiple man: Explorations in possession and multiple personality.* New York: Praeger.

———. 1993. *From Mesmer to Freud: Magnetic sleep and the roots of psychological healing.* London: Yale University Press.

Cross, Whitney R. 1965. *The burned-over district: The social and intellectual history of enthusiastic religion in western New York, 1800–1850.* New York: Harper Torchbooks.

Darnton, Robert. 1970. *Mesmerism and the end of the Enlightenment in France.* New York: Schocken.

Davis, Andrew Jackson. 1854. *Free thoughts concerning religion; or, nature versus theology.* Boston: Bela Marsh.

———. 1857. *The magic staff: An autobiography.* New York: J. S. Brown & Co.

———. 1868. *Memoranda of persons, places, and events.* Boston: William White.

———. 1876. *The principles of nature, her divine revelations, and a voice to mankind.* Boston: Colby & Rich.

———. 1886. Letter of A.J. Davis to H. Furness, March 24. Philadelphia, University of Pennsylvania, Van Pelt Library, Furness Papers.

Deakin, Alfred. 1957. *The crisis in Victorian politics 1879–1881.* Edited by J.A. LaNauze and R.M. Crawford. Melbourne: Melbourne University Press.

References

de Giustino, David. 1975. *Conquest of mind: Phrenology and Victorian social thought*. London: Croom Helm.

Denovan, C. 1785. Eight letters between the people called Buchanites and a teacher near Edinburgh. *Tracts 1757–85*. Edinburgh: n.p.

DeVoto, B. 1957. *The year of decision 1846*. London: Eyre and Spottiswoode.

Dods, John Bovee. 1876. *The philosophy of mesmerism and electrical psychology*. London: James Burns.

Doyle, A. Conan. 1926. *The history of spiritualism*. 2 vols. London: Cassell.

Duss, John S. 1972. *The Harmonist: A personal history*. Philadelphia: Porcupine Press.

E.A.B. 1845. Man a microcosm. *The New Jerusalem Magazine* CCXII (April): 293–306

Eckhardt, Celia Morris. 1984. *Fanny Wright: Rebel in America*. Cambridge, MA: Harvard University Press.

Elkin, A. P. 1977. *Aboriginal men of high degree*. St. Lucia: University of Queensland Press.

Ellenberger, Henri F. 1970. *The discovery of the unconscious: The history and evolution of dynamic psychiatry*. New York: Basic Books.

Elliott, Josephine M. 1969. *To Holland and to New Harmony: Robert Dale Owen's travel journal 1825–1826*. Indianapolis: Indiana Historical Society.

Emerson, Ralph Waldo. 1980. *Representative men*. Malibu, CA: J.Simon. A reprint of 1883 edition.

Fernald, C.E. 1848. Supernaturalism. *The New Church Repository and Monthly Review* 1, no. 5 (May): 259–266.

———. 1858. Spiritualism. *The Monthly Observer and New Church Record* 11 (Jan.–Dec.): 406–412.

Flaxmer, Sarah. 1795. *Satan revealed, or the dragon overcome, with an explanation of the twelfth chapter of the Revelations, and also a testimony that Richard Brothers is a prophet sent from the Lord*. London: n.p.

Fogarty, Robert S. 1990. *All things new: American communes and utopian movements, 1860–1914*. Chicago: University of Chicago Press.

References

Fuller, Robert C. 1982. *Mesmerism and the Americans cure of souls.* Philadelphia: University of Pennsylvania Press.

———. 1986. *Americans and the unconscious.* New York: Oxford University Press.

Gabay, Alfred J. *Messages from beyond: Spiritualism and spiritualists in Melbourne's golden age 1870-1890.* Carlton, Melbourne: Melbourne University Press.

Garrett, Clarke. 1975. *Respectable folly: Millenarians and the French Revolution in France and England.* Baltimore: The Johns Hopkins University Press.

———. 1984. Swedenborg and the mystical Enlightenment in late eighteenth-century England. *Journal of the History of Ideas* 45: 67–81.

Gauld, Alan. 1968. *The founders of psychical research.* New York: Schocken Books.

———. 1995. *A history of hypnotism.* New York: Cambridge University Press.

Gladish, Robert W. 1983. *Swedenborg, Fourier and the America of the 1840s.* Bryn Athyn, PA: Swedenborg Scientific Association.

Goen, C. C. 1962. *Revivalism and separatism in New England, 1740–1800,* New Haven, CT: Yale University Press.

Goldsmith, Barbara. 1998. *Other powers: The age of suffrage, spiritualism, and the scandalous Victoria.* New York: Knopf.

Goldsmith, Margaret. 1934. *Franz Anton Mesmer: The history of an idea.* London: Arthur Barker.

Griffith, Freda G. 1960. *The Swedenborg Society 1810–1960.* London: Chiswick Press.

Grimm, Friedrich Melchior de. 1830. *Correspondance littéraire, philosophique et critique de Grimm et de Diderot,* 10 vols. Paris: Chez Furne, Libraire.

Halhed, Nathaniel Brassey. 1795. *Testimony of the authenticity of the prophecies of Richard Brothers and of his mission to recall the Jews.* London: H. D. Symonds.

Harrison, J.F.C. 1979. *The second coming: Popular millenarianism 1780–1850.* London: Routledge & Kegan Paul.

References

Hempel, Charles Julius. 1848. *The true organization of the New Church as indicated in the writings of Emanuel Swedenborg, and demonstrated by Charles Fourier.* New York: William Radde.

Higginson, T.W. 1968. *Cheerful yesterdays.* New York: Arno Press.

Hilliard, David. 1988. Emanuel Swedenborg and the New Church in South Australia. *Journal of the Historical Society of South Australia* 16: 70–86.

Hindmarsh, Robert. 1832. Anecdote of the late Rev. Mr. Clowes. *Intellectual Repository* XV (May): 123–124.

———. 1861. *Rise and progress of the New Jerusalem church in England, America, and other parts.* London: Hodson & Co.

Hinds, William A. 1878. *American communities.* Oneida, NY: Office of the American Socialist.

Holtved, Erik. 1967. Eskimo shamanism. In *Studies in shamanism.* Edited by Carl-Marin Edsman. Stockholm: Almquist & Wiksell.

Jacob, Margaret C. 1981. *The radical Enlightenment, pantheists, freemasons and republicans.* London: George Allen & Unwin.

———. 1991. *Living the Enlightenment: Freemasonry and politics in eighteenth-century Europe.* New York: Oxford University Press.

Jacoby, John E. 1931. *Two mystic communities in America.* Paris: Les Presses Universitaires de France.

Johnson, Oakley C. 1970. *Robert Owen in the United States.* New York: Humanities Press.

Jones, Silas. 1836. *Practical phrenology.* Boston: Russell, Shattuck, & Williams.

Jonsson, Inge. 1988. Swedenborg and his influence. In *Swedenborg and his influence.* Edited by Erland J. Brock, E. Bruce Glenn, Carroll C. Odhner, et al. Bryn Athyn, PA: The Academy of the New Church.

Keller, Helen. 2000. *Light in my darkness.* 2nd ed. West Chester, PA: Chrysalis Books.

Knox, R.A. 1950. *Enthusiasm: A chapter in the history of religion: with special reference to the XVII and XVIII centuries.* Oxford: Clarendon Press.

Lane, Margaret. 1972. *Frances Wright and the "Great Experiment."* Manchester, England: Manchester University Press.

References

Lang, Bernhard. 1988. Glimpses of heaven in the age of Swedenborg. In *Swedenborg and his influence*. Edited by Erland J. Brock, E. Bruce Glenn, Carroll C. Odhner, et al. Bryn Athyn, PA: The Academy of the New Church.

A Layman. c. 1823. *An examination and defence of the writings and preaching of the Rev. Edward Irving, M.A.* London: John Fairburn.

Lopez, Claude-Anne. 1967. *Mon cher papa: Franklin and the ladies of Paris*. London: Yale University Press.

Manuel, F.E., and F. P. Manuel. 1979. Fourier: The burgeoning of instinct. In *Utopian thought in the western world*. Cambridge, MA: The Belknap Press.

McIntosh, Christopher. 1975. *Eliphas Levi and the French occult revival*. London: Rider & Co.

McLoughlin, William. 1978. *Revivals, awakenings and reform*. Chicago: University of Chicago Press.

McWilliams, Wilson C. 1974. *The idea of fraternity in America*. Berkeley: University of California Press.

Mesmer, F.A. 1957. *Memoir of F. A. Mesmer, doctor of medicine on his discoveries, 1799*. Trans. Jerome Eden. Mt Vernon, VA: Eden Press.

Miller, William. 1842. *Evidence from scripture and history of the second coming of Christ, about the year 1843; exhibited in a course of lectures*. Boston: Joshua V. Himes.

M'Nemar, Richard. 1807. *The Kentucky Revival, or, a short history of the late extraordinary out-pouring of the spirit of God, in the western states of America, agreeably to Scripture-promises, and prophecies concerning the latter day; with a brief account of the entrance and progress of what the world call Shakerism, among the subjects of the late revival in Ohio and Kentucky*. Cincinnati: John W. Browne.

Moore, R. Laurence. 1977. *In search of white crows*. New York: Oxford University Press.

Myers, F.W.H. 1913. *Human personality and its survival of bodily death*. Abridged. London: Longmans Green.

Nelson, Geoffrey K. 1969. *Spiritualism and society*. New York: Schocken.

Newton, Benjamin Wills. 1900. *The antichrist future, also the 1260 Days of antichrist's reign future*. London: Houlston.

References

Nordhoff, Charles. 1961. *The communistic societies of the United States.* New York: Hillary House Publishers.

Noyes, John Humphrey. 1870. *History of American socialisms.* Philadelphia: J. B. Lippincott & Co.

Obituary. 1860. The late professor George Bush. *The New Jerusalem Magazine* XXXII (January): 402–409.

Observations on animal magnetism and the doctrines of Swedenborg. 1842–1843. *The New Church Advocate* (London) 1 (May 1842–December 1843): 35–36.

Odhner, C.T., ed. 1904. *Annals of the New Church.* 2 vols. Bryn Athyn, PA: Academy of the New Church.

———. 1897. The early history of the New Church in Sweden. *The New-Church Messenger* 72: 73–75.

Oppenheim, Janet. 1991. *"Shattered nerves": Doctors, patients, and depression in Victorian England.* New York, Oxford University.

Owen, A. R. G. 1971. *Hysteria, hypnosis and healing: The work of J.-M. Charcot.* New York: Garrett Publications.

Owen, Alex. 1989. *The darkened room: Women, power and spiritualism in late Victorian England.* London, Virago Press.

Owen, Robert. 1971. *The life of Robert Owen.* London: Charles Knight & Co. First published 1857.

Owen, Robert Dale. 1831. *Moral physiology, or a brief and plain treatise on the population question.* New York: Wright & Owen.

Plotinus. 1969. *Plotinus: The Enneads.* Trans. S. McKenna. London: Faber & Faber.

Podmore, Frank. 1963. *Mediums of the nineteenth century.* 2 vols. New York: University Books.

———. 1964. *From Mesmer to Christian Science: A short history of mental healing.* New York: University Books.

The professed revelations of Davis. 1848. *New Church Quarterly Review* II, no.1: 36–62.

Publication of strictures on the case of Davis. 1848. *The New Church Quarterly Review* II, no.1:108–112.

Randall, E.O. 1899. *History of the Zoar Society, from its commencement to its conclusion, a sociological study in communism.* Columbus, OH: A. H. Smythe.

References

Raymond, Henrietta Dana. 1994. *Sophia Willard Dana Ripley, co-founder of Brook Farm.* Portsmouth, NH: Peter E. Randall.

Richet, Charles. 1923. *Thirty years of psychical research.* London: W. Collins Sons.

Rix, R.W. 2003. William Blake and the radical Swedenborgians. *Esoterica* 5 (2003): 96–137.

Roth, Cecil. 1933. *The nephew of the Almighty: An experimental account of the life and aftermath of Richard Brothers, R.N.* London: Edward Goldston.

Rousseau, G.S. 1988. Mysticism and millenerianism: "Immortal Dr. Cheyne." *In Millenarianism and messianism in English literature and thought 1650–1800.* Edited by Richard H. Popkin. Leiden: E. J. Brill.

Sachse, Julius F. 1895. *The German Pietists of provincial Pennsylvania.* Philadelphia: Printed for the author.

———. 1899. *The German sectarians of Pennsylvania 1708-1742.* Philadelphia: Printed for the author.

Sauvage, Micheline. 1960. *Socrates and the conscience of man.* London: Longmans.

Schlesinger, Arthur M. 1945. *The age of Jackson.* Boston: Little Brown.

Scholem, G. 1961. *Major trends in Jewish mysticism.* New York: Schocken Books.

Schuchard, Marsha Keith. 1988. Swedenborg, Jacobitism and freemasonry. In *Swedenborg and his influence.* Edited by Erland J. Brock, E. Bruce Glenn, Carroll C. Odhner, et al. Bryn Athyn, PA: The Academy of the New Church.

Shambaugh, Bertha M. 1932. *Amana that was and Amana that is.* Microfilm. Iowa City: State Historical Society of Iowa.

Silberger, Julius. 1978. The mental healing of Mary Baker Eddy. In *Psychoanalysis, psychotherapy, and the New England medical scene 1894–1944.* Edited by George E. Gifford. New York: Science History Publications.

Singular effects of disease. 1833. *The New Jerusalem Magazine* VI (August): 451–455.

Somnambulism and animal magnetism. 1834. *The New Jerusalem Magazine* LXXVIII (February): 210–231.

References

Stearn, Jess. 1968. *The sleeping prophet: The life and work of Edgar Cayce.* London, Muller.

Struthers, Gavin. 1843. *The history of the rise, progress, and principles of the Relief Church.* Glasgow: A. Fullerton.

Suzuki, D. T. 1996. *Swedenborg: Buddha of the north.* Trans. Andrew Bernstein. West Chester, PA: Swedenborg Foundation.

Swedenborg, Emanuel. 1960. *The Animal Kingdom.* 2 vols. Trans. J.J.G. Wilkinson. Bryn Athyn, PA: Swedenborg Scientific Association. This is a reprint of the 1843 translation.

———. 2000. *Heaven and hell.* Trans. George F. Dole. West Chester, PA: Swedenborg Foundation.

———. 2002. *Divine love and wisdom.* Trans. George F. Dole. West Chester, PA: Swedenborg Foundation.

———. 2002. *Divine providence.* Trans. George F. Dole. West Chester, PA: Swedenborg Foundation.

———. *Secrets of heaven.* Forthcoming. Trans. Lisa Hyatt Cooper. West Chester, PA: Swedenborg Foundation.

———. *True Christianity.* Forthcoming. Trans. Jonathan Rose. West Chester, PA: Swedenborg Foundation.

Tafel, R. L., ed. and trans. 1875–1877. *Documents concerning the life and character of Emanuel Swedenborg.* 2 vols. London: Swedenborg Society.

Taylor, Eugene. 1983. *William James on exceptional mental states: The 1896 Lowell lectures.* New York: Scribner's.

Train, Joseph. 1846. *The Buchanites: From first to last.* Edinburgh: William Blackwood.

Trobridge, George. 1992. *Swedenborg: Life and teaching.* Revised by Richard H. Tafel Sr. and Richard H. Tafel Jr. New York: The Swedenborg Foundation. First published 1907 by Swedenborg Society of London.

Turner, Frank Miller. 1974. *Between science and religion.* New Haven, CT: Yale University Press.

Wallace, Alfred Russell. 1874. A defence of modern spiritualism. *Fortnightly Review*, part 1 (May); part 2 (June).

Walters, Ronald G. 1978. *American reformers 1815–1860.* New York: Hill and Wang.

References

Watts, Howitt [Mrs.]. 1883. *Pioneers of the spiritual reformation*, London: The Psychological Press Association.

Webb, R. K. 1989. *Modern England: From the eighteenth century to the present*. London, Unwin Hyman.

Weisberger, Richard William. 1993. *Speculative freemasonry and the Enlightenment: A study of the craft in London, Paris, Prague, and Vienna*. Boulder, CO: East European Monographs.

White, Hugh. 1785. *The divine dictionary; or, a treatise indicted by holy inspiration*. Dumfries, Scotland: Robert Jackson.

Wiebe, Robert. 1984. *The opening of American society: From the adoption of the constitution to the eve of disunion*. New York: Knopf.

[Wilkinson, Jemima]. 1844. *Memoir of Jemima Wilkinson, a preacheress of the eighteenth century; containing an authentic narrative of her life and character, and of the rise, progress and conclusion of her ministry.* Bath, NY: R. L. Underhill & Co.

Williams, Aaron. 1866. *The Harmony Society, at Economy, Penn'a.* Pittsburgh, PA: W. S. Haven.

Williams-Hogan, Jane. 1988. Swedenborg: A biography. In *Swedenborg and his influence*. Edited by Erland J. Brock, E. Bruce Glenn, Carroll C. Odhner, et al. Bryn Athyn, PA: The Academy of the New Church.

Wisbey, Herbert A. 1964. *Pioneer prophetess: Jemima Wilkinson, the publick universal friend*. Ithaca, NY: Cornell University Press.

Worcester, Samuel H. 1845. *A letter to the receivers of the heavenly doctrines of the New Jerusalem*. Boston: Otis Clapp.

Wright, Esmond. 1986. *Franklin of Philadelphia*. Cambridge, MA: The Belknap Press.

$\mathcal{I}$ndex

Index

Index

Index

Index

Index

Index

Index

Home, Daniel Dunglas, 163
von Höpken, Count Anders, 86
Houghton, Richard, 63
Howitt, William, 73, 77, 212, 235, 236
Hume, David, 155
Hummer, Catherine, 119
Hund, Baron Charles, 58
Husson, H. M., 76, 77, 101
Hypnotism, 71, 74, 78, 79, 160, 242, 247, 249. see Mesmerism
    suggestion school, 248

Influx, 10, 11, 12, 64–65, 90, 181, 198, 208, 223, 236
Ireland, Shadrach, 104, 112, 132

Jacolliot, Louis, 228
James, Henry, 204
James, Henry Sr., 204
James, William, 204, 249
Janet, Pierre, 26, 78, 79, 92, 249, 253
Jefferson, Thomas, 34, 106, 143, 146, 152, 156, 157
Jones, Silas, 206, 207, 210
Jurieu, Pierre, xv
de Jussieu, Antoine Laurent 38
Jung-Stilling, J. H., 72

Kant, Immanuel, 3, 89
Kardec, Allan, 248
Kaufmann, G., 126
Keller, Helen, 5, 10
Kelpius, Johann, 116, 117, 118
Kerner, Justinus, 73
Kornmann, Guillaume, 31, 35
Koster, Henry Bernard, 117
de Krüdener, Baroness Juliane, 71
Lacy, John, xv

Index

Index

Index

Index

Index

Index

About the Author

Dr. Alfred Gabay was born in French North Africa and was educated in France and the United States, where he emigrated with his family. He received a B. A. in Philosophy from the University of California; and following extensive world travel, he settled in Australia, where he completed a Ph.D. in History and Religious Studies at LaTrobe University. He has published widely in journals, including *Australian Historical Studies*, the *Journal of Religious History*, and *New Philosophy*, and has contributed chapters to a volume on the origins of Australian Federation, *Makers of Miracles*, and to a work celebrating the tricentenary of Emanuel Swedenborg's birth, *Swedenborg and His Influence*. Among Dr. Gabay's other works are *The Mystic Life of Alfred Deakin* and *Messages From Beyond*. Dr. Gabay is currently senior lecturer in History and Religious Studies at the LaTrobe University, Bendigo, Australia.

Swedenborg Studies
is a scholarly series published by the Swedenborg Foundation.
The primary purpose of the series is to make materials available for understanding
the life and thought of Emanuel Swedenborg (1688–1772) and the impact his
thought has had on others. The Foundation undertakes to publish original studies
and English translations and to republish primary sources that are otherwise
difficult to access. Currently available in the series are:

The Swedenborg Foundation Publishers
320 N. Church Street • West Chester, PA 19380
Tel: 610-430-3222, ext. 10 • Fax: 610-430-7982
customerservice@swedenborg.com • www.swedenborg.com